ABOUT THE AUTHOR

Jonathan C. Slaght is a world expert on the Blakiston's fish owl. He is the Russia and Northeast Asia Coordinator for the Wildlife Conservation Society and has spent more than twenty years travelling and living in the Russian Far East. His work has featured in the *New York Times*, BBC World Service, *Smithsonian* and *Audubon*. *Owls of the Eastern Ice* is his first book.

PENGUIN BOOKS
Owls of the Eastern Ice

'The remarkable story of one man's heroic quest to save the astonishing fish owl. If only every endangered species had a guardian angel as impassioned, courageous and pragmatic as Jonathan Slaght' Isabella Tree

'Slaght's story reveals the patience and determination of a true conservationist. And the ears and eyes of a poet. Above all, he makes the people, wildlife and landscape of the Russian Far East come alive for armchair travellers. I haven't enjoyed a book on remote Russia as much as this since Ian Frazier's *Travels in Siberia*' Sophy Roberts, author of *The Lost Pianos of Siberia*

'A vivid dispatch from the front line of conservation, *Owls of the Eastern Ice* is engrossing and uplifting; an inspiring story of vital work undertaken with utter determination in wild and distant places' Horatio Clare, author of *Orison for a Curlew*

'True epic. A powerful, passionate and highly readable reflection on the wildness both inside us and out there in the forest' Charles Foster, author of *Being a Beast*

'A stellar example of the fruitful intersection of scientific inquiry, conservation advocacy and wilderness adventure. It belongs to a rare species of nature writing in which facts are delivered with both exactitude and storytelling panache' Heller McAlpin, *Wall Street Journal*

'A gripping account of the author's obsessive quest to save one of the world's most magnificent birds' Dave Goulson, author of *A Sting in the Tale*

'An engaging tale . . . we discover what it feels like to become aware of every little thing, to fully inhabit a living landscape. For this reason and others, this is an unusual (and welcome) book for our times' Tucker Malarkey, *The New York Times Book Review*

'An absolute marvel of a book. Part science narrative, part memoir, part adventure story, it is captivating, thrilling and beautifully written . . . Slaght is a terrific, thoughtful writer, and he tells his story well, with cliffhangers and drama, careful scientific observation and a dash of humor and humility' Laurie Hertzel, *Minneapolis StarTribune*

'From the very first pages, Slaght grips readers with vivid language and tight storytelling . . . The cast of characters he brings to life – both human and avian – illuminate the delicate symbiosis of the natural world and shed a welcome light on the remarkable creatures that are too little known. Top-notch nature writing in service of a magnificent, vulnerable creature' *Kirkus Reviews*

'Unforgettable . . . This is both nature and travel writing at their finest' Joshua Hammer, author of *The Bad-Ass Librarians of Timbuktu*

'Brilliant . . . a gripping tale of his quest to find – and save – one of the world's most magnificent creatures. Along the way, we get a rare inside view of a land, a people, an elusive owl, and ultimately, the human spirit. Anyone who loves birds, science, travel, or just a riveting read will love this book' Jennifer Ackerman, author of *The Genius of Birds*

'I loved *Owls of the Eastern Ice*. It is a riveting adventure with one of the rarest and most fascinating birds in one of the remotest regions of the globe, with most interesting people' Bernd Heinrich, author of *Ravens in Winter*

'Slaght strikes a pleasing balance between science and beauty, never descending into the purple prose that often characterizes nature writing but never losing the lay reader in scientific terminology either. Slaght is often funny, too' Sophie Pinkham, *TLS*

'A thoroughly engaging read which will appeal both to those specifically interested in owls, as well as those with a wider interest in the natural world. Will make armchair and keyboard conservationists envious and uncomfortable in equal measures' John Gray, *The International Owl Society*

'A fascinating account of one man's quest to conserve the magnificent fish owl of Eastern Asia, this is a book that feels both urgent and relevant' Christopher Skaife, author of *The Ravenmaster*

'One of the surprise books of the year: the story of a man's five-year journey into the Russian Far East to preserve the world's most mysterious owl, brought to life by brilliant writing, dashes across thawing rivers and madcap secondary characters' Richard Fitzpatrick, *Irish Examiner*

JONATHAN C. SLAGHT

Owls of the Eastern Ice

*The Quest to Find and Save the
World's Largest Owl*

PENGUIN BOOKS

PENGUIN BOOKS

UK | USA | Canada | Ireland | Australia
India | New Zealand | South Africa

Penguin Books is part of the Penguin Random House group of companies
whose addresses can be found at global.penguinrandomhouse.com.

First published in the United States of America by Farrar, Straus and Giroux 2020
First published in Great Britain by Allen Lane 2020
Published in Penguin Books 2021

001

Printed and bound in Great Britain by Clays Ltd, Elcograf S.p.A.

The authorized representative in the EEA is Penguin Random House Ireland,
Morrison Chambers, 32 Nassau Street, Dublin D02 YH68

A CIP catalogue record for this book is available from the British Library

ISBN: 978-0-141-98726-2

www.greenpenguin.co.uk

MIX
Paper from
responsible sources
FSC
www.fsc.org   FSC® C018179

Penguin Random House is committed to a
sustainable future for our business, our readers
and our planet. This book is made from Forest
Stewardship Council® certified paper.

For Karen

What was happening around us was unbelievable. The wind raged furiously, snapping tree branches and carrying them through the air . . . huge old pines swayed back and forth as though they were thin-trunked saplings. And we could not see a thing—not the mountains, not the sky, not the ground. Everything had been enveloped by the blizzard . . . We hunkered down in our tents and were intimidated into silence.

—VLADIMIR ARSENYEV, 1921, *Across the Ussuri Kray*

Arsenyev (1872–1930) was an explorer, naturalist, and author of numerous texts describing the landscape, wildlife, and people of Primorye, Russia. He was one of the first Russians to venture into the forests described in this book.

Contents

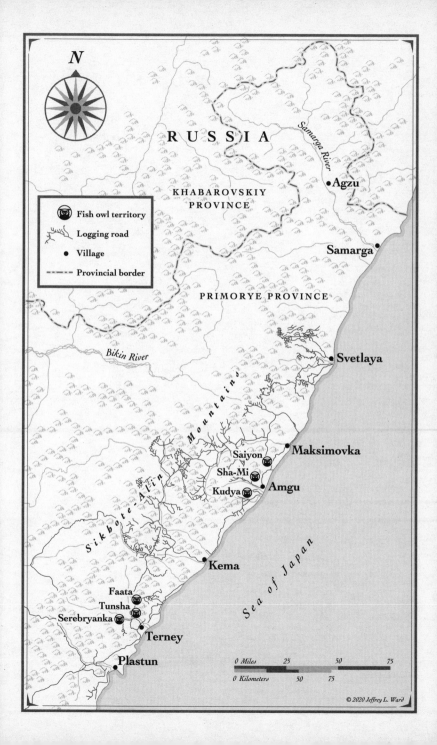

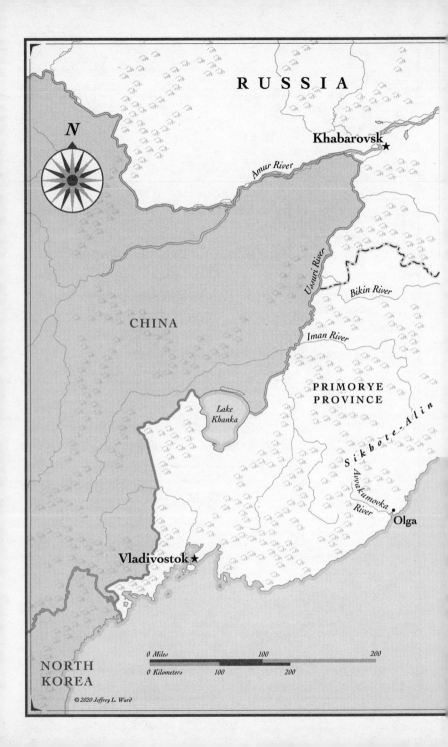

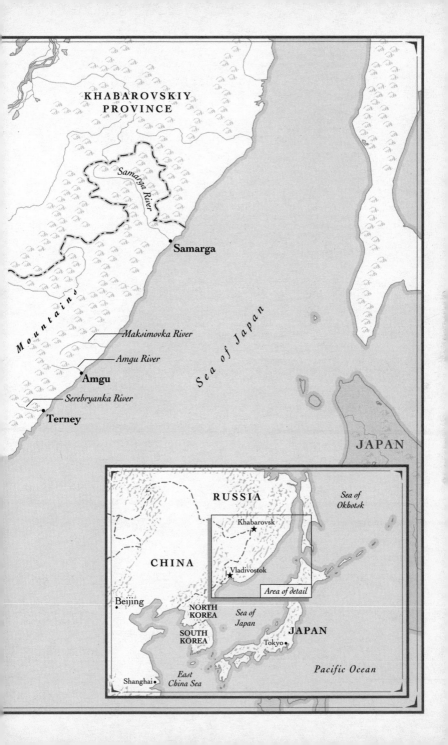

Owls of the Eastern Ice

Prologue

I SAW MY FIRST BLAKISTON'S FISH OWL in the Russian province of Primorye, a coastal talon of land hooking south into the belly of Northeast Asia. This is a remote corner of the world, not far from where Russia, China, and North Korea meet in a tangle of mountains and barbed wire. On a hike in the forest there in 2000, a companion and I unexpectedly flushed an enormous and panicked bird. Taking to the air with labored flaps, it hooted its displeasure, then landed for a moment in the bare canopy perhaps a dozen meters above our heads. This disheveled mass of wood-chip brown regarded us warily with electric-yellow eyes. We were uncertain at first which bird, actually, we'd come across. It was clearly an owl, but bigger than any I'd seen, about the size of an eagle but fluffier and more portly, with enormous ear tufts. Backlit by the hazy gray of a winter sky, it seemed almost too big and too comical to be a real bird, as if someone had hastily glued fistfuls of feathers to a yearling bear, then propped the dazed beast in the tree. Having decided that we were a threat, the creature pivoted to escape, crashing through the trees as its two-meter wingspan clipped the lattice of branches. Flakes of displaced bark spiraled down as the bird flew out of sight.

I'd been coming to Primorye for five years at this point. I'd spent most of my early life in cities, and my vision of the world was dominated by human-crafted landscapes. Then, flying from Moscow the summer I was nineteen, accompanying my father on a business trip, I saw the sun glinting off a sea of rolling green mountains: lush, thick, and unbroken. Dramatic ridges rose high, then drooped into low valleys, waves that scrolled past for kilometer after kilometer as I watched, transfixed. I saw no villages, no roads, and no people. This was Primorye. I fell in love.

After that initial short visit, I returned to Primorye for six months of study as an undergraduate and then spent three years there in the Peace Corps. I was only a casual bird-watcher at first; it was a hobby I'd picked up in college. Each trip to Russia's Far East, however, fueled my fascination with Primorye's wildness. I became more interested and more focused on its birds. In the Peace Corps I befriended local ornithologists, further developed my Russian-language skills, and spent countless hours of my free time tagging along with them to learn birdsongs and assist on various research projects. This was when I saw my first fish owl and realized my pastime could become a profession.

I'd known about fish owls for almost as long as I'd known about Primorye. For me, fish owls were like a beautiful thought I couldn't quite articulate. They evoked the same wondrous longing as some distant place I'd always wanted to visit but didn't really know much about. I pondered fish owls and felt cool from the canopy shadows they hid in and smelled moss clinging to riverside stones.

Immediately after scaring off the owl, I scanned through my dog-eared field guide, but no species seemed to fit. The fish owl painted there reminded me more of a dour trash can than the defiant, floppy goblin we'd just seen, and neither matched the fish owl in my mind. I didn't have to guess too long about what species I'd spotted, though: I'd taken photos. My grainy shots eventually made their way to an ornithologist in Vladivostok named Sergey Surmach, the only person working with fish owls in the region. It turned out that no scientist had seen a Blakiston's fish owl so far south in a hundred years, and my photographs were evidence that this rare, reclusive species still persisted.

Introduction

AFTER COMPLETING A MASTER OF SCIENCE PROJECT at the University of Minnesota in 2005, studying the impacts of logging on Primorye's songbirds, I began brainstorming for a Ph.D. topic in the region as well. I was interested in something with broad conservation impact and quickly narrowed my species contenders to the hooded crane and the fish owl. These were the two least-studied and most charismatic birds in the province. I was drawn more to fish owls but, given the lack of information about them, was worried that these birds might almost be too scarce to study. Around the time of my deliberations, I happened to spend a few days hiking through a larch bog, an open, damp landscape with an even spacing of spindly trees above a thick carpet of fragrant Labrador tea. At first I found this setting lovely, but after a while, with nowhere to hide from the sun, a headache from the oppressive aroma of Labrador tea, and biting insects descending in clouds, I'd had enough. Then it hit me: this was hooded crane habitat. The fish owl might be rare, devoting time and energy to it might be a gamble, but at least I would not have to spend the next five years slogging through larch bogs. I went with fish owls.

Given its reputation as a hearty creature in an inhospitable environment, the fish owl is a symbol of Primorye's wilderness almost as much as the Amur (also called Siberian) tiger. While these two species share the same forests and are both endangered, far less is known about the lives of the feathered salmon eaters. A fish owl nest was not discovered in Russia until 1971, and by the 1980s there were thought to be no more than three hundred to four hundred pairs of fish owls in the entire country. There were serious concerns for their future. Other than the fact that fish owls seemed to need big trees to nest in, and fish-rich rivers to feed from, not much was known about them.

Across the sea in Japan, just a few hundred kilometers east, fish owls had been reduced to fewer than one hundred birds by the early 1980s, down from approximately five hundred pairs at the end of the nineteenth century. This beleaguered population lost nesting habitat to logging and food to construction of downstream dams that blocked salmon migration up rivers. Fish owls of Primorye had been shielded from a similar fate by Soviet inertia, poor infrastructure, and a low human population density. But the free market that emerged in the 1990s bred wealth, corruption, and a covetous eye focused keenly on the untouched natural resources in northern Primorye—thought to be the fish owl's global stronghold.

Fish owls in Russia were vulnerable. For a naturally low-density and slow-reproducing species, any large-scale or sustained disruption to their required natural resources could mean a precipitous population free fall such as the one seen in Japan and the loss of one of Russia's most mysterious and iconic bird species. Fish owls and other endangered species were protected by Russian law—it was illegal to kill them or destroy their habitat—but without concrete knowledge of what their needs were, it was impossible to develop a workable conservation plan. No such approach for fish owls existed, and by the late 1990s, previously inaccessible forests in Primorye were increasingly becoming sites of resource extraction. The need for a serious fish owl conservation strategy was escalating.

Conservation is different from preservation. Had I wanted to preserve fish owls, I wouldn't have needed research: I could have lobbied the government for a ban of all logging and fishing in Primorye. These broad measures would protect fish owls by eliminating all threats to them. But aside from being unrealistic, such a move would ignore the two million people living in the province, a proportion of whom rely on the logging and fishing industries for their livelihoods. The needs of fish owls and humans are inextricably linked in Primorye; both have depended on the same resources for centuries. Before the Russians came to dip their nets in the rivers and harvest trees for construction and profit, Manchurian and indigenous populations did the same. The Udege and Nanai made beautiful embroidered clothing from salmon skins and fashioned boats from enormous, hollowed-out trees. Fish owl reliance on these resources has remained at modest levels over time; it is the human needs that have escalated. My intention was to return some balance to this relationship, to conserve the necessary natural resources, and scientific research was the only way to get the answers I needed.

In late 2005, I set up a meeting with Sergey Surmach at his office in Vladivostok. I liked him immediately, with his kind eyes and small, fit frame capped by a blossom of unruly hair. He had a reputation as a collaborator, so I hoped he'd be open to my proposal of partnership. I explained my interest in studying fish owls for a Ph.D. at the University of Minnesota, and he told me what he knew about these birds. Mutual excitement grew as we discussed ideas, and we quickly agreed to work together: we would learn as much as we could about the secret lives of fish owls and use that information to craft a realistic conservation plan to protect them. Our primary research question was deceptively simple: What were the features on the landscape that fish owls needed to survive? We already had a general idea—big trees and lots of fish—but we needed to invest years to understand the details. Other than the anecdotal observations of past naturalists, we were largely starting from scratch.

Surmach was a seasoned field biologist. He had the equipment necessary for prolonged expeditions into remote Primorye: an enormous, all-terrain GAZ-66 truck with a custom-built, woodstove-heated living compartment on the back, several snowmobiles, and a small team of field assistants trained to find fish owls. For our first project together, we agreed that Surmach and his team would bear the brunt of in-country logistics and staffing; I would introduce contemporary methodologies and secure the majority of the funding by cobbling together research grants. We broke the study into three phases. The first phase was training, which would take two or three weeks, followed by identifying a study population of fish owls, which would take about two months. The final phase was fish owl captures and data collection, which would take four years.

I was enthused: this wasn't retroactive, crisis conservation where overstressed and underfunded researchers battle to prevent extinctions across landscapes where the ecological damage has already been done. Primorye was still largely pristine. Here, commercial interests hadn't taken over yet. While we focused on one species at risk—fish owls—our recommendations for better management of the landscape could help safeguard the entire ecosystem.

Winter was the best time to find these owls—they vocalized most in February and left tracks in the snow along riverbanks—but it was also the busiest time of year for Surmach. His nongovernmental organization had been awarded a multiyear contract to monitor bird populations on Sakhalin island, and he needed to spend the winter months negotiating logistics for that work. As a result, while I consulted with Surmach regularly, I never worked with him in the field. Instead, he always sent Sergey Avdeyuk, his old friend and an experienced woodsman, as his proxy. Avdeyuk had worked closely with Surmach on fish owls since the mid-1990s.

An expedition to the Samarga River basin, the northernmost part of Primorye, was the first phase. There, I would learn how to search for owls. The Samarga River basin was unique—the last completely roadless drainage in the province—but the logging industry was closing in. In 2000, a council of indigenous Udege in Agzu, one of only two villages in the entire 7,280-square-kilometer Samarga River basin, ruled that Udege lands could be opened for timber harvest. Roads would be built, the industry would attract jobs, but the combination of increased access and more people would degrade the landscape via poaching, forest fires, and more. Fish owls and tigers were only two of many species that would likely suffer as a result. By 2005 the logging company, cognizant of the uproar this agreement had caused from local communities and regional scientists, made a series of unprecedented concessions. First and foremost, their harvest practices would be informed by science. The main road would be laid high up the river valley, not next to an ecologically sensitive river like most roads in Primorye, and certain areas with high conservation value would be exempt from harvest. Surmach was part of the scientific coalition charged with environmental assessments of the drainage before the roads were built. His field team, led by

Avdeyuk, was tasked with identifying fish owl territories along the Samarga River, areas that would be excluded from logging altogether.

By joining this expedition, I would help protect fish owls of the Samarga and also gain important experience in the art of searching for them. These were skills I would apply to the second phase of the project: identifying a study population of fish owls. Surmach and Avdeyuk had compiled a list of sites in the more accessible forests of Primorye where they had heard fish owls calling, and they even knew the locations of a few nest trees. This meant we had a place to focus our preliminary searches, and Avdeyuk and I would spend a few months visiting these sites and more within a twenty-thousand-square-kilometer area along much of Primorye's coast. After we'd found some fish owls, we would return the following year and begin the third, final, and longest stage of the project: captures. By outfitting as many owls as possible with discreet backpack-like transmitters, over a period of four years we could monitor their movements and record where they went. Such data would tell us exactly what parts of the landscape were most important to fish owls' survival, which we could use to develop a conservation plan to protect them.

How hard could it be?

PART ONE

Baptism by Ice

1

A Village Named Hell

THE HELICOPTER WAS LATE. I was in the coastal village of Terney in March 2006, three hundred kilometers north of where I'd seen my first fish owl, cursing the snow-storm that grounded the helicopter and impatient to reach Agzu in the Samarga River basin. With about three thousand people, Terney was the northernmost human enclave of any notable size in the province: villages any farther, such as Agzu, had their populations measured in hundreds or even dozens.

I'd been waiting more than a week in this rustic settlement of low, wood-heated homes. At the airport, a Soviet-era Mil Mi-8 sat immobile outside the single-room terminal, its blue-and-silver hull tarnished by frost as the winds and snows raged. I was accustomed to waiting in Terney: I had never flown in this helicopter before, but the buses to Vladivostok, fifteen hours south of the village, ran twice a week and were not always on time or in suitable repair for the road. I'd been traveling to (or living in) Primorye for more than a decade at that point; waiting was part of life here.

After a week, the pilots had finally been given permission to fly. Dale Miquelle, an Amur tiger researcher based in Terney, handed me an envelope with $500 cash as I left for the airport. A loan, he said, in case I needed to buy my way out of trouble up there. He'd been to Agzu and I hadn't: he knew what I was getting into. I got a ride to the edge of town and the airstrip, a clearing cut from riparian old-growth forest. The Serebryanka River valley was 1.5 kilometers wide at that spot, framed by the low mountains of the Sikhote-Alin, and only a few kilometers from the river mouth and the Sea of Japan.

After collecting my ticket at the counter, I inserted myself among the anxious crowd of old women, young children, and hunters both local and from the city, all waiting outside to board, insulated by thick felt coats and clutching suitcases. A storm this protracted was uncommon, and many of us had been stranded in the resulting travel bottleneck.

There were about twenty people in this crowd, and the helicopter could hold up to twenty-four people if there was no cargo. We watched uneasily as a man in a blue uniform stacked box after box of supplies by the helicopter while another dressed the same loaded them on. Everyone in the group was starting to suspect that more people had been sold tickets than the helicopter could carry—the crates and supplies being loaded were taking up valuable room—and everyone was equally determined to squeeze through that tiny metal door. Surmach's team, in Agzu and already waiting for me eight days, would probably travel on without me if I did not make this flight. I positioned myself behind a stout older woman: experience showed that my best chance of securing a bus seat was by tailing such a person, a technique not unlike following an ambulance through traffic, and I assumed this rule held for helicopters as well.

The go-ahead was given almost inaudibly, and as a wall we

surged forward. I battled toward and up the helicopter ladder, climbing among the crates of potatoes and vodka and other essentials of Russian village life. My ambulance moved true and I followed her toward the back, where there was a view out a porthole and a little bit of legroom. As the passenger load swelled to a probably unsafe number, I retained my window view but lost legroom to a giant sack of what I think was flour, upon which I rested my feet. The finite space filled to the crew's satisfaction and the rotors began swirling, languidly at first, then with increasing vigor until their fury commanded all attention. The Mi-8 lurched into the sky, jackhammered low over Terney, then banked left a few hundred meters out over the Sea of Japan and shadowed the eastern edge of Eurasia north.

Below our helicopter, the coast was a strip of pebbly beach wedged uncomfortably between the Sikhote-Alin mountains and the Sea of Japan. The Sikhote-Alin ended almost midmountain here, with slopes of lanky Mongolian oak giving way suddenly to vertical cliffs, some of them thirty stories tall, a uniform gray with the occasional patch of brown earth and clinging vegetation or whitewash stains betraying a raptor or crow nest in one of the crevasses. The bare oaks above were older than they looked. The harsh environment in which they lived—the cold, the wind, and a growing season largely shrouded in coastal fog— left them gnarled, stunted, and thin. Down below, a winter of breaking waves had left a thick, icy sheen on every rock the sea mist could reach.

The Mi-8 descended some three hours after departing Terney, gleaming in the sun through swirls of displaced snow, and I saw a loose collective of snowmobiles massed around the Agzu airport, nothing more than a shack and a clearing. As the passengers disembarked, the crew busied themselves unloading cargo and clearing space for the return flight.

An Udege boy of about fourteen approached me with a serious expression, his black hair mostly hidden under a rabbit-fur hat. I was different and clearly out of place. Twenty-eight years old and bearded, I was obviously not local—Russians my age were clean-shaven almost as a rule, as this was the style at the time, and my puffy red jacket was conspicuous among the subdued blacks and grays that Russian men wore. He was curious to know of my interest in Agzu.

"Have you heard of fish owls?" I answered in Russian, the language I'd be speaking exclusively for this expedition and most of my fish owl work in general.

"Fish owls. Like, the bird?" the boy answered.

"I'm here to look for fish owls."

"You're looking for birds," he echoed flatly and with a note of bewilderment, as though wondering if he had misunderstood me.

He asked if I knew anyone in Agzu. I replied that I did not. He raised his eyebrows and asked if someone was meeting me. I responded that I hoped so. His eyebrows lowered in a frown, and then he scrawled his name in the margins of a scrap of newspaper, holding my gaze as he handed it to me.

"Agzu is not the kind of place you can just go to," he said. "If you need a corner to sleep in, or you need help, ask around town for me."

Like the oaks along the coast, the boy was a product of this harsh environment and his youthfulness hid experience. I did not know much about Agzu, but I knew it could be rough: the previous winter the meteorologist stationed there, a Russian (but still an outsider) and the son of someone I knew in Terney, had been beaten and left unconscious in the snow, where he froze to death. His killer was never publicly identified: in a town as small and tight-knit as Agzu, everyone probably knew who did it, but no one said a word to the inspecting police officers. Punishment, whatever that might have been, would have been handled internally.

I soon saw Sergey Avdeyuk, the leader of our field team, moving among the crowd. He had driven a snowmobile to meet me. We identified each other immediately by the flashy nature of our heavy down jackets, but no one would mistake Sergey for a foreigner—not with his cropped hair, an upper row of gold teeth perpetually clenching a cigarette, and the swagger of someone comfortably in his element. He was about my height—six feet tall—his square, tanned face obscured by stubble, with sunglasses to protect his eyes from the blinding sun's reflection on the snow. Although the Samarga expedition was the first phase of a project I had conceived with Surmach, Avdeyuk was without question the project leader here. He had experience with both fish owls and deep-forest expeditions, and I would defer to his judgment for the duration of this trip. Avdeyuk and two other team members had hitched a ride to the Samarga River basin some weeks earlier on a logging ship from the port village of Plastun, 350 kilometers to the south. They hauled with them a pair of snowmobiles, homemade sleds bulging with gear, and several barrels of gasoline reserves. From the coast they moved quickly to the upper reaches of the river, more than a hundred kilometers away, dropping food and fuel caches as they went, then turned around and were systematically making their way back to the coast. They had paused in Agzu to meet me, planning to stay only a day or two, but had been waiting for the storm to clear as I had.

In addition to being the northernmost human settlement in Primorye, Agzu is the most isolated. Located on the edge of one of the Samarga River's tributaries, this village of about 150 inhabitants, mostly Udege, is a step back in time. In the Soviet era, the village was the hub for a game meat operation, in which the locals were professional hunters paid by the state. Helicopters flew in to collect furs and meat, which were exchanged for cash. When the Soviet Union collapsed in 1991, it did not take the organized game meat industry long to follow. The helicopters stopped coming, and the rapid inflation that trailed the fall of the Soviet Union left these hunters clutching worthless fistfuls of Soviet rubles. Those who wanted to leave could not; they simply lacked the resources to do so. With no other alternative, they went back to subsistence hunting. To some degree, trade in Agzu had reverted to the barter system: fresh meat could be exchanged at the village store for goods flown in from Terney.

The Udege of the Samarga River basin had until relatively recently lived in dispersed encampments all along the river, but in the 1930s, under Soviet collectivization, these camps were destroyed and the Udege were concentrated in four villages, with the majority ending up in Agzu. The helplessness and distress of a people forced into collectivization are reflected in their village's name: Agzu may be derived from the Udege word *Ogzo*, meaning "Hell."

Sergey guided the snowmobile off the packed trail leading through town and parked it in front of one of the huts that was unoccupied at present, as its owner was in the forest for an extended hunt. We'd been given permission to stay there. Like all the other dwellings in Agzu, it was of the traditional Russian style—a single-story wooden structure with a gabled roof and wide, ornately carved frames around double-paned windows. Two men unloading supplies in front of the hut stopped to greet us. It was evident from their modern outfits of insulated bibs and winter boots that this was the rest of our team. Sergey lit another cigarette, then introduced us. The first man was Tolya Ryzhov: stocky and swarthy, with a round face highlighted by a thick

mustache and gentle eyes. Tolya was a photographer and cameraman; there was almost no video of fish owls in Russia, and if
we saw some, Surmach wanted the evidence. The second man
was Shurik Popov: short and athletic, with brown hair cropped
short like Sergey's and an elongated face tanned from weeks in
the field and peppered with the wispy strands of someone who
cannot easily grow a full beard. Shurik was the general fixer of
the group: if something needed to be done, be it free-climb a
rotting tree to investigate a potential owl nest or gut and clean a
dozen fish for dinner, Shurik would do it quickly and without
complaint.

After clearing enough snow to allow the gate to open, we
entered the yard and then the house. I moved through a small,
dark vestibule and opened a door to the first room, which was
the kitchen. I breathed in frigid, stale air, heavy with the stench
of wood smoke and cigarettes. The building had remained sealed
and unheated inside since its owner had left for the forest, and
the cold could suppress only so much of the room's acquired
aroma. Bits of plaster from the crumbling walls littered the floor
and mixed with crushed cigarette butts and spent tea bags around
the woodstove.

I made my way through the kitchen and the first of two side
rooms and into the last. The rooms were separated from one another by filthy, patterned sheets that hung unevenly in the door-
frames. There was so much plaster on the floor in the back room
that it crunched constantly underfoot, and there were small bits
of what appeared to be frozen meat and fur against one of the
walls under the window.

Sergey brought in a load of firewood from the shed and lit the
woodstove, making sure to create a draft first with some newspaper, as the cold inside and relative warmth outside had caused
a pressure seal in the chimney. If he started the fire too quickly,

the draft would not pull and the room would fill with smoke. The woodstove here, as in most huts in the Russian Far East, was made of brick and topped by a thick iron sheet on which one could place a skillet of food to cook or pot of water to boil. The stove, built into a corner of the kitchen, integrated into the wall in such a way that the warm smoke followed a serpentine network through the brick wall before escaping out the chimney. This style, called a *Russkaya pechka* (literally "Russian stove"), allows the brick wall to retain heat long after the fire goes out, which warms both the kitchen and the room on its far side. The slovenliness of our mystery host extended to the stove as well: despite Sergey's careful efforts, smoke seeped through countless cracks and turned the air inside an ashy gray.

With all our belongings inside or in the vestibule, Sergey and I sat down with maps of the Samarga River to talk strategy. He showed me where he and the rest of the team had already surveyed the upper fifty kilometers of the main river and some of its tributaries for fish owls. They had discovered some ten territorial pairs—a very high population density for this species, he said. We still needed to cover the final sixty-five kilometers down to the village of Samarga and the coast and some of the forests here around Agzu itself. This was a lot of work yet and there was not a lot of time to do it: it was late March already and the days we had lost to the weather meant that time was limited. The river ice—our only possible travel route once we left Agzu—was melting. This created dangerous conditions for snowmobiles, and there was some concern we'd be stranded along the river, caught between the villages of Agzu and Samarga, if spring came too quickly. Sergey recommended that we continue working out of Agzu for at least a week—all the while keeping tabs on the spring melt. He thought we could extend farther and farther downriver each day, maybe the next ten or fifteen kilometers, then snowmobile back to Agzu each night to sleep. In this remote environment, it was hard to pass up the guarantee of a warm place to spend the night: if not in Agzu, we would be sleeping in tents. After about a week we would pack up and move to Vosnesenovka, a hunting encampment some forty kilometers downstream of Agzu and twenty-five kilometers from the coast.

Our first night's dinner of canned beef and pasta was interrupted when several of the villagers stopped by and unceremoniously placed on the kitchen table a four-liter bottle of 95 percent ethanol, a bucket of raw moose meat, and several yellow onions. This was their contribution to the night's entertainment—what they expected in return was interesting conversation. As a foreigner in Primorye, a province closed off to much of the outside world until the 1990s, I was accustomed to being seen as a novelty. People liked hearing what I could tell them about real life in television's *Santa Barbara* and knowing whether I followed the Chicago Bulls—two cultural symbols of America popularized in Russia in the 1990s—and they loved to hear my praise of their remote corner of the globe. In Agzu, however, any visitor was seen as a minor celebrity. It did not matter to them that I was from the United States and Sergey was from Dalnegorsk: both were equally exotic places, we both offered entertainment value, and we were both new people to drink with.

As the hours passed, and people came and went, moose cutlets were cooked and consumed, and ethanol was ingested at a steady pace. The room grew smoky from both tobacco and the sieve-like woodstove. I sat in for a few shots of ethanol, eating meat and raw onion, and listened to the men impress one another with stories of hunts and close encounters with bears and tigers and the river. Someone asked me why I didn't just study fish owls in the United States—it seemed like a lot of effort to travel all the way to the Samarga—and was surprised when I said there were no fish owls in North America. These hunters appreciated wilderness but perhaps did not understand how wonderfully unique their own forests were.

Eventually I nodded good night and moved into the back room, pulling the sheet across the doorframe in an attempt to block out the smoke and boisterous laughter that continued into the night. There, I used my headlamp to flip through photocopies of fish owl papers I'd managed to find in Russian scientific journals, my last-minute cramming before tomorrow's test. There was not much to go on. In the 1940s, an ornithologist named Yevgeniy Spangenberg was one of the first Europeans to study fish owls, and his articles provided a basic sketch of where one might expect to find them: rivers with interlacing channels of clean, cold water roiling with salmon. Later, in the 1970s, another ornithologist named Yuriy Pukinskiy wrote a few papers on his experiences with fish owls on the Bikin River in northwestern Primorye, where he collected information about nesting ecology and vocalizations. And last, there were a few papers by Sergey Surmach, whose research focused mostly on patterns of fish owl distribution in Primorye. Eventually I stripped to my long underwear and inserted earplugs, then crawled into my sleeping bag. My mind was electric with anticipation of the coming day.

2

The First Search

THAT NIGHT, somewhere near Agzu, owls fished for salmon. Sound is not so important for fish owls, as their main prey are underwater and indifferent to the auditory nuances of the terrestrial world. Whereas most owl species can track the sounds of their rodent targets flitting unaware among the detritus of the forest floor—barn owls, for example, can do so in complete darkness—a fish owl must hunt prey moving under the water's surface. This difference in hunting strategy is manifested physically: many owls have a distinct facial disk—the characteristic, round feather pattern on an owl's face that channels the faintest sounds to its ear holes—but in fish owls this disk is poorly defined. Evolutionarily, they simply didn't need the advantage, so this feature faded over time.

The rivers that contain the owls' primary prey of salmonid fish are largely frozen for months on end. To survive winters that routinely dip below –30 degrees Celsius, these owls amass thick fat reserves. This once made them a prized food source for the

Udege, who, after consuming the owl, also spread and dried the massive fish owl wings and tails to use as fans to displace peppered clouds of biting insects while hunting deer and boar.

THE PALE LIGHT OF DAYBREAK in Agzu revealed that I was still among rubble and deer meat. I could not smell the stale air of the house anymore, meaning that I had acclimated to it and the odors likely clung to my clothing and beard. In the next room, moose bones, cups, and a drained ketchup bottle cluttered the table. After a bleary-eyed breakfast of sausage, bread, and tea during which we barely spoke, Sergey handed me a fistful of hard candies that would serve as lunch and told me to grab my coat, hip waders, and binoculars. We were going to look for fish owls.

As our two-vehicle caravan of snowmobiles rumbled through Agzu, villagers and packs of dogs ceded the narrow road by sidestepping into the deep snow to watch us pass. Whereas dogs in most of Primorye are chained to guardhouses, dejected and vicious, this was not so in Agzu, where the East Siberian Laikas, a tenacious hunting breed, proudly roamed the village in loose packs. These dogs had been ravaging the local deer and boar populations of late—a season's worth of deep snow was sealed under a late-winter glaze that deer hooves pierced like paper but soft canid pads trod safely. Any ungulate unfortunate enough to be pursued by these Laikas would flounder as though in quicksand and be swiftly eviscerated by their nimble predators. The dogs we passed wore blood matted into their fur as badges of this carnage.

We split up just before the river. The other team members were old hands at this, so there was not a lot of discussion; Sergey told Tolya to show me what to do. Sergey and Shurik aimed their snowmobile south toward the Samarga while Tolya and I went back past the helicopter landing pad, stopping at a tributary that led northeast away from the Samarga.

"This river is called Akza," said Tolya, squinting in the sun and staring up the narrow valley staggered with bare deciduous trees and the occasional pine weighed down by the fresh snow. I could hear gurgling river water and the alarm calls of a brown dipper startled by our arrival. "The man who used to hunt here lost a testicle to a fish owl when he was younger, and he killed them on sight thereafter. He went out of his way to trap, poison, and shoot fish owls. Anyway, what we'll do here is work our way upstream looking for owl sign, like tracks or feathers."

"Wait . . . he lost a testicle to a fish owl?"

Tolya nodded. "They say he went out one night to take a dump in the woods—it must have been spring—and he apparently squatted right over a flightless young fish owl that had just left the nest. When fish owls are vulnerable they flop on their backs and defend with their talons. The bird just grabbed and squeezed the closest bit of flesh, the lowest-hanging fruit, you might say."

As Tolya explained, looking for fish owls takes patience and a careful eye. Since the owls tend to flush at great distances, it's best to assume you won't see one even if it's around—better to focus on what it may have left behind. The basic protocol was to walk slowly up a valley looking for three key things. First, a patch of open, unfrozen water on the river. There are only so many sections of flowing water in fish owl territory in winter, so if an owl is present, it probably will have stopped by such a spot. The snow along river edges needs to be carefully scrutinized for tracks where the bird may have walked while stalking fish or marks left by primary feathers as the bird landed or took flight.

The second thing to look for is feathers: these birds are always losing plumage. This occurs most actively during the spring molt, when fluffy, down-like semiplume feathers up to eight inches long release and drift, their barbs reaching like a thousand tentacles to cling to branches near fishing holes or nest trees—little flags that shimmer gracefully in the breeze as quiet announcements of fish owl presence. The third sign is a massive tree with a huge hole in it. Fish owls are so big that they need true forest giants—typically old-growth Japanese poplar or Manchurian elm—to nest in. There are usually only so many of these Goliaths in a given valley, so anytime such a tree is spied it should be approached immediately and examined. Find one with semiplume feathers nearby and you've all but certainly found a nest tree.

I spent the first few hours wandering the river bottom with Tolya, observing as he indicated good trees to inspect and promising patches of water to scrutinize. He moved deliberately. I had noticed that Sergey, who made decisions in an instant and acted on them unwaveringly, chided Tolya for this perceived indolence. But Tolya's unhurried approach made him a good teacher and a pleasant companion. I also learned that Tolya often worked for Surmach to document the natural histories of Primorye's birds.

We stopped to brew tea in the early afternoon. Tolya made a fire, then boiled some river water, and we crunched on our hard candies and sipped tea while Eurasian nuthatches chirred inquisitively in the trees above. After lunch Tolya suggested I lead, using my instincts and what I had learned that morning, while he observed. One stretch of water I thought we should explore Tolya dismissed as too deep for the owls to fish, and another was too overgrown with willows for the enormous birds to realistically approach on the wing. After I fell through the ice on a slow backwater, albeit only to my knees, my rubber hip waders keeping me dry, I learned the value of Tolya's ice pole—a stick tipped with a metal spike that he used to test the integrity of the ice before walking on it. We followed the stream until the valley narrowed to a sharp V and the water disappeared under the snow and ice and rock.

We found no fish owl sign that day. At dusk we lingered to see if any owls might call, but the woods were as silent as the snow along the river was undisturbed. I took my cues from Tolya on how to react to the day's lack of tangible result. He explained that even if fish owls inhabited the very patch of forest we stood in, it might take a week of searching and listening to actually detect them. This was disappointing news. It was one thing to sit comfortably in Surmach's office in Vladivostok and talk about finding fish owls; the reality of the process—the cold and the darkness and the silence—was another thing entirely.

It was well after dark, perhaps nine o'clock, when we returned to Agzu. The uneven window light on the snow outside our cabin alerted us that Avdeyuk and Shurik had already returned. They had made soup using some potatoes and moose meat gifted by a neighbor and had been joined by a skinny Russian hunter in an oversized parka, who introduced himself as Lësha. He appeared to be around forty years old; his thick glasses distorted his eyes, but not enough to mask his considerable intoxication.

"I have been drinking for ten or twelve days," Lësha announced matter-of-factly, without rising from the kitchen table.

As I exchanged impressions of the day with Sergey, Shurik ladled soup and Tolya emerged from the foyer with a bottle of vodka, which he placed ceremoniously at the center of the kitchen table along with some cups. Sergey glowered. Russian social customs typically dictate that once a bottle of vodka is on the table for guests, it is not removed until empty. Some vodka distillers don't even put caps on their bottles—opting for a thin layer of aluminum to puncture instead—because what do you need a cap for? Either a bottle is full or it is empty, with only a short period between those two states. On a night that Sergey and Shurik were hoping for respite from drink, Tolya had just committed them to a bottle of vodka. There were five of us, but Tolya had put only four cups on the table. I looked at him quizzically.

"I don't drink," Tolya replied to my silent question. This made him exempt from the suffering associated with yet another night of heavy drinking, and I found that this was a habit of his—to offer vodka on our behalf to guests, without consulting the group and often at inopportune times.

We talked about the river over soup and shots. Sergey explained that the Samarga River was not particularly deep, but the current commanded respect. Someone unlucky enough to go through the ice might not have time to claw himself free; the flow threatened to suck him under and away toward a quick, cold, and disorienting death. Lësha added that this had already happened once that winter; the tracks of a missing villager had been found leading to a small, dark gash in the ice that revealed the rushing Samarga. Human skeletons were occasionally discovered downstream by the river mouth: the Samarga's victims from years past, tangled and askew among logs, rocks, and sand.

I saw that Lësha was eyeing me.

"Where do you live?" he asked, slurring.

"Terney," I answered.

"Are you from there?"

"No, I am from New York," I answered. It was easier than explaining Minnesota and the Midwest to people with likely no comprehension of North American geography.

"New York . . . ," Lësha repeated, then lit a cigarette and glanced at Sergey. It was as though an important realization were trying to penetrate the thick cloud of uninterrupted alcohol consumption. "Why do you live in New York?"

"Because I am an American."

"An *American*?" Lësha's eyes bulged and he looked at Sergey again. "He's an *American*?"

Sergey nodded.

Lësha repeated the word several times while staring at me incredulously. He had apparently never met a foreigner and certainly hadn't expected one to speak fluent Russian. To be sitting at a table with a Cold War foe in his hometown of Agzu was not something easily reconciled. We were distracted by a noise outside, and a small group of men entered; I recognized many of them from the night before. I wanted to be fresh for the morning, so I took that as my cue to disappear to the back room, while Tolya ducked out to play chess with Ampleev, a local Russian retiree who occupied a house across the street. I recorded some notes from the day by headlamp, then got into my sleeping bag, once again wincing at the pile of meat and fur, red, glistening, and neglected in the corner. Like the river ice we depended on, it was softening.

3

Winter Life in Agzu

THE GRAY LIGHT of the next morning found Sergey awake with cigarette in hand, crouching next to the smoldering woodstove. He exhaled clouds that folded upon themselves before meeting the draft and disappearing into the stove. Sergey swore at the massive and empty ethanol bottle on its side by the table and said we had to get out of Agzu soon—the alcohol was killing him. There was no free will in the matter: as long as we were in Agzu, we had to please the villagers.

As we prepared for the field, Sergey warned that a fish owl might slip away before I got close enough to see it, given how wary they are of humans, so I should be vigilant. One thing we had on our side, he said, was that fish owls were loud in flight, a characteristic that distinguishes fish owls from their owl relatives. Most birds are noisy when they fly, and some species can even be identified solely on the sounds their wings make as they flap. A typical owl, however, is almost completely silent. This is because their flight feathers are fringed with miniature, comblike protrusions that act almost like a cloaking device to displace the air before it reaches the wing, thus muffling the sound. This gives owls an advantage when stalking terrestrial prey. It was unsurprising, then, that the flight feathers of a fish owl were smooth and lacked this adaptation: their primary prey was underwater. Especially on a quiet night, one could often hear the air vibrate in resistance as fish owls labored past on heavy wings.

The plan for our day was largely the same as before. A lot of fish owl fieldwork was repetitive action: search and search again. We had to dress sensibly, in layers, because we'd be in the field all day, then linger past sundown. The fleece jacket I wore unzipped as I hiked under an afternoon sun wouldn't be enough to keep me warm after dark, when I sat immobile listening for owls in the dropping temperatures. Other than a pair of hip waders, no special equipment or gear was needed for this work. Tolya had some camera equipment, but he would keep that at our base and bring it with him only in the event we discovered something worth filming.

I was paired once more with Tolya, who had promised to give Ampleev, his chess partner, a ride to the river to fish. We attached one of our empty sleds to Tolya's green snowmobile and moved it a few houses down to idle in front of Ampleev's cabin. He soon emerged in a massive fur coat carrying an ice pole and a wooden fishing box that would double as a stool for sitting on the ice. He stretched out on the sled as though reclining on a daybed, joined by his old dog, a Laika, who curled up against him and looked at me. Both were too old to hunt, but they could still fish.

"Fiishhhowwwl!" Ampleev said to me in English, grinning, and we were off.

Tolya drove the sled where the old man commanded, cutting the engine just south of Agzu at a section of river where the ice was pocked with frozen-over auger holes. This was clearly a popular fishing site.

Ampleev and dog eased off the sled while Tolya used our auger to drill clear a selection of the holes. Each sudden and satisfying puncture forced slush and water to upwell and spill onto the surface ice. On this early April day, signs of spring shone through the frozen world around us: thawed patches here and there, the harbingers of violent change soon coming. This was my first time on the Samarga proper, and I felt a certain amount of trepidation and awe. The stories I'd heard of the river gave it legendary dimension: the Samarga brought Agzu life, but it was also an unforgiving, jealous force that battered, maimed, and even killed anyone cavalier enough to let their attention drift while within its influence.

Tolya unhooked the sled and told me he was going back upriver to look for owls, then suddenly seemed to realize he had no plan for me.

"Why don't you, uh, check out all these patches of open water for owl tracks," he said, waving his ice pole vaguely and in a wide arc. "I'll be back in an hour or so."

He handed me the pole and told me to use it liberally.

"Whack at the ice, and if it sounds hollow or the pole pokes through, don't walk there."

He departed in a cloud of exhaust and roar of engine clatter.

Ampleev removed a short fishing pole and a filthy dirt-and-grease-stained jar packed with frozen salmon roe from his fishing box, which he closed to use as a seat. The old man dipped his hand into one of the ice holes to massage some of the dull orange orbs and soften them in the water. He baited his hook with an egg and dropped his line out of sight into the Samarga. I pointed to the open water that Tolya suggested I examine and asked Ampleev if the ice around it was safe. He shrugged.

"This time of year, no ice is really safe."

He turned his attention back to the hole, gently flicking his wrist so the hook and its bait danced in the half-light below. The Laika wandered arthritically.

I inched across the ice, smacking it soundly as I went, as though afraid to spring some hidden trap. I made sure to keep a wide berth of any sections of open water, using my binoculars instead to scan their snowy fringes for fish owl tracks. I didn't find a thing. I walked slowly, perhaps a kilometer or so downriver, moving from open patch to open patch before hearing the snowmobile return about ninety minutes later. When I arrived back up at the fishing spot, I saw that Tolya had picked up Shurik, and both had joined Ampleev on the ice, where their twitching rods pulled masu salmon and Arctic grayling from the hidden waters.

As they fished, Shurik told me he was from the same small agricultural town as Surmach—a place called Gaivoron—just a handful of kilometers from the edge of Lake Khanka in western Primorye. Villages such as Gaivoron were economically depressed, with few jobs and considerable poverty, which resulted in a high prevalence of alcohol abuse, poor health, and early death. Surmach had rescued Shurik from this fate by taking the village boy under his wing: he taught Shurik how to use mist nets to band and release birds (or prepare skins for museum collections) and how to properly collect tissue and blood samples from them. Shurik had no formal education, but his bird skins were exquisitely prepared, he took careful field notes, and he was an expert at looking for fish owls. His ability to climb towering and rotting old-growth tree trunks to examine cavities for fish owl nests—which he felt most comfortable doing in his socks—was a true asset to the team.

We lingered at the fishing hole until nightfall, hoping to hear some owls. I kept my eyes on the tree line, eager to discern movement among the branches. My ears pricked at any distant sound. But I didn't really even know what a fish owl sounded like. Sure, I'd studied the sonograms in Pukinskiy's papers from the 1970s and heard Surmach and Avdeyuk mimic the territorial call of a fish owl, but I had no way of knowing how true those sounds were to real life.

Fish owl pairs vocalize in duets. This is an uncommon attribute recognized in less than 4 percent of bird species globally, most of which are in the tropics. The male usually initiates a fish owl duet, filling an air sac in his throat until it's swollen like some monstrous, feathered bullfrog. He holds that position, the white patch of his throat now a conspicuous orb contrasting against the browns of his body and the grays of the gathering dusk, a signal to his mate that the vocalization is impending. After a moment he exhales a short and wheezy hoot—the sound of someone having the breath knocked out of him—and she answers immediately with one of her own, but deeper in tone. This is unusual among owl species, where females usually have the higher voice. The male then pushes out a longer, slightly higher hoot, which the female also responds to. This four-note call-and-response is over in three seconds, and they repeat the duet at regular intervals for anywhere from one minute to two hours. It is so synchronized that many people, hearing a fish owl pair vocalize, assume it is one bird.

But we heard no such thing that night. We returned to Agzu after dark, chilly and disappointed, where we cleaned and fried our catch and shared our table with whoever stopped by. My companions shrugged off the frustrations of the day, quickly shifting focus to food and drink, and I realized that for Sergey, Shurik, and Tolya this was just a job. Some people work construction, others develop software. These guys were professional field assistants, pursuing whichever species Surmach found money to study. Fish owls, for them, were just another bird. I did not judge them for this, but for me the owls meant much more. My academic career and perhaps the conservation of this endangered species depended on what we found and how we applied this information. It was up to me—and Surmach—to parse out the data we collected and make sense of it. And from my perspective it was not starting well. I went to bed worried about our lack of progress and the steadily melting river ice.

FOR MY NEXT TRIP to the forest, the following day, I was paired with Sergey. We were to search for fish owls only slightly farther south than where I had been the day before, and Sergey was shooting for an early afternoon departure from the village. This would give us a few hours to look for evidence of fish owls before focusing on listening for vocalizations at dusk. Before we left, Sergey wanted to review plans for our upcoming trip downriver and to make sure we had enough chopped firewood for the remainder of our stay in Agzu.

Late in the morning, I was alone in the kitchen with a cup of black tea, examining maps while Sergey chopped wood outside. Suddenly an absolute bear of a fellow burst through the door of the hut and strode up to the table. The man was massive and hairy. He wore a thick coat of tanned hide, insulated with felt and possibly of his own construction. The left sleeve dangled empty. I assumed that this was Volodya Loboda, the only one-armed hunter in town. He was extolled by the locals as one of the best shots in Agzu, despite the hunting mishap that left him maimed.

The huge man sat down, unceremoniously pulled two half-liter cans of beer from his coat pockets, and plunked them on the table. The cans looked warm.

"So," Volodya began, meeting my eyes for the first time, "you hunt."

This was said more as a statement of fact than a question. Volodya looked at me as if anticipating the kind of response that one hunter might give another: what I liked to hunt, where I hunted, what type of rifle I used. Or so I assumed, because I am not a hunter, and I told him so. He shifted weight on his stool and rested his stump on the table, not taking his eyes off me. I could tell that his arm was gone below the elbow.

"Then, you fish."

Also a statement, but said with less certainty. I replied somewhat apologetically in the negative. He broke eye contact and abruptly stood up.

"Then what the hell are you doing in Agzu?" he growled.

Although finally a question, this one was clearly rhetorical. He returned his two cans of still-unopened beer to his coat pockets and left without another word.

Loboda's dismissal stung. In one sense he was correct: the Samarga was a deadly serious place; the wildness here and his lost arm were evidence of that. But on the other hand, my purpose in Agzu—to learn what I could about fish owls to help keep this place as pristine as possible—would ensure that Loboda and those like him would always have deer to hunt and fish to catch.

After lunch, Sergey and I packed snacks of hard candy and sausage and set out for the river in the early afternoon. Sergey slowed the snowmobile to an idle on the edge of Agzu, in front of a hut unfamiliar to me. There was a man inside, standing at the door, waving at us frantically through the small glass pane. He looked panicked, his eyes wide, and he was motioning for us to approach.

"Stay here," said Sergey.

He dismounted and entered the yard through a gate, then

followed a wooden plankway to the porch. The man inside was pointing down at something and yelling, and I then noticed the padlock hanging outside on the door, unlocked but in place and thus preventing the door from being opened from the inside. Sergey stood there, staring, as the trapped man continued to implore and point. Something in what he was shouting didn't sit well with Sergey, because he hesitated before lifting the lock free and turning back toward the snowmobile. The man exploded out like a long-caged beast. The jerky, frenzied motions of his dash past Sergey, through the yard, and into the street indicated a mind too hysterical for any coordination.

I looked back at the door still ajar and saw a young boy standing in the dark space within. I'd guess he was about six years old. I pointed him out to Sergey, who whipped around and cursed.

"His old lady locked him in so he wouldn't go out drinking," Sergey explained. "He didn't say there was a child . . ."

The boy peered into the cold in the direction his father had fled, now out of sight, then reached up and quietly pulled the door closed.

4

The Quiet Violence of This Place

WE EASED OUT OF THE VILLAGE, down a gentle bank, and onto a frozen tributary that took us past columns of gangly willows to the river, just as a crowded side street would lead to a main thoroughfare. In a matter of weeks this would all change: ice breakup was coming. Since the Samarga River was the sole route between Agzu and the village of Samarga, the dangerous conditions of breakup tethered the villagers to Agzu. This was an annual, involuntary exile that lasted until the spring floods washed the last ice into the Strait of Tartary. Breakup gave these hunters and fishermen time to retire their snowmobiles, pack away their ice augers, and ensure their boats were in working order.

Sergey followed the beaten snowmobile trail down the middle of the frozen waterway, knowing that if others had traveled before us, the ice would likely not yield. We passed the spot where the old man had fished the day before, then curved a sharp bend around a mountain spur—I recalled this long, rocky, fingerlike protrusion from the helicopter flight in—and the valley widened considerably once past it. Here, the Sokhatka ("Little Moose") River joined the Samarga, and forests of conifer and broadleaf trees, some of them quite large, were intersected by mingling channels of the two rivers. Though I did not recognize it yet due to inexperience, this was perfect fish owl habitat.

Fish owls must choose their territories carefully: a perfect stretch of river for fishing in summer might be a block of solid ice in winter, so they need to find channels with upwelling spring water or natural hot springs that increase the water temperature enough to keep a vital patch reliably ice free year-round. This is a resource that fish owl pairs tie themselves to and defend from other fish owls.

Sergey and Shurik had been here the day before, and although they had found no evidence of fish owls, Sergey thought it was promising enough for further examination. He wanted to explore the Sokhatka a little more, then listen for owl vocalizations at dusk. We stopped the snowmobile and strapped on our skis. These were Russian hunter skis—short things about a meter and a half long and twenty centimeters wide, and functionally similar to snowshoes. The point is more to shuffle along the surface than to pick up any speed, and their simple bindings, nothing more than a loop of fabric to kick a foot into, allowed for limited maneuverability. Hunters traditionally secured strips of red deer hide to the undersides of their skis for increased traction, but the skis we used had light, synthetic ski skins I'd brought with me from Minnesota.

I was awkward on the hunter skis in the meter-deep snow and still new to searching for fish owls, so I shadowed Sergey as he moved deftly among the trees. We wandered the forest in a wide, meandering circle that led us away from, then back toward, the Samarga. It was a beautiful afternoon, but my spirits were diminished by the lack of fish owl sign. Sergey had seemed sure we would find something here. Back again where the Sokhatka's channels merged with the Samarga, we moved along a low rise between two barely frozen river channels. I happened upon the weathered remains of a small songbird nest from last season, deep in the protective branches of a now bare shrub, and I leaned in for a closer inspection. The cup of grass and mud was carefully lined with soft feathers the songbird had found somewhere to insulate the nest. I removed one, a breast feather weathered with time and exposure: large and certainly from a raptor and possibly an owl. I showed it to Sergey, who smiled gold.

"It's from a fish owl!" he said, holding the prize aloft so the afternoon light shone through it. "I knew they were here!" The feather, half the length of his hand, was old and dirty: debris clung to it and the vane was broken. But it was important evidence.

We inspected the nest more closely. It held multiple fish owl feathers, likely found somewhere close, as songbirds typically collect construction materials near their nests. With renewed encouragement we decided to split up to listen for owls. Dusk was about an hour off and Sergey wanted to listen downstream, from the far side of the river valley, in order to maximize the coverage of our survey. He would follow the river another two to three kilometers south, then collect me on the way back. The sound of his receding snowmobile carried far in the clear winter air, and I could hear the high whir of its engine long after it was out of sight.

A light wind moved through the treetops, rattling the bare canopies of aspen, birch, elm, and poplar and occasionally gathering strength and dropping to gust brashly just above the frozen river. I listened under the sound of the wind for the distinctive call of the fish owl. Fish owls hoot at frequencies in the low-two-hundred-hertz range, in the same ballpark as a great gray owl and twice as low as a great horned owl. In fact, the frequency is so low that the sound can be difficult to capture well with a microphone. On the tapes I'd later make, the owls always sounded far away, muffled, lost, even if they were close by. The low frequency of the vocalizations served a purpose: it ensured that sound passed cleanly through dense forest and could be heard some distance away, up to several kilometers. This was especially true in winter and early spring, when there was little tree cover and the crisp air facilitated movement of sound waves.

The duet is both a territorial call and a pair bond affirmation. The frequency of duets follows an annual cycle, with the most active vocalizations occurring in February during the breeding period. Duet bouts can be long during this time, lasting for hours, and can be heard throughout the night. Once a female is incubating eggs, however, in March, these calls are most often heard only at dusk, perhaps because the birds are reluctant to advertise their nest location. Duets increase again as their young hatch and fledge but, by summer, begin to diminish in frequency again until the next breeding season.

I had some concern that the strengthening wind might cut through my insulation as I waited, still and exposed. I spotted a massive log half-buried in snow about a hundred meters away, a large tree that had been uprooted in some storm and carried there by flood. I used my feet to dig out and pound down a shallow depression in the snow by the tree's base and crouched there to take shelter from the wind, largely concealed by roots and shadow.

About a half hour later, focused on the joy and crunch of my last hard candies, I did not hear the roe deer approaching. It burst into view not more than fifty meters off, finding purchase on the hard crust of river ice and bounding upriver, a hunting dog at its heels. The gasping deer approached a section of deep, open river, about three meters wide and fifteen meters long, and without pausing plowed into the water. Perhaps it had intended to jump clear across but too late realized it lacked the strength to do so. The dog, a Laika, stopped short and bayed with exposed teeth. I was frozen in place. From my low vantage point among the roots, I could see only the deer's head—snout held high and nostrils flared—bobbing above the clean line of the river surface. The deer pushed briefly against the flow and then succumbed to it, drifting like a rudderless boat, then disappearing from view at the downstream lip of ice. I stood up for a better view and saw only the open wound of quiet, rushing water. I envisioned the deer in the darkness beneath the ice, water likely filling its lungs, another of the Samarga's victims floating serenely seaward, the winter and village dogs now irrelevant. The Laika noticed my movement and pivoted toward me with ears erect and a quivering, questioning muzzle. It dismissed me as an unknown human, then refocused its attention on the exposed river, sniffing at it before trotting back downstream.

I returned to my tree hole, stunned by the quiet violence of this place. Primeval dichotomies still outlined existence on the Samarga: hungry or satiated, frozen or flowing, living or dead. A slight deviation could tip the scales from one state of being to the other. A villager might drown because he went fishing in the wrong spot. A deer evaded capture by a predator only to find death anyway because of a misstep. The line between life and death here could be measured in the thickness of river ice.

A muted tremor in the air pulled me from my thoughts. I sat up and took off my hat to expose my ears. After a protracted silence I heard the sound again: a distant, muffled quiver. But was it a fish owl? It must have been quite far up the Sokhatka River valley, and I could really hear only one note, maybe two, not the four I was expecting. I had a sense of what a fish owl sounded like only from Sergey's and Surmach's coarse mimicries, and it was hard to evaluate the quality of their hoots without the real thing to compare it with. What I was hearing now didn't really match. Perhaps this was just a single fish owl—not a pair? Or maybe a Eurasian eagle owl? But those owls had higher voices than what I was hearing and did not duet. The sound repeated every few minutes or so, until the gradual, almost imperceptible transition from day to night was complete. In the dark, the vocalizations ceased.

An undulating, high-pitched whine from downriver told me that Sergey was returning, and I soon saw the snowmobile's single headlight casting its pale beam on the snow.

"Well?" he said triumphantly as I came out to meet him. "Did you hear them?"

I told him that I thought so, but maybe only one bird. He shook his head. "There were two—it was a duet! The female call is even lower than the male's and harder to hear, so maybe you missed it."

Sergey possessed a highly perceptive sense of hearing—he could confidently discriminate far-off duets when all I could make out was the breathy higher voice of the male. Later, even when I was sure there was just one bird, we would sneak closer, and only then could I make out the female as well. Fish owls are nonmigratory, enduring the summer heat and winter frosts in the same places, so if we heard a duet, that meant the pair was resident to that patch of forest. These were long-lived birds— there are records of wild fish owls more than twenty-five years old—so duetting owls were likely to be in the same place year in and year out. If we heard just one bird hooting, however, that might mean it was a bachelor owl looking for a territory or a mate. If we heard one today, it did not mean it would be there tomorrow, much less the next few years. We needed resident pairs for our study population: birds we could track.

I told Sergey about the deer and the Laika.

He spat and shook his head incredulously. "I passed that dog! I met its owner fishing downriver. He said his team of dogs had killed five roe deer and three red deer today alone! He complained that rich city folk have been flying into Agzu all winter and shooting the deer; that's why the woods were empty. Meanwhile, his unattended dog was drowning one!"

We rode back to Agzu in silence.

THAT EVENING, we had a few guests but not as many as the previous nights. Among them was Lësha, the bespectacled hunter who was once again visibly shaken to learn that I was an American, just as he had been two nights prior. He had forgotten that we'd already had the conversation—and then confided that he had been drunk for ten to twelve days.

"That's what he said two days ago," I whispered to one of the village leaders, an unshaven Russian in fatigues.

He laughed. "Lësha's been saying 'ten to twelve days' for a week! Hard to say how long he's really been drinking."

I stepped outside for some fresh air. The unshaven village leader came out with me and lit a cigarette. He stood next to me, almost shoulder to shoulder, on the narrow path leading to the outhouse, swaying almost imperceptibly in the dark from the vodka and the uneven snow underfoot. He spoke about his years in Agzu: how he came to this wild place as a young man and never left, how he could not imagine life elsewhere. Stars were strewn across the clear sky, and howls of village dogs sounded in waves above the constant rumble of a nearby diesel generator.

As the man spoke, I heard a curious soft sound and saw with some disbelief that he had unbuttoned his fly and urinated not more than a pace or two away from me, one hand on his hip and the other holding his cigarette and scratching his neck, all the while continuing to describe his love for the Samarga.

5

Down the River

THE TEAM had been working out of Agzu for nearly two weeks, both while waiting for my helicopter to arrive and then in my company. There was more we could do here, but citing satisfaction with the local search, a melting river, and his overtaxed liver, Sergey gave the call to pull up stakes. Before I joined them, the team had met and arm-wrestled a hunter named Chepelev in the forest upriver, who had invited us to work out of his cabin some forty kilometers south of Agzu, a place called Vosnesenovka. We'd relocate there, where Sergey thought the atmosphere would be more peaceful. It was only my fifth day in Agzu, and I would have benefited from more time on the Sokhatka River looking for the nest tree of the fish owls we knew were there. But just because the birds were residents of a certain territory was no guarantee of nesting. This is because unlike most birds, fish owls in Russia typically attempt to breed only once every two years and typically raise only one chick, more rarely two. In Japan, just across the sea, fish owls tend to breed every year and usually have two chicks.

The reasons for the discrepancy in breeding output remain unknown, but I now believe it has to do with how many fish are in the rivers for the owls to catch. In Japan, where fish owl extinction was narrowly avoided by concerted government intervention and significant financial investment, nearly a quarter of the fish owl population is artificially fed in stocked ponds. This might mean that the Japanese birds are better fed and thus in better physical condition to reproduce. In Russia, a pair concentrates on a single chick that often stays with its parents for fourteen to eighteen months after hatching—an astonishingly long period for any bird species—before it leaves to find its own territory. In contrast, a young great horned owl of North America, a dwarf at only a third the weight of an adult fish owl, seeks its own territory after only four to eight months.

But simply confirming the existence of a pair in the area was enough for the purposes of this expedition, which was designed only to identify key locations along the Samarga River where fish owls were found to prevent logging there. I could understand Sergey's sense of urgency: I had been in Agzu for only a few days, but the others had been weathering local hospitality for nearly two weeks. We would be heading south as soon as the sleds were ready.

It took us several hours to prepare. Tolya carefully packaged all of our food in a giant watertight barrel. Shurik filled the snowmobile tanks with gasoline from our diminishing supply. Sergey consulted with some locals about the route. We piled the majority of the weight on the wooden, yellow-painted sled that Sergey had constructed in his garage in Dalnegorsk, and we hitched it to the black Yamaha, which was the larger of the two machines we had at our disposal. The smaller, green Yamaha was recreational, designed for speed, and pulled an aluminum sled with some of our lighter gear. We boxed and wrapped our supplies, covering them in several concentric layers of blue tarp before cinching everything down tightly on the sleds with rope to keep anything from flying off and to keep any water out.

Tolya rode alone, helming the spry green snowmobile, while I straddled the long bench of the black Yamaha behind Sergey. Shurik assumed a dog-musher stance on the back rails of the yellow sled we towed. Our positioning was purposeful: if we started to flounder in deep snow, Shurik and I could pop off and push to keep the Yamaha's momentum going. We led and Tolya followed.

We departed Agzu without fanfare. A few locals came out to wish us well, including the unshaven Russian and Loboda, the one-armed hunter. However, Ampleev and most of the faces I'd seen around the table the previous few nights were absent.

As our caravan sped south, I recognized the forests we had surveyed in the days before; we passed the spot where Ampleev had fished, then where I had dug a hole to hide from the wind and where the deer drowned. A little farther south, Sergey slowed the snowmobile and leaned back, his eyes shielded like mine by ski goggles and a hood cinched tight around his head. The ice surface was uneven here, with a small disk from some disturbance where the ice had ruptured and then refrozen.

"This is where that guy went through," he yelled so Shurik could hear in the back, "the one they told you about in Agzu. This is the spot."

We continued on.

Every so often someone would point a gloved hand, and we'd all look to see deer after deer, some red but mostly roe, resting on the thawed southern banks or chewing at the newly exposed vegetation. There were so many deer that eventually we stopped pointing and passed them without announcement. These were gaunt creatures with hides of matted fur pulled tight around arching ribs. Exhausted from the punishing winter, the deer did not flee—some did not even stand—and they paid only cursory attention to the thunderous, curious spectacle we made. These animals were on the tail end of a season's long decline, and as the days grew warmer and the nights shorter, their perseverance would reward them with snowmelt and deliverance into spring. God forbid some Laikas strayed this far south, I thought. It would be a massacre.

Sergey suddenly slowed the machine and stood, looking ahead intently. Tolya pulled up behind. About fifty meters up we could see open water—a light blue snake of slush that contrasted sharply against the surrounding whiteness of solid ice. The slush meandered narrowly before slowly spreading to envelop the entire river from bank to bank for perhaps five hundred meters, beyond which we could again see solid ice.

"Naled," said Sergey in assessment, and Shurik and Tolya nodded their agreement. I did not know what a naled was, but I certainly did not think the best plan forward was to pick up steam and head straight into it, which was exactly what we did, with Tolya lingering behind to watch and wait his turn.

A naled, literally meaning "on the ice," is a phenomenon common to the rivers here in late winter and early spring. In the awkward between-season months of March and April, the combination of warm days and subzero nights turns surface water into a slushy mass known as "frazil ice." This dense ice sinks, causing blockages downstream that dam the river's flow. These stoppages cause pressure to build and force the slushy water–frazil ice mixture out of any fissure in the surface ice, where it flows atop uninhibited. The trouble with any naled is that without close inspection, there is no way of knowing how deep the soupy mush is. In fact, instead of solid ice underneath, a naled could be hiding free-flowing water. If the latter case was true, we were essentially careening to an abrupt end to the expedition: we'd never get the snowmobile out if the naled was concealing a deep, open river.

At the time I didn't know any of this, only that we were barreling toward what seemed to be cloudy water, pulling a heavy anchor of a sled. I suppose Sergey and the others assumed this naled was only a few centimeters deep and we would continue largely unfettered, but when we slammed into the water and immediately lost all momentum, we discovered that it was, in fact, meter-deep slush. The snowmobile listed in the water, belching black exhaust, while the sled sank into the icy bog and sat half-submerged, suspended in the mire and immobile. We moved quickly to unhitch the sled; I followed Shurik's lead, and when he dropped into the thick soup of the naled so did I, my feet finding the still-frozen ice hidden underneath. The slush was above my hip waders, and I could feel the water saturating my pants and quickly soaking through my socks. We threw our weight behind Sergey, engine straining, to push the snowmobile in a tight arc back to the solid ice only a few meters away. We then wheeled the suspended sled around and rehitched it to the snowmobile. With solid ice underneath it, the Yamaha had the traction to pull the sled free.

Too frantic from the flurry of sudden activity, I had not registered the cold until then. I was soaking from the waist down. Tolya, who had remained dry during this adventure, started a fire on the bank as Shurik and I put on fresh clothing and began drying our soaked pants and boots. I examined our situation. As little as a few days ago, this had all likely been solid ice, but with the warmer days of early April contributing to ice melt, the river was no longer a viable route forward, at least not here. We had barely tested the naled: from what we could see, there was half a kilometer of it to go.

Shurik scouted downriver, following the riverbank, and returned to say the naled eventually disappeared. The only realistic course of action was to cut a trail through the forest and bypass it altogether. The forest was fairly open here, consisting mostly of willow, so we had cause for optimism. As our boots dried Shurik unpacked the chain saw, then he and I went ahead to clear a trail while Sergey and Tolya followed on the snowmobiles. We moved slowly, cutting trees where necessary, and made it back to the solid river ice downstream.

Some fifteen kilometers after we returned to the ice, the Samarga transitioned from one side of the valley to the other, and we followed it briefly east past branching tributaries before reaching a cliff base, which forced the river to curve south again. Past the bend, in a clearing opposite a towering slope of the Sikhote-Alin, I could see two wooden structures high on the Samarga's west bank. This must be Vosnesenovka.

6

Chepelev

I WAS ASTONISHED by what I saw as we approached Vosnesenovka. The closest structure was likely a *banya*—a Russian
sauna—but it was the second building, offset some fifty meters from the bank, that caught my attention. Still under construction, the house rose two stories high, extremely rare for the
wilderness here. It was a mansion of a cabin, with walls of carefully planed logs, squared and butt ended, under a gabled roof. It
was flanked by green-painted shed roofs on the north and south
sides that sloped down to lead rain or snow away from the building; a storage room to the north that shared a wall with the
cabin; and a porch and the cabin's entrance to the south. The
hunting cabins I was accustomed to seeing in Russia were hap-
hazard one-story, one-room amalgamations of whatever materials could be scraped together in a pinch. But here, someone had
put considerable time, money, and thought into this structure.

The riverbank directly in front of the cabin, cut sheer by the
rasp of rushing water, was too tall and steep to mount by snow-

mobile. We left our convoy on the river ice and went back for our belongings after greeting Chepelev, our host, the man that Sergey and Shurik had arm-wrestled some weeks earlier at a cabin north of Agzu. Though the ice had melted along the river edge and water ran freely, the ice in the center was still thick, and we had no worries parking there.

We ascended a drooping tongue of compacted snow that joined land and river like a drawbridge above a moat of open Samarga water. This ice bridge likely formed when, after some early snowfall, Chepelev descended a snowdrift to the river, then followed that same path again and again all season. This packed and condensed the slender track so that now, on the cusp of spring, all the softer snow around it had melted and fallen; only this precarious span of ice remained. The bridge was intimidating, steep, and narrow, and after some hesitancy we climbed it one at a time. The river under the ice bridge was only about waist deep, I could see the pebbly substrate beneath, but it surged past with a turbulent ferocity. Given the high bank on one side and the thick ice rim on the other, it would be difficult to climb out of the river if the ice bridge failed or one of us lost his balance.

Up on land, I walked the fifty-odd meters to the house and onto the porch past neatly stacked supplies. The cabin was a work in progress inside as well. To my immediate right past the foyer was a small bathroom with a door not yet hung and a toilet still wrapped in protective packaging. Out of all the surprises I would encounter in this place, and there were many still to come, it was perhaps the toilet that amazed me the most. Even houses in Terney—the county seat—didn't have toilets. Everyone used outhouses. In fact, this was possibly the only toilet within a several-hundred-kilometer radius, and to find it in a hermit's cabin on the edge of the Samarga River was most unexpected. The hall opened past the bathroom to a modest kitchen. Pots, mugs, and a meat grinder hung on nails pounded into planed log walls, with socks and boots crowding any free space by the woodstove to dry. A large window dominated the east wall, revealing the river, our snowmobiles, and the mountains beyond. A wide archway joined the kitchen to a living room that lacked any furniture but had several icons of Russian Orthodox saints on the wall and a fireplace in the corner—another rarity in a land where most preferred the heat efficiency of a woodstove. A steep staircase rose to the second floor.

Viktor Chepelev was in the kitchen, hunched on a low stool by the stove with his back to me, where he skinned and quartered potatoes with a hunting knife. Wearing nothing but long-john bottoms and slippers, he was stocky yet lean, with ropy muscles under coarse skin and wild, shoulder-length hair. It was hard to say how old he was—perhaps in his late fifties? As he turned, I noted a striking resemblance to the musician Neil Young.

"So you're the American," he said, glancing up from the pile of potatoes, and I nodded.

I heard reluctant acceptance in his voice. Chepelev mistrusted me, and it would take days to understand why.

We hauled perishables and personal items up the ice bridge, leaving behind anything not immediately needed: our skis, the chain saw, an ice auger, and gasoline. Chepelev finished with the potatoes and added them to a pot of boiling water. He then stood outside in his long johns, watching us teeter up the ice bridge laden with backpacks and clutching cardboard boxes that had become soft with travel and threatened to rupture.

Once inside, there was a flurry of activity as food was unpacked and items misplaced during our hasty exit from Agzu were looked for and found. I asked Chepelev if I could tour the upstairs and he nodded his consent. I was unprepared for the curious sight that awaited me. The second floor was a single room, sparsely furnished as below but dominated by a large, four-sided plywood pyramid standing askew in its center. One of its sides had a hinged door, and I approached to peer inside. Bedding. Chepelev slept inside a pyramid on the second floor of his cabin. There was a metal mug holding a liquid next to his pillow, and I tentatively picked it up and sniffed, relieved to conclude it was water. For some reason I had feared urine. I walked back downstairs.

Everyone was in the kitchen, working on the final stages of dinner preparation; Chepelev was stirring the stew of potatoes and boar meat and listening to news about Agzu from Sergey, who smoked by the stove. Tolya was digging out our plates and spoons from the boxes we'd brought in, and Shurik was cutting some fresh bread we had acquired in Agzu. I asked Chepelev about the pyramid, why he slept in it.

"Uh, energy?" he responded, stupefied, looking at the others as if I were crazy. Pyramid power, a pseudoscience with some popularity in western Russia that promised enhancement of everything from the taste of food to physical well-being, had apparently reached the forests of the Russian Far East.

As Chepelev ladled out stew to our eager bowls, Tolya emerged from the foyer and put two bottles of vodka on the table. Sergey clenched his jaw; Shurik licked his lips. After dinner, Chepelev, Sergey, and Shurik drank vodka and arm-wrestled, while Tolya and I laid out our sleeping pads in a long row in the living room.

AFTER A BREAKFAST OF MILLET GRUEL and instant coffee, I hurriedly put on my boots and hat and headed for the outhouse in the early light of the morning, following a short trail that forked just shy of the banya. I saw movement on the hill across the river and paused to watch the dark shape of a wild boar ambling cross-slope through the lines of trees, highlighted against the back-drop of snow. Wild boar have short legs that carry heavy bodies and cannot hope to posthole in the snow as deer might—this beast plowed through it like an icebreaker tearing a line across a fro-zen ocean.

On my way back to the cabin I noticed a small shed behind it and, compelled by the unexpected rewards behind so many of the doors here, stopped to investigate. This one did not disap-point. Inside hung row after row of . . . something, but I was not sure what. There were several dozen brownish-tan things, each about twenty centimeters long and skinny like dehydrated fin-gers, carefully hung to dry by a short length of string. I had no idea what they were or why he needed so many.

Later that morning, we set out as before. We descended the ice bridge, unhooked the sleds, and got underway on the unen-cumbered snowmobiles. Given that we had left Agzu somewhat prematurely, Sergey and I backtracked north to examine a net-work of tributaries near where the Zaami River merged with the Samarga some five kilometers from Vosnesenovka. Tolya and Shurik remained closer to our base. As we walked through the forest, I asked Sergey if he knew anything about Chepelev's background and how he could have financed his cabin. His one-word response made everything much clearer:

"Ratimir."

This was one of the biggest meat distributors in the province. As Sergey explained, the land where Chepelev lived on the Sa-marga was leased to Aleksandr Trush—a sausage magnate and one of Ratimir's founders—and Chepelev was the caretaker of this hunting lease. The sausage magnate also owned a helicopter—one Trush would crash and die in two years later—which explained how Chepelev could transport luxuries such as a toilet and a gas stove to that remote location. The Ratimir revelation also explained the mystery sticks hanging in the shed, which Sergey had noticed as well.

"Red deer penises," he said. "Those are just evidence of the males—I can't imagine how many they've actually killed . . ."

"But what does he do with them?"

"I asked him about that," said Sergey. "Chepelev soaks them in alcohol, and he drinks the concoction for virility."

We returned to Vosnesenovka in the late afternoon, frustrated. We hadn't located any fish owl sign. Was I gaining any useful knowledge on this expedition? Or was I just burning grant money while the team choked down ethanol? Would this experience help me find fish owls for my study population? My plan for a Ph.D. project, catching a bunch of fish owls, seemed unrealistic at this point, given that I had not even seen one on this trip. And my proposition to develop a fish owl conservation plan seemed arrogant. I was heartened, however, when Tolya and Shurik returned with news of some old fish owl tracks along a tributary north of Vosnesenovka. I would explore the area more with Tolya the following day to get a better sense of the types of places where fish owls hunted.

Chepelev announced that the banya was warming up. While Tolya abstained, the rest of us took full advantage of the opportunity to steam and bathe. There are two reliable ways to get a Russian man to respect you: the first is to consume voluminous amounts of vodka and bond over the honesty exposed by the subsequent drunkenness, and the other is to go toe-to-toe in a banya. I had long ago stopped trying to keep pace with Russian men and their drinking, but in those days, I could steam with the best.

We stripped, then ducked into the low, narrow steam room,

crowding onto the short bench. The only light inside was an uneven glow escaping the edges of the stove door and reflecting off the gold in the grimacing mouths of my companions. After allowing a brief moment of acclimation, Chepelev leaned over, scooped up a ladleful of water richly tinted from soaking oak leaves, and cast it onto the rocks that lined the stove. The resultant hiss warned of an impending wave of intense heat: one that billowed through the room, then settled on us heavy and still, thick with the earthy aroma of oak. Even the opening salvo was too much for Shurik, who disappeared with a curse and closed the door behind him. Then another ladle of water, followed by another, and another. We sat in silence: breathing, anticipating, relaxing, enduring.

Chepelev eyed me carefully throughout the experience; he appeared to expect me to balk at the intense heat or somehow mishandle the ritual. As I emerged naked and steaming onto the banya's icy porch, I could sense him still watching me, perhaps surprised that I had made it that far without complaint or capitulation. Had I been alone, at this point I probably would have stood silently enjoying the quiet of the night and my temporary imperviousness to the deep cold, but instead I scooped up handfuls of snow and rubbed them vigorously on my face, neck, and chest. When I finished, Chepelev was nodding his approval. "A strange American you are," he said, "one who knows how to banya."

We repeated the cycle of concentrated steam and short breaks for more than an hour, before finally washing and heading back to the cabin for some dinner and sleep. Tomorrow I'd see my first fish owl tracks.

7

Here Comes the Water

ARLY THE NEXT MORNING, I watched the sunrise pour gold onto the Sikhote-Alin mountains. Tolya was anxious to look for more owl sign, and I was eager to see real fish owl tracks—all I knew was that they looked like the letter *K*. I would go with Tolya, while Sergey and Shurik motored south on the black Yamaha toward the abandoned village of Unty. The ice bridge appeared to have lost some of its girth in the past day, but it still bore our weight as we descended. We did not have a long commute—the tributary Tolya led me to was only a kilometer and a half upriver. We parked the snowmobile on the ice of the main channel and shuffled up the snowy fringes of the flowing tributary on skis. The waterway was mostly open: a shallow creek with clear water bubbling over a smooth pebbly bed interspersed with large boulders. Like the riverbanks, these rocks were topped by thick crowns of snow that made them seem much larger than they really were.

Suddenly Tolya stopped short. We were not more than two hundred meters from where we'd started.

"Fresh tracks!" he breathed, jutting his ice pole upriver in excitement.

They were huge—the size of my palm—suggesting that the bird that made these tracks must have been massive. The right foot made an impression like the letter K and the left imprint was its mirror image. It is thought that, like the osprey's, this toe configuration helps a fish owl better grip its squirming aquatic prey. The frost overnight had formed a crust on the deep snow, bearing the owl's weight and yielding just enough to leave clear, crisp indentations on the sparkling surface. The owl had walked with a calm swagger, each toe pad clearly articulated and its two hind talons raking lines in the snow like a spur-heeled cowboy in the rodeo dust. The sun glistened brilliantly off the marks, scars on a field of diamonds. It was beautiful, and I felt almost like a voyeur: the owl had been here in darkness and secret, but the snow left evidence of its path for me to marvel at.

Tolya was ecstatic, smiling and busying himself with his camera before the pristine evidence of our discovery disappeared. He had never seen such perfect tracks. Very soon, perhaps within the hour, they would soften in the sun, and the details would fade.

Fish owls typically hunt alone. Sometimes the pair will hunt near each other, but like people, they have different preferences. One bird might prefer a particular bend in a river, and another might favor a certain riffle. And when the female is on the nest—incubating eggs or warming a young chick—the male fishes for both himself and his mate, bringing her fresh fish or frogs as often as he can.

We followed the tracks upriver, seeing where the owl paused to loom over the water, perhaps waiting for fish, then saw where it must have waded into the shallows. Once in the water, all evidence disappeared. We continued upstream about a kilometer but saw no more tracks, then followed a smaller tributary that led us back to the Samarga, upriver of where we'd left the snowmobile.

Within a few meters of reaching the tributary, we saw enormous prints that moved upriver with patient purpose. They intersected a ski trail, then ascended the bank and continued into the forest. Tiger tracks.

"I was here yesterday evening," whispered Tolya, claiming the human ski tracks as his own. "These tiger tracks were not."

What an enthralling place, I thought, where humans, Amur tigers, and Blakiston's fish owls move past one another in a matter of hours. I wasn't worried about this tiger: I'd been working in their habitat for years and trusted them to be harmless to humans, if respected. Or at least as harmless as a massive carnivore can be. "Siberian" tiger is a misnomer: there are no tigers in Siberia. Rather, since these animals live in the Amur River basin, east of Siberia, the name "Amur" tiger is more accurate.

When we returned to Vosnesenovka later that afternoon, Chepelev was outside chopping wood, wearing his familiar long johns with boots and a light wool shirt. He paused his work to ask of our successes. Tolya proudly described the fish owl tracks, detailing the bird's gait along the waterway, holding his hands palm out with jutting thumbs to explain how he framed some of his shots. Chepelev listened politely but clearly without interest. Then Tolya mentioned the tiger tracks.

"Definitely fresh too," Tolya drawled. "I would have noticed them yesterday for sure."

Chepelev put down his ax.

"Damned tigers," he muttered, and went inside, having forgotten about the woodpile, Tolya, and fish owls.

He emerged again a few moments later, still in his long johns and boots, but also wearing a coat and fur hat and carrying one of his rifles. He leaped onto his tractor, a rusty ancient thing, and started up the engine while eyeing the forest line with loathing. There is a belief shared by some in the Russian Far East that tigers are roaming gluttons, systematically eliminating deer and boar populations with their unappeasable appetites. For a portion of the hunters who rely entirely on the forest for survival, tigers are a menace to be shot on sight. Recent scientific data have demonstrated that Amur tigers usually kill only one animal a week, and since they live at very low densities (occupying massive home ranges between 400 and 1,400 square kilometers in size), they certainly do not have a significant impact on deer or boar populations. The reality is that human overhunting and destruction of habitat are the true culprits behind dipping ungulate numbers. But tigers are easy scapegoats, and it can be difficult to change the hard-set opinions of hard-living people, irrespective of how statistically defensible one's argument might be.

Chepelev guided the tractor onto the rutted path leading north toward the woods, his narrowed eyes peering out from under the fur of his hat, scanning the horizon. He drove with one hand clutching the jerking tractor wheel and the other his rifle. The sight parodied a tiger hunt from imperial India: a royal riding proudly upon an elephant's back in search of his elusive striped prize. Only here it was an eccentric Russian straddling a wheezing tractor in his underwear. Chepelev's steel elephant was not likely the mobile fortress he thought it to be: in one of only a handful of recorded tiger attacks on humans in twentieth-century Russia, a tiger easily pulled a farmer off his tractor and killed him.

Chepelev circled back to Vosnesenovka an hour or so later,

still agitated. He had seen the tracks and concluded the tiger had moved north early that morning, out of reasonable range for his tractor. I hadn't been too worried that he would actually find it: tigers here know to avoid people and are usually caught only when surprised. Chepelev bumping along on an antique tractor would be easy to hear and escape. With luck the predator would steer clear of all humans, but the draw of frail prey lining the river was probably too much for it to resist, bringing it closer and closer to unsympathetic adversaries in Agzu. If seen by a silent hunter, one on foot, the encounter might be fatal. The fact was that tigers did not tend to live long on the Samarga.

It was starting to get dark, and Tolya and I were still excited about the fish owl tracks. We put our skis back on and glided slowly upriver, hoping to hear a call to determine if the territory was occupied by a pair of birds or just one. We were a few hundred meters shy of the tributary by dusk when a massive form dropped from a tree. Despite the failing light, its shape was pronounced against the river's frozen surface near the cliffs opposite the tributary's mouth. I'd seen other owls in shadow before, so I knew immediately that's what this was, only this was much bigger than any other owl species I'd ever seen. It was a fish owl. I found myself holding my breath as this truth washed over me. The bird did not make any unnecessary movements; it floated on extended wings at a descending angle over the water, then disappeared up the tributary where it had hunted the night before. Tolya and I looked at each other, grinning. We'd seen only a profile, but it felt like a victory. Given the location from which the bird had flushed, it had probably been watching us the whole time as we neared. Not wanting to disturb it any further, we cut our approach short and waited a little longer for vocalizations but heard none. We shuffled back downriver to Vosnesenovka and were joined soon after by Sergey and Shurik, who also returned triumphant. They had heard a fish owl duet near Unty. The distance between the bird Tolya and I had seen and the area where the Unty pair vocalized was about four kilometers—not terribly far for an owl to fly—but given that our detections had been nearly simultaneous, we guessed that we'd encountered birds from two different territories, with Vosnesenovka the dividing line between them.

CHEPELEV WAS STILL IRRITABLE, and this lingered into dinner. Perhaps he was already getting tired of our company; four strangers for three days can be a trying experience for someone accustomed to solitude. Toward the end of a second bottle of vodka, he complained of the "homosexual–Jewish conspiracy" in Moscow to erode Russian values in favor of Western ones, slowly and almost imperceptibly through cultural and social subversion. I finally began to understand the source of his icy attitude toward me; his paranoia brought to mind Anthony Burgess's novel *A Clockwork Orange*, in which the postmodern West was corrupt, violent, and influenced by the Soviet Union both in ideology and in language (Burgess's invented language, Nadsat, was English infused with Russian words). But it was the reverse that had proved true: global Soviet influence had waned and English words had become entrenched in the Russia lexicon, with Western ideals permeating Russian culture. Some, like Chepelev, were alarmed and embittered by this.

Shurik changed the subject by asking Chepelev if he ever wished he could share this beautiful place with anyone else. A woman, perhaps.

"I had a woman live here with me for a few months." Chepelev shook his head at the memory. "But I kicked her out. She used way too much water in the banya."

I found it very interesting that the man who consumed red deer penises for virility also shunned companionship, and I saw Sergey's gaze dart to the window as if to measure the few meters of distance from the banya to the Samarga River, the largest source of fresh water in northern Primorye. But he said nothing, and Chepelev continued.

"What do you need a lot of water in the banya for? There's only three important parts that need an occasional rinse anyway." He pantomimed a brisk wash of his groin and each one of his armpits. "Anything else is vanity, pure and simple. So I sent her to the coast when a boat came by."

After Chepelev coursed through the decline of the Russian Man and meandered through feminine vanity, his displeasure settled locally. He was upset that we were only just getting to the Samarga for an endangered species survey. He knew that our goal was to find fish owls to help protect them from logging and described meeting other groups of biologists passing through with the same purpose, some counting salmon and others looking for tigers.

"Where were you five years ago?" he seethed, slapping his palm on the table so hard that the small amount of vodka left in the bottle heaved against the glass. "Where were you last year? When the Samarga really needed you? The logging is already coming. Now, it's too late."

From the other room came sounds of a fish owl calling. Tolya had connected his video camera to the television and was reviewing some of the footage he had shot at a fish owl nest earlier on the expedition, prior to my joining the group in Agzu. Chepelev went to join him. We all followed, sitting shirtless and in silence on the floor in our long johns, watching the grainy, hooting shadows on the small screen. This would be one of our last nights on the banks of the Samarga River.

THE NEXT DAY, Sergey and Shurik wanted to see the fish owl tracks we'd found yesterday, so they went upriver while Tolya and I headed south to search a network of channels for sign of the Unty pair that Sergey and Shurik had heard the night before. We had no success. As we approached Vosnesenovka upon our return, we could see the black Yamaha parked next to the two sleds. Tolya stopped the snowmobile, and we dismounted but then stopped short, staring at the empty space where the ice bridge had been just a few hours ago. For a brief moment I wondered if Sergey and Shurik had gone with it, but then Shurik came out of the cabin, pointing and indicating we should follow their tracks about a hundred meters to the left to detour around the moat and up the bank. We emerged near the banya and followed its trail to the cabin.

Once inside, I saw that Sergey and Shurik were also rattled by the disappearance of the bridge. Shurik laughed it off, but there was concern in his eyes. He told us that he and Sergey had seen multiple ungulates in the forest and had even posed with both a red deer and a roe deer—the animals were simply too exhausted to run off in the deep snow. On the drive back downriver to Vosnesenovka, sheets of ice had cracked and then slid into the Samarga behind their snowmobile.

"I'm actually really surprised you guys are still here," Chepelev observed, sitting by the woodstove and cupping a warm mug of black tea. "If it was me, I would have left two days ago. You might not even make it at this point."

The loss of the ice bridge underscored the fact that we had outstayed not just Chepelev's welcome but winter's as well. We began gathering our things almost immediately, with a plan to gun it for the coast at first light, unsure if the ice downriver would be thick enough to support the weight of our heavy snow-mobiles and sleds. We asked Chepelev what supplies he was short of and replenished what we could from our own stores. We carried everything but our sleeping bags and pads down to the sleds. The detour around the moat made the task take four times as long. Eventually, Tolya and Shurik simply stood by the sleds while Sergey and I tossed what we could across the moat for them to pack. Our singular focus was to reach the village of Samarga: we could not risk being stranded on the river between seasons. Only when we reached the safety of the coast could we consider resuming the fish owl surveys.

8

Riding the Last Ice to the Coast

T HE SUN that crested the spine of mountains to the east found us on the ice with snowmobiles idling. It was April 7, and a deep frost overnight held a thin promise of ice integrity for the morning. Chepelev had provided us with a satiating breakfast of rice topped with sautéed onions and cubed deer meat, which we washed down with instant coffee mixed with the last of our *sgushonka*, the sweetened, condensed milk sold in squat blue cans and consumed by Russians with un-abashed enthusiasm. Perhaps knowing we would never be back that way, given the remoteness of the site, Chepelev said his door was always open to us. After parting words and firm hand-shakes, he wished us luck. Tolya was once again piloting the green snowmobile. Shurik straddled the bench behind Sergey on the big Yamaha. I assumed the standing position on the wide tracks of the yellow sled hitched to them and turned to watch Vosnesenovka disappear behind us.

The route ahead seemed fairly straightforward, but given the collapsed ice bridge and the seasonal naleds, we didn't know how far we'd make it before encountering an obstacle. Almost immediately after leaving Vosnesenovka, we faced a naled. This was a stretch of river Tolya and I had easily crossed not twelve hours before, but in that time a thirty-meter band of calf-deep slush had formed to block our path. Sergey investigated on foot and decided that gumption and brute force might be enough to push through to the other side, and we sped at it full bore with shoulders hunched and jaws clenched.

"Here comes the water!" Sergey screamed over the shrieking snowmobile.

I tightened my grip on the sled just as we plowed into the naled. The snowmobile's back track ground into the soupy mess, propelling a wall of heavy slush that hit me in the face and chest like an open-handed slap. I wondered if this was why Shurik had been so eager to cede his place on the sled to me—he must have been similarly soaked the last time we encountered a naled, but I had been too frantic then to notice.

"Push!" bellowed Sergey, not looking back and pressuring the engine.

Shurik and I leaped off and sank into the icy slush. I gripped the back of the sled and heaved forward, once again ignoring the ice and water that found the opening in my hip waders and slowly saturated my pants, then my socks. Sergey barked commands like a coxswain and slid off the bench to help push, all the while maintaining his grip on the throttle. Our momentum propelled us to the far side of the naled, where, finding hard ice underneath, the spinning rubber track gripped the surface and pulled us clear. I looked back to see Tolya and his lighter load churn through the naled with only marginal difficulty. We didn't stop to change clothes or dry off, even though water was pressing the wool of my socks tight to my feet. We were worried about more naleds ahead—a worry soon to be validated—and did not have the luxury of time for a break. From here the Samarga River flowed southwest all the way to the coast. A second snow-mobile trail from the west converged with ours at the base of the wide floodplain some six kilometers from Vosnesenovka—this must be the trail to the abandoned village Unty. Just past it, the river split into multiple channels. Chepelev warned us to pay attention every time the river forked, to ensure we followed the correct route, but he was confident we would see the beaten trails of a season's worth of hunters and trappers passing on their snowmobiles and sleds. In summer this was more challenging and local knowledge was essential; what seemed like the obvious route to guide a boat might prove deadly when a logjam abruptly swallowed that channel.

After a kilometer or two without incident, I heard a sudden, sharp crack reverberate behind us. I looked back. A broad sheet of ice in between our snowmobile and Tolya's had separated from the rest of the river ice, darkening as water spread across it. Tolya slowed his machine and stood for a better view.

"You need to move *now*!" screamed Sergey, catalyzing Tolya into action. He pushed the engine and streaked across the wet surface as the displaced ice continued to shift. The floating sheet pressed down under him but held his fleeting weight, and he pulled up alongside us, panting and swearing. From that point on, each meander in the river brought with it a dread of what the far side might bring. We continued on, besting naleds, enduring slush waves, skirting holes that had once been trail, and watch-ing the river devour ice in our wake.

We finally took a break at the burned shell of a hut called Malinovka, where we dried our saturated socks above hissing wood on the skeletal remains of a woodstove. Back in Agzu we had at one point considered staying here, but that was before seeing its condition and before ice breakup. Sergey and Tolya had been to the Samarga before, but only in summer, so no one was sure how long the ice would hold. We remained at Malinovka only as long as we needed to and had just started off again when suddenly the water before us flowed free in the main current, hugging the left bank and then crossing the entire riverbed to continue flowing down the right bank and out of sight around a bend. The snowmobile trail drove into the water, then picked up on the far side of a thick ice shelf. This was no naled to fumble through. We were trapped.

"Good a place as any for lunch," said Sergey, lighting a cigarette and staring pensively downriver. The day had already been strenuous, and we were probably still fifteen kilometers shy of Samarga. Tolya started a fire on the thick ice for tea, and Shurik followed the right bank on foot to see what came ahead. He moved with difficulty, as the forest floor, not subject to the same melting influences of naleds and direct sun exposure as the river ice, was still under close to a meter of snow. Shurik was back in twenty minutes, reporting that just as we had north of Vosnesenovka several days ago, we could probably cut a trail through the snowy forest to reach solid ice on the far side of the meander. He estimated the distance at approximately three hundred meters.

The floodplain was crowded with vegetation; trees and shrubs broke through the snow cover, and its surface was uneven from multiple small streams that joined the Samarga here. Cutting a path would not be as easy as last time. However, it was evident that this was our only viable option forward—the alternative was to abandon the snowmobiles on the bank and make it to Samarga on skis, carrying what we could on our backs. Sergey and I trudged ahead with the chain saw, cutting a path as straight as possible from one side of this blockage to the other.

In some places all four of us worked, swearing and straining to wrestle each snowmobile and sled down and then back up some narrow gully or through the vegetation-free chute we had cleared. We were exhausted and drenched with sweat by the time we were back on the ice an hour later. But the urgency of our flight and absence of an alternative proved sufficient motivation.

Some kilometers later we passed through a tight gap between mountains, then the trail veered unexpectedly off the river and Sergey slowed to a stop. We were on the edge of a vast, snow-covered field flecked with the occasional slender stalk of last year's grass exposed by wind and thaw. A crescent of low hills of oak and birch rose in the west and curved north around us before sinking again to our east. The flatlands to the south ahead held promise of Samarga, the Strait of Tartary, and the culmination of our exodus.

"Friends," Sergey said triumphantly as he swung his leg over the bench and leaned back on the handlebar with a satisfied sigh, "we made it."

He and Shurik lit congratulatory cigarettes while Tolya removed his ski goggles and stretched his arms and groaned. A group of five horses eyed us distrustfully from afar; I approached for a closer look, but they shied away to keep a healthy distance. These were feral horses, part of a herd descended from those brought to the region during Soviet collectivization in the 1950s. They had outlived their original purpose and had been released to outsmart floods and tigers on their own rather than continue burdening whatever farmer no longer needed their services. While these horses had propagated in modest numbers and to some degree even thrived, this winter had been hard on them as well: they stood deep in the snow with pronounced hip bones and ice clinging in clumps like Christmas ornaments to the long strands of their tails.

We sped toward Samarga, emboldened by solid ground underfoot. Tolya nearly crashed his snowmobile by racing off trail and unintentionally lifting airborne from a hidden rise. Sheepishly, he fell back in line.

We reached the first houses of Samarga and saw few signs of life. The wind rolled off the Strait of Tartary like a tsunami passing low and unstoppable through the village and forcing all but those with pressing business indoors. Unlike Agzu, which was a tight collection of houses, here the buildings were widely dispersed in loose groups. I suspected that the snow and ice under the wooden bridges between these clusters hid river channels and wetlands, so the homes were relegated to what dry land their builders could find, giving Samarga an air of disassociated aloofness.

The first Russians known to visit the mouth of the Samarga River were three fur traders in the year 1900. Their survival rate was a modest 66 percent; one trader lost his feet to frostbite and subsequently died there. The village was founded eight years later by Old Believers, members of a Russian Orthodox sect that eschewed seventeenth-century church reforms and were persecuted violently for it. Old Believers fled the populated corners of Russia, some going as far as Alaska and South America, with hundreds relocating to the remote forests of Primorye to practice their religion in peace.

The explorer Vladimir Arsenyev was there to document Samarga's birth. In 1909, he described two houses at the mouth of the Samarga River with eight human inhabitants along with two cows, two pigs, seven dogs, three boats, and ten guns. Since then, the village has undergone several failed vitalization attempts, including a collective farm called Samarga-Fish that opened in 1932 and closed an even three decades later, possibly due to a massive earthquake that changed ocean currents and shifted the herring fishery away from the coast sometime in the 1950s. A second initiative, the game meat industry that also supported Agzu, failed in 1995. The logging company had recently built their port a short distance up the coast, and the 150 or so residents of Samarga once again held hope of a comfortable future grounded in stable employment.

We passed sun- and wind-beaten homes of gray wood and peeling paint and moved clear through Samarga to stop at a row of houses facing the Strait of Tartary itself like a line of first defense. The wind was an oppressive thing, reminding us that while we had survived the river, the elements still ruled here. Sergey showed us to one of the houses, a compact three-room structure maintained for guests by the local administration. Typically this meant police officers, teams of two who flew in from Terney (the closest police station) ostensibly to maintain law in the outlying villages, but in reality such trips were often drinking binges thinly disguised as official business. Sergey had made arrangements with Samarga's mayor for us to stay there as we awaited transport back south. I glanced at my watch. Although it seemed as if we had been on the river for an eternity, we had left Vosnesenovka only six hours earlier.

Our temporary accommodations were surrounded by a slovenly fence with pickets of varying widths and heights and some of the more prominent gaps blocked by green nylon fish netting. A mottled, sullen cow stood nearby in the snow; it watched us approach and stop but did not move, only stared. The yard we passed through to reach sanctuary from the wind was tiny and cluttered with debris and snowdrifts. I would have to scramble over and among these obstacles to reach the outhouse in back, which had no door and tilted down as though ashamed of its many shortcomings. We were forced to clear a snowdrift from the front door of the house in order to enter; this led through a vestibule jumbled with boxes and rusted things that someone did not have the heart or opportunity to discard. The interior door, painted a dull orange, opened to reveal a small kitchen and two satellite rooms: one straight ahead beyond the woodstove and the other to the left, past a water dispenser nailed to the wall over a sink and slop bucket. I noticed considerable graffiti on the interior of the orange door, most conspicuously the words *Close the door—preferably from the other side*, followed by a series of ramblings about life and fate, most of which were indecipherable. The upkeep of this house was not high on anyone's list of priorities, although it was modestly tidy. A cursory search found no rubble or meat piles in the back rooms, just bare mattresses on single bed frames, a desk with a telephone that produced a weak, static-filled dial tone, and a bookcase full of well-worn books and periodicals from the 1980s.

Shurik began preparing the woodstove while the rest of us unpacked the sleds and moved everything inside. We had passed a well near our house, so I gathered two empty buckets from the corner and backtracked. I was suspicious of village wells; a friend in Terney once found a drowned cat in one. But this was our sole option, as all other water around us was brackish. When I returned, I put one bucket on the stove so we would have warm water for washing and cleaning, then split the other bucket evenly between our teakettle and the water dispenser. The plan was to rejuvenate with a short rest and some sausage. Then, as it was yet early afternoon, Sergey would take us to the fish owl nest tree he had discovered the previous summer on an island among the channels of the Samarga River's mouth.

9

Village of Samarga

WITH ABOUT TWO HOURS TO SPARE before sundown, Sergey and I climbed onto the snowmobile while Tolya and Shurik settled on the sled, their legs dangling over the end so that their backs were to the wind. We followed a snowmobile trail toward the river, then parked the machine near a footbridge, which we crossed to an island. After a pause to put on our skis, Sergey moved ahead of us with uncharacteristic hesitation in search of the nest tree. After some time, he confessed that he was not seeing the landmarks he expected. The same forest, made familiar by searching in summer, can look entirely new in winter. In addition to changes in foliage, river courses can shift overnight in a flood and fundamentally alter any points of reference.

Tolya volunteered that he had found the nest tree independently the previous month, when they had just arrived in Samarga, and he offered to lead the way as his memory was still fresh. Sergey begrudgingly ceded his position, and Tolya curved

us in a new direction. We pushed our way through the low vegetation, beating back branches that snagged our skis and hooked
our hats and regularly stopping to remove our skis in order to
wade through the shallow channels that divided these willow-
dominated islets of the river mouth. This was my first true trudge
through fish owl habitat. Up to this point, I had mostly shuffled
along the branch-free, flat expanse of the frozen Samarga River,
dipping into the floodplain forest only if I saw a tree that war-
ranted further investigation. This day's struggles turned out to
be the standard rather than the exception: there are poking
thorns, prodding branches, and unexpected falls in the future of
anyone who chooses to study fish owls.

Our odyssey stretched on for nearly an hour as we crossed
the delta, then looped back east, at which point Sergey's escalating grumblings erupted into outright accusations of leadership
by the blind.

"No way I was this off track," he growled, just as Tolya raised
his ice pole and pointed to an old chosenia tree, a type of willow
that grew thick like a Greek column to thirty meters tall. A slit of
a cavity showed where a large limb had once extended skyward.

"There it is," Tolya said quietly.

Sergey's eyes narrowed in concentration as he regarded the
tree for a moment. "This is not the nest tree I found. Shurik, go
up there and have a look at that hole."

Shurik assessed his ascent route up and along the massive,
gnarled knobs of the trunk, then skied to its base, removed his
boots, and without hesitation began scaling the tree. He quickly
reached the cleft and peered down at us, shaking his head.

"Too shallow and too narrow for a fish owl nest."

We had finally located the tree Tolya was looking for, but it
was not the one we needed to find. Tolya began apologizing, but
Sergey cut him off with a wave of his hand.

"No matter. I'll keep looking. You three head back to the sled, and if I am not there by dusk, split up and see if we can hear these birds vocalize."

According to my GPS, we were about a kilometer from the snowmobile. We headed toward it directly, following the gray-scale arrow on the device's screen rather than backtracking along our serpentine snow trail. As we walked, I saw the cigar-shaped outline of what looked like a Ural owl perhaps fifty meters ahead, sitting on a branch with its back to me. This is a species that seems to coexist with fish owls—they are a regular sight in fish owl habitat. I raised my binoculars for a closer look, then mimicked the sound of a distressed rodent to draw its attention. The owl's head pivoted toward me and the yellow eyes that bored into mine caught me off guard. This was no Ural owl, a common bird with brown eyes; this was a great gray owl, a species found in lonely taiga forests throughout northern climes from Alaska and Canada to Scandinavia and Russia. With only a few known records in Primorye, great gray owls are quite rare this far south, and to date this bird remains the only one I've seen in the Russian Far East. For a bird-watcher, it's always exciting to see something rare and unexpected; and for an owl enthusiast, it's always a pleasure to see a great gray. It was gone before I could pull my camera from my backpack.

Sergey returned to the sled not long after we did. He had finally stumbled upon the nest tree and would take us back there in the morning. As he drove the snowmobile back into Samarga, the machine's lights illuminated a man outside our house, waiting for us. This was Oleg Romanov, a remarkably Russian name for the Udege hunter who answered to it. He was thin and in his late forties, with large, brown-framed glasses and a smoking habit that kept pace with Sergey's. Oleg was regarded as a local authority on the Samarga River and had helped Sergey plan some of the logistics of our fish owl surveys by suggesting where we could stay along the river and where we should drop fuel caches. He was eager to hear about the expedition.

"When you didn't show up last week I started to worry," he said, shaking Sergey's hand. "I can't believe you were on the river so late in the season."

He said that villagers in both Agzu and Samarga had entertained themselves by tracking our progress and were wondering if we would reach the coast before ice breakup. We were the last to travel the river that winter—we would later learn that a hunter from Agzu attempted to make his way to Samarga a day or so after we departed but was forced back home by the rushing waters. Because of these conditions, communication between the villages ceased for several weeks until all the ice had cleared. We'd ridden the last ice of the season to the coast.

Oleg, Sergey, and Shurik sat by the woodstove, smoking and talking. While we still had a little more searching for fish owls to do around Samarga, Oleg informed us that the mayor of Samarga expected to stop by early the next day to help us plan our return trip to Terney. Indeed, it was not yet eight o'clock the following morning when a rumbling engine alerted me to a tractor outside. The mayor was young, in his midthirties, and in the morning light his bright blue eyes reflected what could have been the glossy sheen of the bottle's influence. The wafting aroma of spirits deepened my suspicions when he climbed down to shake hands. Intoxicated or not, he was lucid and quite helpful. Tolya and I were planning to book tickets on the next helicopter, and he advised us to instead consider traveling on a ship called the *Vladimir Goluzenko*, which was scheduled to depart in two days' time. The *Goluzenko* was a transport ship used by the logging company to shuttle employees to and from isolated ports along the coast and the company's hub in Plastun, a port just south of Terney. This was the method by which Sergey and other team members had reached Samarga at the start of the expedition. The mayor could help arrange our passage, and we could probably travel for free.

"It'll take you seventeen hours to reach Plastun by boat," he conceded, "but you never know how long you'll be stuck in Samarga if you rely on the helicopter. The ship is a safer bet."

The mayor sat with Sergey, discussing how much space we needed for our gear on the next cargo ship, which was scheduled for later in the week. We had to coordinate with the logging company to transport our snowmobiles and other equipment back south, and Sergey and Shurik would stay on in Samarga to chaperone this load.

The conversation wrapped up, and the mayor said he was late for another meeting. He seemed surprisingly busy for a man whose primary form of transportation was a tractor and who represented a mere 150 constituents. As he left, the mayor offered us the use of his banya that evening. Anyone in town could point us to his home, he said, should we wish to take him up on it.

We ate a quick breakfast, then Sergey, Shurik, and I nestled tight on the bench of the black Yamaha, while Tolya went to examine some possible fish owl habitat north of town. We followed our path from the day before back across Samarga to the river mouth. One of the proposed goals of my five-year study was to learn how and why fish owls selected the nest trees they did. Was it all about a suitable cavity, or did the surrounding vegetation play a role in selection as well? I had adopted a standardized methodology to describe the structure and vegetation at nest sites for scientific analysis and comparison, which required quite a bit of measuring. I wanted to practice this methodology on a nest tree to work out any kinks. I brought my tape measure and other instruments along. We found the nest tree very quickly; Sergey had been quite close the day before. He blamed his previous confusion on the fact that the river channel he'd been orienting by had shifted during some storm over the past year, and by following it, he'd gone in the wrong direction.

When tree species such as Japanese poplar, Manchurian elm, and chosenia reach maturity—twenty or thirty meters tall, more than a meter around, and two or three hundred years old— their size and age become liabilities. Typhoon winds snap them at their crowns, leaving the trunks standing like chimneys. Sometimes only a limb cracks off, exposing the soft wood inside. Over time, the resulting decay creates a space big enough for a fish owl to clamber inside and make itself a comfortable nest.

Fish owls seem to prefer the "side cavity" nest—a hole in the side of a tree—because these offer better protection from the elements than the alternative. Chimney cavities—depressions formed at the top of a tree—leave an incubating owl much more vulnerable. The female must sit tight to protect her eggs or young from exposure to wind, snow, and rain. Surmach once observed an incubating female on a chimney nest in a blizzard, remaining immobile in the swirling storm until only her tail was visible, sticking out under a puff of snow.

There are, of course, exceptions to these rules. In places where fish owls have long forgotten (or never had) the luxury of a tree cavity, they make do in other ways. In Magadan, on the northern Sea of Okhotsk coast, a juvenile fish owl was recently seen peeking from an old Steller's sea eagle stick nest high in the crook of a young poplar. And in Japan, where old trees are now rare, one pair fledged chicks on a cliff ledge.

Shurik pocketed the tape measure and a small digital camera and climbed the target tree, a large chosenia with ample branches and knobs leading to a broken-top cavity about seven meters up the main trunk. He proceeded to measure and photograph the cavity while I busied myself with other measurements, such as nest tree diameter and condition and counting the number of trees nearby and their size. One obvious shortcoming of our work here was that it was still winter—we were on top of several feet of snow and the trees and shrubs were bare. Not only was it awkward to maneuver on skis, but a number of the measurements I took (such as canopy cover and understory visibility) were clearly inaccurate. Regardless, it was good to practice. The exercise took about four hours to complete. Eventually, once I had the hang of it, this procedure would take about an hour.

We returned to Samarga intent on finding the mayor's residence for a banya. We stopped by our house first to collect Tolya, but he had not yet returned, so we went on without him. A passing ice fisherman told us where the mayor lived, and we were pleased to find on arrival that the banya had been stoked. It was a small, low structure with rotting floorboards that could hold only two people at a time. I steamed and bathed first, after which Sergey and Shurik took their turn. While I waited for them to finish, the mayor invited me inside his home for tea and dessert, then promptly begged off on business. I sat at a table opposite an older man and a young girl I had not been introduced to but presumed was the mayor's father or father-in-law along with the mayor's daughter. These slight, gray figures observed me gloomily from across a table crowded with bread and jars of jam, honey, and sugar. After several unproductive attempts to stimulate conversation, I drank my tea in silence and endured their stares, occasionally wiping my brow free of the sweat still trying to normalize my body temperature following the heat of the banya.

In the morning, we received word that Tolya and I were confirmed on the *Vladimir Goluzenko*, scheduled to set sail midafternoon the next day. We would embark from Adimi, the logging port some twelve kilometers up the coast. The mayor reported that the road there was passable, so we should have no problem making it if we left before the midday sun turned the surface to mud. This news initiated the countdown: we had twenty-four hours left on the Samarga, time we all wanted to fill looking for more fish owls. After all, we'd had to largely abandon surveys along the final stretch of the river due to the melting ice. We could not get too far up the Samarga without encountering open water, so Tolya and I took one of the snowmobiles to the general area he had searched the day before, while Sergey and Shurik left early to make it to the mouth of the Edinka River just down the coast where Sergey had heard a fish owl the previous summer. As Tolya and I made our way along trails crossing the valley, he suddenly lifted his gloved hand off the throttle to point at a plump brown spot the size of an eagle a good hundred meters away among the trees—it was a fish owl, one of the pair that lived at the Samarga River mouth. This was the first time I'd had a clear view of a fish owl since my first sighting in 2000.

Tolya slowed the snowmobile so we could get a better look, but the moment we hesitated in our trajectory the bird flushed, first receding and then disappearing among the bare branches. While I was thrilled by this brief sighting, it also worried me: captures were absolutely essential to my research project, but fish owls seemed to actively avoid attention from humans. How on earth did we think we could catch one if they were never closer than a football field away?

We continued on, with ice regularly cracking and falling into the waters of the narrow, shallow channels behind us as we passed over them. Had this been my first experience with snowmobiles and ice melt, I would have been alarmed, but it was at most an annoyance and a far cry from the life-threatening hurdles we had encountered upriver. The forest around us seemed ideal for fish owls, but we were able to examine only a portion of it. We returned to the village with only that brief owl sighting, and sometime later Sergey and Shurik returned. They had found no evidence of owls. Sergey recounted passing a starving horse on the rocky beach south of Samarga.

"It lay on its side, all bones and twitching, dying slowly," he said, wincing from the memory. "If I'd had a gun I would have shot it."

10

The Vladimir Goluzenko

THERE WAS GOOD ENERGY in our hut the morning of April 10. It did not take Tolya and me long to pack, and we strapped our bags to the yellow sled. Sergey drove us up the coast to Adimi on the snowmobile along a trail that alternated between slush and mud, with both of a similar consistency. As we approached the edge of town, we could see a massive transport vehicle idling; we were at the border of the logging camp, and private vehicles were allowed no farther. I scrambled up into the back of the waiting truck while Tolya and Sergey handed me bag after bag. As I expected to see Sergey a week later in Terney, our parting here was a simple handshake and a curt nod. Tolya climbed up the ladder into the truck and slapped the metal roof so the driver knew we were ready to go, and we rolled into Adimi. Sergey stood next to the mud-caked snowmobile and empty sled to watch us leave.

Like a frontier town in the nineteenth-century American West, Adimi was a tight concentration of wooden buildings of freshly hewn lumber lining a main road of calf-deep mud. Logging company employees bustled past on hastily raised boardwalks. The truck led us to the pier where loggers, at the end of their months-long shifts, were shouldering bags of belongings and lining up to cross a gangway to board the *Vladimir Goluzenko*.

The ship, which looked to me like a cross between a tugboat and a ferry, was built in 1977 and had been owned by the logging company since 1990. It had a small forward deck, crowded from behind by a perky pilothouse, a larger aft deck, and a cabin below with enough seats for a hundred passengers, although maybe only twenty loggers were aboard. The seating compartment was arranged much like an airplane cabin, with rows of comfortable seats divided by two aisles. There was a small cafeteria toward the aft deck with a tank of perpetually hot water for tea or instant coffee and several booths with tables and benches. The front corner of the main cabin was occupied by a television set blaring a low-budget sitcom about life on a Russian army base. From what I could tell, and I was trying my best to ignore it, the plot revolved around a gang of good-hearted but inept conscripts routinely flummoxing the person in charge, a hefty officer with a tall hat. His catchphrase was *"Yo-mayo!"*—"Oh my!"—a statement repeated with some regularity and a palm firmly slapped against his forehead.

Most of the loggers were congregated toward the front of the cabin, near the television, so I selected a quieter spot closer to the back corner and spread some of my belongings across several adjacent seats in order to have space to lie down later. Seventeen hours was going to be a long time on this boat. Then I returned to the aft deck, where Tolya was busy photographing the slaty-backed gulls that hung in the air behind our ship, the pelagic cormorants that fled as we approached, and the rafts of long-tailed ducks that bobbed on the waves as we passed.

As in Agzu, Tolya and I were met with considerable interest from those around us. Adimi was an isolated settlement where everyone knew one another. Suddenly, a pair of strangers appeared in their midst, seemingly out of nowhere: the first one short and olive skinned and photographing everything and the other tall, bearded, and clearly a foreigner. Curiosity and boredom got the best of these loggers with seventeen spare hours on their hands, and throughout the trip we were often approached with questions about who we were and why we'd been to Samarga.

Somewhere near hour five, Tolya and I went into the cafeteria for some hot water to steep our tea bags and to eat some snacks we had packed in Samarga, a half loaf of uncut bread and some sausage jostling loosely in a black plastic shopping bag. Two men were having their own snacks a table over: one of the loggers was slim and the other enormous. They shifted to our booth to join us as soon as we sat down.

"So," said the giant, who introduced himself as Mikhail, "what's your story?"

We had a pleasant conversation with these men, telling them why we were on the Samarga and learning about their roles with the logging company. Mikhail, whose blue-and-gray flannel shirt was unbuttoned low to give the yeti of hair on his chest a taste of freedom, operated a harvester. He told us of his horror when he beheld the vast clear-cut forests near the village of Svetlaya. Russians were more accustomed to selective harvest, where only some trees were removed, but a joint venture in the early 1990s with the South Korean company Hyundai savaged the hills of the Svetlaya plateau and left them bare. Hyundai also had eyes on the Bikin River basin, an Udege stronghold like the Samarga, but the locals protested, and Hyundai was denied their timber prize. Not long after, Hyundai and their Russian partners accused each other of corruption and the partnership in Svetlaya imploded.

"I bet we can rustle up some vodka," said Mikhail with a broad smile, but then a member of the crew approached and stated that the captain wished to have a word. I was glad to have escaped what was likely to spiral into a vodka vortex. On the forward deck, I listened as the captain spoke with unabashed enthusiasm of his time along Primorye's coast, naming mountains and river valleys as we motored slowly past them, a kilometer or so west across the placid waters of the Sea of Japan. He spoke of the fishing villages that had once dotted the coast but had atrophied to nothing following the herring collapse fifty years prior. One village, he said, pointing, was called Kants.

"There's still a tractor there," he continued wistfully, "it's the only thing left—a rusting relic just sitting there among the birch and aspen in what was once a field."

We were approaching Svetlaya, the coastal logging town that Mikhail had referenced earlier. The ship slowed and moved closer to shore. The village itself sat on the north bank of the Svetlaya River opposite a black, jutting cliff to its south that stabbed into the Sea of Japan like an ebony knife. Perched high upon this steep mass of rock stood a lighthouse, backlit by the setting sun, surveying the carcass of a pier below. The structure must have been destroyed in a terrible storm, and waves moved among its skeletal fingers and washed impotently against the rocks below the cliff. I was thankful the sea was calm—shipwrecks here seemed inevitable. Given the absence of a functioning pier, the *Vladimir Goluzenko* waited as a small craft bobbed toward us from the direction of the village, delivering the dozen or so Svetlaya loggers also destined for Plastun. I stayed with the captain to watch them board, then went back below as we continued our journey south. It was getting dark, and I was going to try to get some sleep.

There were approximately thirty loggers aboard now, which

meant about seventy empty seats. I returned to find mine occupied by a drunken logger, passed out and widely splayed over the coat I had draped to mark my territory. After a modest attempt to rouse him, I abandoned my corner space. Displaced, I could only move closer to the television, and my foam earplugs were no match for the sound effects complementing the antics on-screen, which, amazingly, still featured the exasperated platoon captain repeating his catchphrase: *"Yo-mayo!"* Around hour nine and unable to sleep, I wandered, maintaining as wide an arc as possible around the cafeteria. I did not know what was going on in there, but the animated shouting suggested I did not want to know. I encountered Tolya on the aft deck. It was midnight, and we were the only two outside, surrounded by darkness and a cold wind. I remarked that the ship must own the whole collection of that army base sitcom—they were still playing it.

"Haven't you noticed?" he whispered. "It's the same episode. They have been looping the same, hour-long program since we've been on this boat. Why do you think I'm out here?"

Yo-mayo, indeed.

I managed to get a few hours of sleep and woke in early dawn to see a familiar cape just north of Plastun. The ship maneuvered into the sheltered bay there, and we disembarked. Zhenya Gizhko, an acquaintance from Terney, had been given word to expect us and was waiting, reclined and smoking in the cab of a white Range Rover, listening to synthetic dance music.

The Samarga expedition was over. I was surprised to realize it had been less than two weeks since I'd left Terney. It had been a thirteen-day roller coaster of ice and eccentrics, with seemingly more time devoted to logistics than to finding fish owls. But I was off to a good start: field study in the Russian Far East is a constant negotiation between the research, the local inhabitants, and the elements. For the next week or so, the team would take a short break; Tolya would join me in Terney as we waited for Sergey to come south from Samarga. Then Sergey and I would initiate the second part of the exploratory phase of this five-year project—searching for possible owls to capture in the Serebry-anka, Kema, Amgu, and Maksimovka River drainages of Ter-ney County. A six-week excursion, this next stage would provide the groundwork for our fish owl telemetry study.

PART TWO

Fish Owls of the Sikhote-Alin

11

The Sound of Something Ancient

FTER A FEW DAYS in Terney, Tolya and I began to recover from the whirlwind of ice and chaos that had defined our time on the Samarga River. Sporadic phone calls came in from Sergey, who was still there and barked updates over the static. The supply ship scheduled to take him and Shurik back south had been delayed due to rough seas, so they were stuck in that windswept frontier village for five days longer than expected. To make matters worse, a group of officials had moved into the house with them—it was the only guesthouse in town, after all—and they had brought vodka. Sergey agonized in this inescapable position. He told of an ice-fishing trip to the river mouth where he languished under his coat on the snowmobile sled, hungover and hiding from the glaring sun, while his impervious drinking companions jostled their lines around him and smoked.

Then several days passed and the telephone was silent. We finally heard from Surmach in Vladivostok that Sergey and Shurik had left on a logging ship but were forced to take shelter in the port of Svetlaya for two nights. The coastal waters had been violent, everyone was vomiting, and cargo broke loose and crashed about as the waves heaved the ship where they pleased. Sergey and Shurik had eventually arrived in Plastun, and then each drove south to their respective homes for some rest.

Tolya and I occupied ourselves with this unexpected free time by searching the Serebryanka River valley, near Terney, for owls. The Samarga trip had shown me what to focus on when looking for a fish owl—the type of forest, the silvery shimmer of a snagged feather within it, the scrape of a track in the snow by the river, or the tremor of a vocalization at dusk—and I needed to start generating a list of individual owls that I might be able to use in my telemetry study. These would be the owls critical to the third and final phase of the project, capture and data collection, scheduled to start next winter. It was the information we collected from these specific owls that would allow us to create a conservation plan to protect them. However, I had misgivings about how many owls I could expect to find in the Terney area. I'd spent several years bird-watching here in my Peace Corps days and had even accompanied the local ornithologist on his survey routes through the riparian forest of the Serebryanka River valley. It was specifically this kind of habitat—the forests lining the river full of large, water-loving trees such as poplar and elm—that was home to fish owls. But I'd never seen or heard one there. I assumed most of my luck would be farther north in the more remote Amgu area, where I was planning to go in a few weeks with Sergey, but it made sense to at least look near Terney. I had nothing better to do and could use the practice.

I conducted my searches for owls mostly with Tolya but was occasionally joined by John Goodrich, then the field coordinator for the Wildlife Conservation Society's Siberian Tiger Project, based in Terney. John had been in Russia for more than a decade, and I had known him for six years. He was tall, blond, and action-figure handsome. So much so, in fact, that for a while New York City's Bronx Zoo, the headquarters of the Wildlife Conservation Society, sold an articulated doll rumored to have been made in his likeness. It came with binoculars, a backpack, snowshoes, and a little plastic tiger for the character to track.

John thrived in the rustic environment of village life in Terney and had even Russified to some degree, as anyone would after living so long in the country. He wore a traditional fur hat in winter, kept his face strictly clean-shaven, and waited impatiently for the mushroom- and berry-picking seasons to begin. But there was not enough vodka in Russia to fully leach the rural Americana from him. In addition to introducing fly-fishing to Terney, in summer John drove around town in his pickup truck wearing wraparound sunglasses and a sleeveless T-shirt: a vision teleported from the country back roads of the American West.

John was deeply inquisitive when it came to wildlife, and even though he was a tiger researcher, he was eager to assist with fish owl surveys when he had the free time to do so. On an evening in mid-April, lacking any of the recordings from the Samarga River, I mimicked fish owl vocalizations for John's benefit, including the four-note duet and a two-note call by a single bird that I'd learned from Sergey. I wouldn't be fooling any fish owls with my crude hoots, but the most important thing to know was the cadence and the deep pitch—nothing else in the forest sounded like it. The common owl there, the Ural owl, had a higher three-note call, and the other owls likely to be heard in the region—Eurasian eagle owl, collared scops owl, Oriental scops owl, brown hawk owl, Tengmalm's owl, and northern pygmy owl—all had higher and easily recognizable calls. The fish owl was unmistakable.

Once John had a good understanding of what to listen for, we headed out. He drove Tolya and me ten kilometers west of Terney to the confluence of the Serebryanka and Tunsha Rivers. The road split here to follow each river, and the habitat looked perfect for fish owls, with plenty of shallow river channels and large trees. Given the ease of access, this would be a great location for us to study owls, should we be lucky enough to find them.

There wasn't a lot to initial fish owl surveys like this. In contrast with the Samarga, where we had to reach and then travel along the frozen river, here we simply drove the dirt roads parallel to rivers and paused to listen for the characteristic calls. We did not need to get too close to the river itself; in fact, it was better if we didn't, as the rush of flowing water would make it harder to hear anything else. John left Tolya and me by the bridge, then continued some five kilometers farther up the Tunsha. We agreed to meet back at the confluence forty-five minutes after dark. I wore a camouflage jacket and pants, more to blend in with the locals than with my surroundings. I walked the dirt road in one direction and Tolya headed in the other. I felt my pocket to make sure I had my hand flare. This was for protection: it was spring and the bears were out. As a foreigner I could not carry a firearm, and bear spray was difficult or impossible to find. Hand flares, designed for distressed Russian sailors and reliably available in Vladivostok, were activated by pulling a string to release a deafening, meter-long pillar of molten fire and smoke that lasted several minutes. In most cases, this shock-and-awe approach was enough to deter any dangerously curious bear or tiger. But if it wasn't, the flare could also be used as a weapon. John Goodrich had once used one in this way: on his back and pinned by a tiger chewing holes in one hand, John used his other hand to press this knife of fire into the animal's side. It ran off and he survived.

I'd gone maybe half a kilometer when I heard the duet. It echoed from upriver, in the direction I was walking, a four-note hoot perhaps two kilometers away. This was the closest I'd been to vocalizing fish owls and the clearest duet I had yet heard. The sound rooted me to the spot. Certain noises in the forest—a deer bark, a rifle shot, even a songbird warble—are sonorous eruptions that catch one's attention immediately. The fish owl duet was different. Breathy, low, and organic, the call pulsed through the forest, hiding among the creaking trees and bending with the rushing river. It was the sound of something ancient and in its place.

A reliable way to pinpoint the location of a distant sound is triangulation, a simple process that requires only a few bits of information and enough time to gather it. In my case I needed a GPS to record where I was when I heard the owl, a compass to note the direction the hoot came from (called a "bearing"), and the time to collect multiple bearings before the owls stopped calling or moved. Later, on a map, I could plot my locations with the GPS points and use a ruler to draw a line to follow each respective bearing. Where these lines intersected was the general location the owl had been calling from. In principle, three bearings are often considered the minimum number needed, putting the sought-after location within a triangle of space formed where the bearings cross (hence "triangulation").

I had to work fast: breeding fish owls often start their duets at the nest but soon move off to hunt. If I could gather three bearings, I'd have a good chance of finding the nest tree. I took a quick bearing, recorded my location with my GPS, and ran up the road. A few hundred meters up the dirt track I stopped short, heart pounding, and listened again. Another duet. I took another compass bearing and GPS location, then ran some more. By the time I reached a third location, the birds were quiet. I waited longer, ears straining, but the forest was still. I finally understood how I had been living in Terney near fish owls for so long and hadn't registered their presence: I had to be outside at just the right time under just the right conditions. Given how the duet folds into other sounds, if there had been some wind or even someone talking nearby, I might have missed it.

I was heartened by my two bearings. Depending on their accuracy, they might lead me to a nest tree. I waited a little longer for another vocalization, which did not come, then backtracked along the road, gravel crunching underfoot as I walked in the dark, elated. Tolya and John both wore their own smiles, as both reported hearing owls. The birds Tolya detected were certainly the same Serebryanka pair I had heard, based on his descriptions, but the owls John had heard were different: he had heard a duet from the opposite direction. My list of potential study animals had, in the course of an hour, gone from zero to four birds. The fact that we heard pairs, not just single birds, was most encouraging. A single bird might be a transient, but pairs were territorial. These were owls we could possibly catch and study next year.

That night, I plotted my bearings on a map, then entered the coordinates of their intersecting lines into my GPS. The next morning, Tolya and I drove the dusty and potholed road back to the Serebryanka River to follow the gray arrow on my GPS wherever it might lead. Progress was soon blocked by the wide, fast-flowing river, which we had not reached the night before. The owls must have called from the far side of it. We wrestled into our hip waders and approached the main channel of the Serebryanka, which was about thirty meters across. Both upriver and downriver the water was too deep to wade across, but here it was not, varying in depth between the knee and the waist, clear water rushing over a substrate of smooth, fist-sized stones and smaller pebbles.

In Primorye, a river even only knee-deep can deceive the un-initiated into the expectation of an easy crossing—the Serebry-anka's current, like those of the Samarga and other coastal waterways here, can be formidable. Its swiftness manhandled us as we waded through it. Pebbles eroded underfoot if we paused too long in one place to scout the course forward. Once we had reached the far bank, we found ourselves among a network of small islands interlaced by lesser channels; covered by lush, old-growth forest of pine, poplar, and elm; and fringed in the most flood-prone areas by curtains of willow. The GPS led us to the largest of these islands, one encircled by lazy backwaters more swamp than stream, its upland dominated by a grove of colossal poplars rising from a bed of shrubs tangled among the decaying remains of their wind-fallen brethren. My binoculars scanned from one gaping cavity to the next among them; the number of potential nests was almost overwhelming. At the center of these gangly trees stood a graceful pine, like a belle surrounded by intimidated suitors. It was a robust and healthy beauty with a stout trunk of red bark that rose and then disappeared under a green skirt of branches. There, clinging to a bough, I saw a fish owl feather trembling in the imperceptible breeze.

I waved to attract Tolya's attention, and we walked toward the pine, transfixed. Although its dense branches should have shielded the tree's base from the elements, there was something underneath that blended with the surrounding and melting snow. This was the carpeted whitewash of fish owl excrement—a lot of it—intermingled with the bones of past prey. We'd found a roost tree. Fish owls prefer roosting in conifers like this pine, a place that provides some shade during the day when they sleep and protection from wind, snow, and the attention of roaming crows eager to harass. I saw instantly that fish owl pellets were unique: these were not the gray, sausage-like regurgitations that other owls produce. As most owl species eat mammals, their pellets are made of bone wrapped in a tight package of fur. When a fish owl regurgitates the indigestible remains of its prey, however, there is nothing to keep the bundle of bones together. They were pellets in name only.

Roused by our find, Tolya and I gave each other the Russian version of a high five, which was a handshake. Fish owls do not use habitual roosts as reliably as some other owl species, and to find one so well used was a rarity indeed. However, a roost was also a strong indication that a nest tree was nearby; when the female sits on the nest, the male is usually somewhere close to guard her. We spent the rest of the morning craning our necks at the cavities high above, all cavernous and ranging in height from ten to fifteen meters, looking—without luck—for some clue of which tree might hold a fish owl nest. We had stumbled upon a secret place for these fish owls, well protected from prying eyes among the river islands and the swamp.

Over the next few days, we continued to search the Serebryanka and Tunsha River valleys for fish owls. We heard the pair that John had found but were unable to find any physical sign. These nonmigratory birds had been here all winter, but now that the snow was melting and leaf buds were emerging, both their tracks and their feathers were becoming more and more difficult to see. After a few more days, Tolya headed to the Avvakumovka River some two hundred kilometers due south, where Surmach had found an occupied fish owl nest with a freshly hatched egg. Surmach wanted Tolya to monitor the nest, recording how much food the parents brought the chick, what prey species were delivered, and when the chick fledged. I finished out the week listening for owls with John and searching a few more potential territories for occupancy, including the Sheptun River, where

Surmach and Sergey had found a nest several years prior. John and I found the tree, a girthy poplar, only it lay on its side, felled in a storm and almost hidden by the shrubs that had flourished since its demise. We heard no fish owls there.

Since my return from the Samarga, I had been living with John in Terney. He occupied a comfortable, bright home painted blue and yellow and buttressed by a modest garden on the hill above town. I stayed in his guesthouse, a musty room just large enough to fit a brick woodstove, a low bookcase, and a compact couch that pulled out to an uneven bed, located in an outbuilding that shared a wall with his banya. John had an expansive front porch built around an apple tree that overlooked the low wooden homes of Terney and the Sea of Japan in the distance. This spot had been almost a second home to me on warm summer evenings in years past: we'd drink beer, eat smoked sockeye salmon, and never tire of the spectacular view. We were sitting there on a similarly pleasant night that spring not long after Tolya departed, eating mollusks that had washed up on shore by the same storm that marooned Sergey and Shurik in the village of Svetlaya. John shifted the conversation to Tolya.

"Do you know why Tolya doesn't drink?" John asked quietly, peering at me inquisitively over the mouth of his half-liter bottle of beer. I replied that I did not. John nodded and continued.

"He told me he was in the Altai Mountains some years back, visiting some family, and he drank too much wine on a picnic. He was reclining on the grass, looking at the blue sky above, when something inside made him wish for rain. To his amazement, the drops started falling. Tolya realized then that he had power over the weather, and decided to quit drinking because he needed to shepherd this dangerous responsibility."

I stared at John, unsure of how to respond.

"Just when you think someone's right in the head," said John, drawing on his beer, "they go and say something like that."

SPRING CAME LATE in 2006, and most of the rivers we had expected to ford in hip or chest waders were still swollen from snowmelt and brown from runoff, making any foot crossings dangerous. After discussions with Sergey, it was decided that we would head south, to join Tolya on the Avvakumovka River, giving the rivers some time to relax before we headed north toward Amgu. I would spend some time watching fish owl behavior at the nest with Tolya and also help Sergey look for other owls in the Avvakumovka area to possibly include in our telemetry study. In late April, I took a bus from Terney to Dalnegorsk, where Sergey lived, four hours south. From there we would drive farther down the coast to the Avvakumovka River in Sergey's pickup truck.

12

A Fish Owl Nest

ALNEGORSK IS A CITY of forty thousand inhabitants tucked between the steep slopes of the Rudnaya River valley, founded as a mining camp in 1897 by the grandfather of actor Yul Brynner. The city, river, and valley were all called Tyutikhe until the early 1970s, when thousands of rivers, mountains, and towns across the southern Russian Far East were abruptly given new, non-Chinese names in light of deteriorating Sino-Russian relations. When explorer Vladimir Arsenyev and his men passed through the Rudnaya River valley in 1906, they were spellbound by its beauty: the rugged cliffs, dense forests, and near-unimaginable numbers of salmon left their mouths agape. Sadly, a hundred years of intensive mining and lead smelting have deeply tarnished its luster. The epic salmon migrations are a thing of the distant past—lost to degraded river habitat and overfishing—and the valley is a grotesque shell of its former self. Some of its once striking hills have been decapitated by mountaintop-removal mining and others eviscerated for the minerals found within. The scarring is internal as well. Four directors of the lead smelter in a row died of cancer, and at a nearby village playground, soil samples revealed lead at eleven thousand parts per million, more than twenty-seven times the threshold that triggers mandatory cleanup in the United States. Inhabitants of one village in the Rudnaya River valley have cancer at a rate nearly five times that found in residents of Terney.

SERGEY MET ME at the bus station and we left Dalnegorsk the next morning. He drove the *domik* ("little house"): an early 1990s Hilux with a custom-built camper cab on back, the whole thing uniformly painted a shade of light violet. The back compartment, all brown carpet and plush inside, had a booth with a table and benches and could sleep two comfortably. The truck was poorly heated, so it was not particularly suitable for winter work, but it was ideal for spring owl surveys: we'd work until we were too tired, then park and sleep where we pleased. While elsewhere in the world this vehicle might be considered an unremarkable sight, in central Primorye it garnered considerable attention. Passersby craned their necks and village boys hollered to one another to look before we passed from view.

After about two hours of driving we paused in the coastal village of Olga, where we ate a late lunch with Sergey's brother, Sasha, who lived there. We continued a short distance to Vetka, one of the oldest Russian villages in Primorye, settled by immigrants arriving from southeastern Russia in 1859. Vetka may have prospered at some point in the century and a half since its founding, but considerable time had passed since fortune shone on this corner of the Russian Federation. The village was a small assemblage of single-story homes in extensive disrepair occupied by stern pensioners and surrounded by vast yards of rust. We turned off the main road, bounced down a hill, then moved past crumbling shells of a failed Soviet collective farm, one of the many that did not survive perestroika. On its far side was the village dump, a wide swath of garbage and broken bottles, which abutted and spilled into a shallow tributary of the Avvakumovka River. We crossed this waterway and could see a figure on the trail about two hundred meters ahead. It was Tolya standing outside his camp. He'd set up a tent at the edge of a field bordering a riparian forest, and drawn a large blue tarp over a small firepit. He'd been here for more than a week. After a cup of tea, Tolya walked us to the nest tree by following a trail used by fishermen to reach the river.

The tree that Tolya brought us to was a chosenia like the nest tree I had seen near the Samarga River mouth, with deeply rutted bark and twisted limbs stretching skyward like the arms of a sea monster. Tolya pointed up the crook to where the main trunk had once continued but now ended abruptly with a ragged line of splintered wood. A storm had likely brought it down. There was a depression there, which held the nest cavity. A few meters to the right, a small camera and ultraviolet illuminator stood on the end of a long pole—several willows that Tolya had stripped and bound together, then held erect with rope. Black wires descended in tight spirals down the pole, snaking along the ground and then disappearing under a camouflaged dome nearby: the observation blind.

Tolya had become nocturnal here. He slept during the day so he could huddle silently in the blind all night to watch the nest and record activity.

"She just sits there all day," Tolya said. "Doesn't flush. Just stares."

"You mean she's on the nest?" I said in a whisper, looking up.

"Of course," said Tolya, surprised I was only now under-standing. "She's looking at us as we speak."

I raised my binoculars. After a moment I saw her: first just a patch of brown that was her back blending with the surrounding bark. The rest of her seemed obscured, then I focused on a thin fissure in the front lip of the depression and spotted the yellow of one eye staring sternly back into mine. This bird of mystery was a half-dozen meters up a tree only paces away. I was exhilarated. I was reminded again how much fish owls seemed part of, not just something in, the forest: her camouflage made it hard to tell where the tree ended and she began. It also felt surreal. After all the effort to search for fish owls in the pristine forests near Sa-marga and Terney, here I was, standing on a fisherman's trail at the edge of a village dump, with a fish owl looking down on me.

I STAYED WITH TOLYA for a few days while Sergey took the domik up the Sadoga River, a tributary of the Avvakumovka, looking for fish owls. As I set up my own tent near Tolya's, he suggested that I take watch that night in the blind. I eagerly accepted, and he enumerated the basic rules of life in the blind.

"Don't make any noise and move as little as possible," he said solemnly. "We don't want the parent owls to stay away from their chick because of us. We are trying to observe natural behavior, not behavior influenced by human proximity. And don't leave the tent until morning. If you need to pee, use a bottle."

With that, he bade me good luck. I gathered my pack and set off through the forest back to the blind. Wedged within the under-story a dozen meters from the nest tree, it was a two-person, three-season camping tent covered by sound- and light-dampening fabric and camouflage netting that Tolya had sewn. The blind inside was cluttered by twelve-volt car batteries, various adapt-ers and cables, and a small, grayscale video monitor. I unpacked my stakeout snacks: a thermos with black tea and a few table-spoons of sugar, and bread with cheese. Next I turned on the monitor, which illuminated the tent interior with its soft light. My movements were deliberately slow and noiseless. I was terri-fied of spooking the female, who was on the nest and certainly saw me approach. As the screen focused I could see she was in place, and to my relief she sat still with an air of calm. Toward dusk she perked up, catching sight of something, and I heard a noise in the tree above—probably the male landing nearby. This suspicion was validated when the female ambled out of the nest and walked along a branch out of view. Then the duet began, deep and resonant and loud, just overhead.

I sat mesmerized as I listened to the owls above me, hushing the sound of my heart pounding in my ears, reluctant to swallow or twitch for fear the owls would hear me and break off this cap-tivating ritual. Even at close distance the sounds seemed muf-fled, as though the birds were hooting into pillows. The juvenile fish owl, clearly visible on the monitor, was a small gray sack of potatoes that waddled to and fro in the wide and flat nest cavity, shrieking. He knew food was soon coming, and unlike me, he had no patience for all this hooting.

The duet ceased, meaning the pair had left to hunt. The night was long and fascinating. The adults brought food to the nest five times before midnight, each time heralded by the shudder of hefty wings slapping canopy branches as they careened closer. One dislodged branch even hit the top of the blind. I conceded that it can be difficult for anything with a two-meter wingspan to maintain poise in the tangled jungles of the river bottom at night.

The angle of all prey deliveries was poor and the video grainy, so I could not determine what food had been brought for the chick. I was also unable to discern which of the adults was male and which was female: both looked quite similar, so I could not isolate which (if either) was doing more of the feeding. Years later, I would understand that females have much more white in their tails than males do, and this is a reliable way to distinguish the sexes. But on this evening I could tell only that it was an adult who approached, sat on the lip of the cavity, and offered food to the squawking nestling, who would shuffle forward and accept it. Then the adult would disappear in flight.

After the fifth delivery, one of the adults stayed in the nest for nearly ten minutes before leaving again, and I did not see another adult for more than four hours. The interim was punctuated by the near-incessant shrieks of the nestling; I counted 157 of these grating vocalizations between two-thirty and four-thirty alone, making a tick mark in my journal every time it called.

I left the blind and returned to camp in the stillness and chill of dawn. The long-extinguished fire indicated that Tolya had not yet woken. I ducked into my own tent, wrapped my sleeping bag around me, and quickly fell asleep.

I WAS ROUSED only a few hours later by Tolya, who had an urgency in his voice that brought me to quick attention. I leaped from the tent to find the sky black and the land aflame. A ground fire, about a hundred meters off, was seething toward us, devouring the dry grass of the pasture to our south and goaded onward by a stiff wind.

"Grab a bucket!" Tolya screamed, and ran to the meter-wide backwater between us and the fire. "Get everything wet!"

We stood there, the two of us in shallow water muddy from

the agitation, casting scoop after scoop on the vegetation on the far side of the stream, this line we had to hold. If the fire broke past it, our camp was lost. The flames swelled several meters high in some places, drunk on the desiccated plants. If it surged close enough to the stream, the fire would likely jump across without pause. The flames were closer, maybe thirty meters.

"Are you scared?" Tolya asked me without looking, continuing to cast his windmill spray of water and mud as far as he could.

"Hell yeah I'm scared," I responded. Moments before I had been blissfully and deeply asleep, and now I was standing in mud in my underwear and rubber boots, trying to save my tent from a wildfire with a bucket.

The flames reached the fringe of our water buffer and tentatively tested the damp grasses and shrubs. They licked searchingly, but the vegetation did not burn: the line held. The fire died an unimpressive death a few meters shy of the stream, a battle charge stopped short of total victory by our intervention.

I stared at the field, ashy and smoldering, and asked Tolya what was going on. He said that he had seen someone drive up to the far side of the field, idle for a minute, then drive away. Tolya had not thought anything of it until he saw the smoke, then realized what had happened. It was common practice for villagers to burn their fields in spring—an action thought to promote new growth, kill ticks that might otherwise plague grazing livestock, and add nutrients to the soil. But these fires were usually left untended and, as had been the case here, could extend into the forest and do real harm. In fact, had this blaze happened a few weeks later—after the fish owl chick fledged from the nest but was still unable to fly—the bird could easily have been killed by the flames. These fires are particularly destructive in southwest Primorye, where they are slowly and systematically converting

the dense forests—the last corner of habitat in the world for critically endangered Amur leopards—into an open oak savanna.

Sergey returned the next morning. Our plan was to leave
Tolya in a few days, making our way back to Terney, then continue north to Amgu, but first we would search more of the Avvakumovka River. We surveyed for fish owls by listening
along the Avvakumovka road, similar to how Tolya, John, and
I had listened for owls near Terney, and heard a duet along a small
tributary some twenty kilometers upriver from Vetka. Sergey
and I scoured the forest for signs of a nest there, spending
two nights in a tent next to the river. The birds called from
different places each evening, and since fish owls do not breed
every year, this suggested they were not nesting. We did, however, find what we thought was an old nest tree and evidence of a
nearby roost. We would have spent more time at that site, but
one morning we woke to heavy rains that flooded the river and
our tents. We moved down the Avvakumovka to explore another
tributary closer to the coast, where Sergey had found a nest a
few years prior. Now, though, the nest was empty, and the forest
was quiet.

The morning that Sergey and I left for the north, Tolya asked
that we deliver some fresh supplies before we disappeared. The
nearby village of Vetka was too small to have any shops, so
Sergey and I drove the purple domik into Permskoye, a slightly
larger village about five kilometers away, looking for the potatoes, eggs, and fresh bread Tolya asked for. I sat in the back,
jostling about on one of the soft benches of the domik, and looked
out the tinted, curtained windows. Villages the size of Permskoye,
although they often had stores, sometimes did not advertise them
with storefronts or signs. My theory was that local merchants
felt that anyone who really needed to buy something was a local
who already knew where the store was. We drove up and down

Permskoye's only road, but nothing stood out as obviously a store, so we pulled over and Sergey rolled down the window near two stocky, middle-aged women sitting on a bench. They indicated where we could buy eggs and potatoes—there was a woman selling wares out of a shipping container on the far side of town—but we were out of luck for bread. Apparently, daily deliveries of piping-hot loaves arrived every morning from Olga and quickly sold out: just enough was brought to meet Permskoye demand. Sergey climbed in the domik with this news and we were discussing if it was worth our time to drive into Olga for Tolya's bread when there was a knock at the domik's back door. Sergey opened it to reveal the two women from a moment before, who looked in at us curiously.

"So," one of them started uncertainly, "how does it work with you guys? Do we make an appointment or do you go door-to-door?"

We looked at them blankly. Sergey politely asked for clarification.

"You guys are doctors, right?" the other woman interjected. "People have been talking about the purple truck with X-ray equipment . . . doctors giving free X-ray exams to needy citizens?"

I frowned. Sergey had driven this road back and forth the past week as he moved from one potential owl site to another, and the people of Permskoye and Vetka had come to the logical conclusion that we were a mobile team of freelance X-ray technicians? Odd, but I suppose no stranger than the truth, which was clear from their faces when Sergey explained we were not doctors but ornithologists looking for rare owls. For villagers who had poured their lives and health into these fields and vegetable gardens and were only barely making ends meet, the idea that people might look for birds and call it work was perhaps more bizarre a notion than roaming doctors with a spare X-ray machine on their hands.

We purchased some eggs and potatoes from the shipping container, went into Olga for bread, and delivered all this to Tolya before turning back and heading north. I fell asleep stretched out on the comfortable back bench of the domik while Sergey drove. Once in Dalnegorsk, we parked the domik in Sergey's garage and switched it for his other Toyota Hilux, this one red and souped-up; a field-hearty pickup truck with thick green vinyl covering the bed and all of our field gear that was crammed into it. It looked like something a warlord would drive and was quite suited to negotiate the punishing roads and frothing rivers that awaited us in Terney County. We were heading back into the wild.

13

Where the Mile Markers End

WE MADE OUR WAY SLOWLY, pausing to listen for fish owls. Near Terney, not far from where Tolya, John, and I had heard two pairs, Sergey and I located a third by following distant hooting down a logging trail along the Faata River. We continued over Beryozoviy Pass along the only road north. The hills here still bore the marks of a decades-old forest fire that burned more than twenty thousand hectares of dense, old-growth Korean pine forest. The aftereffects of this catastrophe—rolling hills evenly carpeted by charcoal bristles of standing trunks—gave the impression of driving through an ancient burial field with sentinel trees watching over the lifeless forest. The scarring was less noticeable in winter when everything was bare, but among the optimistic green of spring, a funereal air hung heavy in these barren highlands.

We descended to and crossed the Belimbe River, a narrow and boisterous waterway that grows wider and deeper nearer the coast. I had visited the river mouth some years prior, dumb-founded to find a line of salmon poachers taking turns blocking the river with gill nets, then casting fist-sized grappling hooks into the river and yanking indiscriminately. They were after the valuable roe within the engorged abdomens of pink salmon fe-males, fish that were intent on sprinkling their eggs among the soft pebbles in the river's lower reaches. I could not fathom how any made it past that gauntlet of net and hook.

We followed the Belimbe River east only briefly before drop-ping to low gear and ascending the Kema Pass. The muddy road split at the top, where a bullet-riddled sign pointed straight for Kema and left for Amgu. We turned left. We would not see an-other road sign or mile marker until passing this same one on our drive south: farther north, a labyrinth of logging roads stretched hundreds of kilometers all the way to the logging port of Svet-laya, with no indicators suggesting which of the forks led to the few isolated settlements and which to logging camps or dead ends. As with the absent store signs in Permskoye, it's assumed that if someone ventures onto a road north of Kema, they know where they're going.

Sergey slowed the vehicle on the far side of the pass, as we approached the Tekunzha River. He swung off the road into what I thought was shrubbery but in fact was a long-overgrown logging trail. We bounced along it as though through a car wash, crowded by branches of dry leaves that slapped, massaged, and scraped every surface of the vehicle. We emerged at a clearing, the old logging staging area, and parked there. It was near dark and the ideal time to listen for fish owls, but the evening was windy and we could hear nothing above the noise.

We set up our tents by flashlight and quickly boiled some water on my camp stove for an unsatisfying dinner of "Business Lunch," a dehydrated and prepackaged meal consisting of mashed potato powder and some grizzled bits of beef. The young professional on the packaging seemed far more enthused about his portion than we did about ours, which we drowned in Vietnamese hot sauce and swallowed in silence. Four years prior Sergey had found a nest tree near here, probably only three hundred meters from our camp, that we would visit at first light. This would be an ideal pair to include in our telemetry study, if they were still here, given how close to the road this territory was.

THE TALL GRASSES were still wet with dew the next morning when we followed an overgrown skid trail—a temporary road that loggers use to remove timber—to reach the river. Sergey was in the lead. Although he often recorded the GPS coordinates of notable fish owl locations, such as nest trees or hunting areas, he rarely used his GPS to find them again. His reasoning was sound: there was no better way to understand fish owl habitat than to navigate by feel—walking the rivers and the forest. If we were ever really in a hurry, then by all means turn on the GPS, but staring at a battery-operated box as a matter of routine resulted in the forest becoming a secondary focus; it was easy to miss important details. Sergey led us upriver, paused at a wide beach of water-smoothed pebbles, then peered into the forest.

"If you look hard," he said, leaning to the side and squinting, "you can see the cavity from here."

There was an elm nearly twenty meters tall, poking out of the surrounding willows some forty meters from the riverbank. About halfway up the tree, the trunk split; one half continued up to form a leafy crown, while a gouge remained where the other branch had once been. In the resultant space was the nest cavity of the Tekunzha pair.

Like the other fish owl nests I'd seen, this was a chimney

cavity nest. It was hard to tell if the birds were using it or not. Looking through my binoculars, I could not see any of the telltale signs I'd learned to look for, such as down feathers hooked to the bark near the nest or recent claw marks left when an adult perched on the cavity edge. Sergey figured that if the pair was breeding, the female would be sitting firm and the male would be hidden somewhere nearby on guard; we just needed to cajole him into revealing himself. We moved toward the tree and away from the river's din, then sat on a fallen log in the understory. The green vegetation around us was so thick, it was almost suffocating. Sergey began mimicking the sound I'd heard from the Vetka nestling, a begging shriek also sometimes made by adults, by forcing air through his teeth in a hoarse, descending whistle. He made for a convincing fish owl, and we received a response almost immediately. From downriver the pair vocalized resonantly, a jumbled and poorly synchronized duet that betrayed their fluster. We knew now that the territory was still occupied, but the resident pair was not breeding: otherwise the female would have been on the nest above us.

The birds were incensed that an unknown fish owl had just called from the region of their nest tree, the center of their territory, and one of the spruces overhead swayed suddenly with the burgeoning weight of a fish owl in its crown. Judging from its order in the duet that followed, this was the male. The female had moved closer as well but remained hidden. Both were highly agitated and intent on rooting out the intruder. Sergey, grinning and statue still, was still obscured from them in the understory and whistled again to fan some air on the fire of their hostility. The male transitioned to a horizontal branch of the nest tree opposite us, scouring the ground with his yellow eyes like a glowering dragon. Everything about this bird was striking. The buffy brown plumage of his chest, speckled with darker lateral stripes, made the bird seem almost like an extension of the tree itself, a stout protrusion come alive and vengeful. When he hooted, the white patch on his throat bulged, and his ear tufts, erect and ragged and massive and comical, swayed with every movement.

Suddenly, out of the azure sky above, a Japanese buzzard tucked its wings and plummeted at the fish owl, veering away just before impact. The owl ducked and spun its head to watch the departing hawk and in doing so detected and avoided a carrion crow that was coming in next. I was stunned. We had drawn the fish owls out of hiding, and their vocalizations had in turn attracted this hawk and crow, which alternated mobbing runs at the fish owl. Both attackers must have nests nearby and they possibly mistook this bird for a Eurasian eagle owl, a species that kills and consumes both crows and hawks. The buzzard and the crow, mortal foes themselves, had entered into an uneasy alliance to drive their common enemy away. I had never seen anything like it. The owl's attention was torn: Search the ground below for the intruding owl or avoid blows from above? Sergey and I realized that things were getting out of hand. We thought the best way to de-escalate the situation was by leaving, so we retreated to camp. Despite this, the Tekunzha pair remained in an agitated state and several hours passed before they finally relaxed and their calls ceased.

For the time being, we had all the answers we needed here: the territory was occupied, the pair was not nesting, and we had another pair of birds to add to our potential capture list. We were up to six pairs: two in the Avvakumovka River basin near Olga, three in the Serebryanka River basin near Terney, and this pair in the Kema River basin. After lunch, we packed up the truck and returned to the dust of the road, continuing north as the track traced the Kema River.

We did not go far that day—less than twenty kilometers—before reaching our next stopping point. There was a small valley on the far side of the river that Sergey had always wanted to explore for fish owls but had never had the time to spare. This was his opportunity. We put on chest waders and moved across the fifty-meter-wide waterway, using heavy poles to help keep our balance in the difficult crossing. Similar to my experience at the Serebryanka River some weeks earlier with Tolya, the river here had no patience for hesitation and blasted me with surging water whenever I paused and my body created eddies downstream. The more experienced Sergey scouted ahead, indicating the shallowest and safest route and shouting instructions back to me. Once ashore, we abandoned our waders: we did not want to haul them with us while we searched the forest for owls, and quite frankly, anyone willing to cross that menacing river to steal them was worthy of the prize. Besides, we'd hardly seen another car all day—there were not many people on these roads—and the few vehicles we did see were usually logging trucks.

Almost immediately we stumbled upon a narrow path that led us through a dark forest of young fir and spruce. Sergey was disappointed—this was not fish owl habitat at all. Up ahead we spied a small clearing with a hunter's cabin and followed the trail to it. The hut appeared to have been unoccupied for some time, so we were startled when a domestic cat dropped from the eaves, a long-haired tabby with dirty, matted fur. It howled at us, a desperate, mournful sound. I suspected the cat was starving, but we had no food to offer—we had not brought any with us across the river. Hunters commonly kept cats with them at their cabins to limit the number of hantavirus-carrying rodents that penetrated the wooden walls and porous floors, but sadly, sometimes these creatures were abandoned at the end of the season. On occasion I'd find a cat carcass in an empty hut. We moved past the cabin with the imploring cat at our heels and found that the valley narrowed even further and the trees in this coniferous forest tightened their ranks until there was no understory growth, only a soft bed of aromatic needles. There was nothing for us here. We looped off-trail to the other side of the valley and headed back toward the Kema River. The cat followed. Sergey cursed the hunter who left the creature there and threw sticks to drive the cat back in the direction of the cabin. The animal understood what we were doing and its emphatic wailing turned despondent and bitter. It continued to follow us for about a kilometer, but at a distance—out of sight but still audible. Eventually, we got close enough to the river that the sounds of the water muffled its pleading cries. We forded across without looking back.

WE SOON REACHED the most impressive of the mountain passes of our drive north: the Amgu Pass. The road, a series of narrow, sharp switchbacks, demanded complete attention. Any driver with eyes wandering to the surrounding mountain views risked careening off the road's soft shoulder or plowing headlong into an oncoming logging truck obscured by the many turns. At the bottom of the pass, the road found and then followed the middle reaches of the Amgu River and passed through a lush, mixed-species forest. I assessed the river and was troubled to find it an angry, seething brown. We had delayed our trip to Amgu precisely to avoid this: we intended to drive the Hilux across this river near its mouth sometime in the next week to look for fish owls. I asked Sergey what he thought our prospects of safe passage were.

"Won't be a problem," he responded, dismissing my concern without hesitation. "I know a guy with a tractor in Amgu. If the water's too high we'll latch our truck to it and be towed across. It'll be fine."

Although we still intended to make it to the village of Amgu that night, we first stopped sixteen kilometers from it. It was nearly dusk, and we were at the confluence of the Amgu River and the Sha-Mi, one of its tributaries. Here, Sergey had heard a pair of fish owls calling for years. He'd devoted countless days and nights to hunting down the nest tree but had absolutely nothing to show for it except sweat and frustration. He was itching for closure and wanted to see if they would call tonight. He dropped me off along the muddy, uneven path that led up the Sha-Mi. There had been a village up there once, abandoned for decades, but the road remained. Sergey drove up it. He would go as far as conditions would allow, then pause to listen before turning back. I would walk up the road, ears alert, until we intersected.

I strolled quietly in the waning light, content in the pleasant evening and hearing the plummeting trill of a rufous-tailed robin, the chipper clucks of Oriental scops owls, and once, a bout of energetic hoots from a brown hawk owl. But no fish owls. I had walked perhaps two kilometers when I spied Sergey's truck up ahead, parked on the far side of a shallow river crossing where the water only just submerged the pebbly substrate. I found him there, silent and smoking. He had not heard any fish owls either.

Sergey pointed toward the dark river water and suggested I test its temperature. I dipped in my finger, suspicious, and it was warm. It should have been near freezing. Sergey revealed that this was where natural radon gas bubbles seeped from underground into the current, warming it. Radon gas—perhaps best known as the cancer-causing, odorless substance lurking in basements around the world—is formed naturally when radioactive metals break down. The resultant gas leaks into the atmosphere through cracks in the ground. In this case, the radon leaked directly into the water, which was why this stretch of river remained unfrozen in winter and consequently why fish owls were able to survive here, as they had open water in which to hunt. Sergey said many of the rivers in this part of Primorye were warmed by radon, which meant our prospects to find fish owls were good.

We climbed into the Hilux, returned to the main road, and continued to Amgu. Sergey had a friend there, Vova Volkov, who had offered us a room in his house while we searched the area. As the Sha-Mi River was so close to town, we would stay with Vova and commute. We soon reached the low fences of the first houses and then descended a hill to the center of Amgu. There were no streetlights here, so the village was dark. Sergey stopped the car in front of one of the few houses that still had light in the windows.

Despite the late hour, Vova Volkov was behind a gate outside his house under a floodlight, repairing what looked like a grocery truck. When Sergey and I entered the yard through the wrought-iron fence, the short and rotund figure beamed at Sergey, hustled over, and extended his right arm with a limp wrist—the Russian signal that his hand was too dirty for a proper handshake. Sergey and I took turns grasping Vova by the forearm and shaking vigorously. Vova, whose last name means "of the wolves" in Russian, was in his midforties and jovial, cussing as though under contract to do so. He led us inside, where he washed his hands under the water dispenser nailed to the wall near the door while Sergey greeted Alla, Vova's wife, then introduced me. She was older than Vova by maybe a decade but shared his round form and, as I would soon learn, his vulgar tongue. Alla and Vova ushered us to the table in their kitchen and began unloading their culinary arsenal, a battle I was thoroughly unprepared for. Plates of deer cutlets, seaweed salad, and fresh bread were pushed aside to make space for volleys of boiled potatoes, a skillet of six freshly fried eggs, and bowls brimming with salmon soup. The Volkovs took their food seriously and once they began cooking were a near-unstoppable force. Protests of satiation were ignored or outright mocked, then countered with a fresh dish. Russians are famous for their hospitality around a kitchen table and in my experience none more so than the Volkovs.

Vova produced a bottle of vodka. The social bond to drink until the bottle was empty was not enforced among close friends, so we learned a little about one another over a few shots. Vova was formerly a professional hunter, part of the same Soviet program that funded the hunters and trappers of Agzu. Although he still maintained a hunting territory up the Sherbatovka River, land that he and his father had hunted for decades and where we later planned to look for fish owls, Vova no longer spent as much time in the forest as he would have liked. The majority of his days were consumed by commerce—he and Alla owned one of the three or four stores in town. Alla handled the business side while Vova oversaw daily maintenance: everything from building construction to generator operation during one of Amgu's frequent power outages. However, his biggest and most time-consuming role by far was keeping the store supplied: this required driving the truck south to Ussuriysk every six weeks, a four-day round-trip journey along nearly 1,200 kilometers of largely terrible road.

Vova asked us our intentions in the area, and Sergey explained that we envisioned beginning our fish owl search with a weeklong investigation of the Amgu and Sherbatovka River drainages to the west, before shifting farther north to the Saiyon and Maksimovka River drainages. As we would have to cross the Amgu River near its mouth to reach the Sherbatovka River,

Sergey inquired about water conditions. I realized then that Vova was the tractor-owning friend Sergey had touted earlier, should the river current prove too formidable for the pickup truck.

Vova winced. "The river's terrible. The other day someone was trying to cross with their tractor and the current knocked it over."

We decided to work out of town as planned, then head north to the Saiyon and Maksimovka areas before risking a crossing of the Amgu River to reach the Sherbatovka. We spent the majority of a week investigating the Sha-Mi territory. We found considerable fish owl sign there, from a molted primary feather the length of my forearm to an incredible roost littered with dozens of pellets containing fish and frog bones. But despite this, and hearing the pair call vigorously every night, we were unable to pinpoint the center of their territory—that is, the nest tree. The first night they had called from the far side of the Amgu River, opposite the confluence with the Sha-Mi, so the following evening we donned our chest waders and endured a harrowing nighttime river crossing only to then hear them call from far up the Sha-Mi. And on the third night, when they hooted from the mountain slope between those two locations, we threw up our hands. Clearly they were not breeding this year and were not amenable to leading us to their nest. One positive development came as we made our dejected return to the village one night: we heard another pair vocalizing from the Kudya River valley, across the Amgu. We did not have the time to investigate, but this discovery meant that we were up to eight pairs in our pool of potential birds to capture the following year. In mid-May, we loaded up the red Hilux and stopped by the bakery for a few loaves of fresh bread. We tore off hunks of its warm, crispy crust as we headed north for the Saiyon and Maksimovka Rivers.

14

The Banality of Road Travel

THE SAIYON RIVER was about twenty kilometers north from Amgu. We took the Hilux on the lone track that led that way, passing between the only gas station within hundreds of kilometers and the logging company headquarters, a complex of several one-story structures with cream-colored vinyl under maroon roofs on the hill above the tsunami zone. The tidiness of these buildings was out of place in this frontier town: an artificial rose conspicuous among the briars. From there the road skirted the wide and sandy beach on the north side of Amgu Bay, a flat expanse scattered with gray driftwood, weather-beaten marine debris, and the occasional shrub bowed inland in submission to the coastal wind. After crossing a low pass of spruce and fir, the road split. The more maintained thoroughfare headed northwest toward timber concessions, the Old Believer village of Ust-Sobolevka, and the logging town of Svetlaya. The second road led northeast another eighteen kilometers to Maksimovka, a collection of 150 people at the mouth of the river that

A Blakiston's fish owl, the Sha-Mi female, alert and with ear tufts erect, is about to flush upon my approach in March 2008. (Photograph © Jonathan C. Slaght)

TOP: Terney, Primorye, a village of about three thousand people encircled by mountains, forest, river, and sea, in March 2016. (Photograph © Jonathan C. Slaght)

ABOVE: Our base camp by the Saiyon hot spring in 2009. We lived in this truck, a GAZ-66, for weeks while trying to capture the resident pair of fish owls.

(Photograph © Jonathan C. Slaght)

ABOVE: After a long day scouting for fish owl hunting locations in March 2009, I cross a channel of the Serebryanka River. (Photograph © Andrey Katkov)

BELOW: Sergey Avdeyuk (right) and I attach a color leg band to a juvenile fish owl, the third one we caught in the span of an hour in the Kudya territory in March 2009. The band allowed us to identify this owl as an adult years later, some forty kilometers away, on the other side of a mountain range. (Photograph © Andrey Katkov)

The plumage of an incubating fish owl blends almost seamlessly with the blacks, browns, and grays of the surrounding bark. She is further cloaked by a veil of smoke from a spring fire, in 2014. (Photograph © Sergey G. Surmach)

ABOVE LEFT: Stacks of birch and fir logs in Amgu, destined to become lumber and wood veneer, then shipped to China, Japan, and South Korea, in 2011. (Photograph © Jonathan C. Slaght)

ABOVE RIGHT: Andrey Katkov as a blizzard sets in, right before we enter the forest to look for a fish owl nest tree in March 2009. (Photograph © Jonathan C. Slaght)

BELOW: The Saiyon nest in April 2008, with a just-hatched, still-blind chick. The narrow Saiyon River is visible below. The second egg never hatched. (Photograph © Jonathan C. Slaght)

ABOVE: The Vetka female, roosting and relaxed, while her now chicken-sized offspring rests in the nest nearby, in 2006. (Photograph © Sergey G. Surmach)

BELOW: A fish owl pauses in shallow river water with its fresh kill, a young masu salmon, before swallowing it whole, in 2017. (Photograph © Sergey Gafitski)

ABOVE: The nestling fish owl at Vetka, threatened by Sergey Surmach's approach in 2006, ruffles its feathers in an attempt to intimidate him into backing off.
(Photograph © Sergey G. Surmach)

RIGHT: Shurik Popov, having free-climbed an adjacent tree amid the tangles of the Kudya River valley, confirms he's found a fish owl nest in an old-growth chosenia—the largest tree on the right side of the image.
(Photograph © Jonathan C. Slaght)

TOP: The hermit Anatoliy, with the word любовь ("love") tattooed on his left hand, hangs pink salmon to dry under the eaves of his cabin in 2008. Anatoliy hosted us during portions of our fieldwork for most seasons of the telemetry project.

(Photograph © Jonathan C. Slaght)

MIDDLE: With cans of fish, peas, corn, and some sips of moonshine, Sergey Avdeyuk (right) and I celebrate the end of our telemetry project's final field season in 2010.

(Photograph © Jonathan C. Slaght)

BELOW: This valley near Terney, photographed in 2004, represents the Goldilocks of habitat for fish owls: a partially unfrozen river for hunting, adjacent old-growth deciduous trees for nesting, and intermingled conifers for roosting.

(Photograph © Jonathan C. Slaght)

bore the same name. In winter, the locals just as often drove on the river ice or across frozen swamp to reach this village—it was much faster that way—but for the majority of the year, motorists were confined to the banality of road travel. We slowed and turned up the Maksimovka village road, stopping soon after in front of a radon hot spring.

In contrast with the hot spring at Sha-Mi, which was nothing more than a warm stretch of water where radon gas seeped into the cold river, this one had been dug out at the source and lined with timbers, resulting in a waist-deep pool sunken into the earth. There is a belief—particularly among those from former Soviet republics—that exposure to radioactive radon, when the gas is dissolved in water, can cure a range of maladies from high blood pressure to diabetes and infertility. Here, a massive wooden Russian Orthodox cross loomed over this pit of warm water, and a small log cabin had been constructed a few paces away.

As we drove closer, we saw a battered white sedan with no license plates parked nearby. Few vehicles were legally registered this far north, as there were no police to enforce the law—the closest police station was in Terney—so no one bothered. A scrawny naked form, attracted by the sound of our motor, crawled lethargically out of the radon-infused waters. Sergey parked the Hilux and we walked over to greet the man; I could sense by his sway that he was intoxicated.

"Who the bloody hell are you guys?" he asked, dripping and slurring. Locals were sometimes protective of their resources, and here just about everybody knew everybody. We were strangers, and snooty types with license plates, no less.

"Ornithologists," answered Sergey, eyeing this wet creature birthed from radon. "Do you know what a fish owl is? Have you ever seen or heard one?"

The man looked at us uncertainly; the response and counter-question seemed to knock him a little further off balance. Then his eyes darted over to the Hilux, where they settled on the "AC" in Sergey's license plate—the mark for Dalnegorsk. All legal vehicles could be identified by a two-letter code to the county in which they were registered.

"Zemlyak!" he cried, recognizing Sergey as a product of his own hometown. Then, perhaps following an unstated rule that underclothes were the minimum dress code for hugs with strangers, he hastily legged his way into boxer shorts, grabbed Sergey by the neck, and pressed their foreheads together, grinning. The man gushed about his childhood in Dalnegorsk and the various failures and opportunities that led to his subsequent exodus to the village of Maksimovka, where he worked as a logger. They exchanged stories of shared acquaintances. After some minutes, as if for the first time, his hazy gaze fell on me.

"And who's the quiet guy?" this mostly naked, still-wet gentleman inquired of Sergey, looking at my camouflaged, cross-armed, bearded figure. A large knife hung from my belt. "Is he your bodyguard?"

I had learned that silence was the best policy when encountering strangers, especially drunken ones, as the most common reaction to meeting a foreigner was demands of communal vodka ingestion to facilitate a lengthy exploration of cultural differences. I'd done my time and was not volunteering for more. Sergey was aware of this danger as well, so he simply said I was not his bodyguard, then returned the conversation to this family or that, who moved where, and who died of what. Eventually the man put on pants and a shirt, and after beseeching Sergey to pass along his regards to a variety of Dalnegorskers, he climbed into his car and drove off.

We walked to the Saiyon River. Sergey had a spot where he

usually camped on a wide and pebbly bank, adjacent to a sharp river bend with a deep hole and reliably good fishing. It was about half a kilometer from a fish owl nest tree, the first he had ever discovered, sometime in the late 1990s. It was still too early to listen for owls, so we walked there to find it. The lower Saiyon River valley was different from most fish owl habitat I had encountered thus far: the landscape was largely open and wet, more swamp than forest, with larch trees and grassy hummocks dominating the center of the valley and deciduous species clinging tightly to the thin line of flowing water. The sparse vegetation offered little cover for a roosting fish owl—they must regularly be harassed by crows here. I learned from Sergey that Saiyon had been the site of a political prisoner work camp during the Second World War. Human bones were still occasionally found among the curtains of sedges.

We soon reached the nest tree, only a few meters from the edge of the river. We discovered the nest itself empty, with no signs of recent use. It was an exposed cavity surprisingly low in a chosenia, only four meters off the ground, and with a decaying frame that made this nest more of a platform than a cavity. The resident pair had likely moved on to something better. When we returned to the Hilux, Sergey told me he thought I was ready for a solo nest search. We had been working closely for nearly two months and always together. He believed it would do me good to explore the forest completely on my own, without the crutch of his expertise. I was up to the challenge. Our camp was at the confluence of two small river valleys, the Saiyon and the Seselevka, and I elected to spend that day walking the former. I packed a bag with enough snacks to hold me over and filled a thermos with hot water for tea. Sergey volunteered to spend his time that day estimating fish owl prey density, a terribly masked but earnestly stated euphemism for fishing. He wished me luck, then opened the back of the Hilux and began rummaging for his pole and tackle box.

I was back before he was done baiting his hook.

"Found it."

"Already!?" Sergey was astounded but proud, as a father might be.

I had walked northwest up the valley and had not gone more than sixty meters from camp, passing the cut stump of a huge Japanese poplar. This tree had likely been felled to build a nearby bridge, and although I couldn't say for sure if there had been a cavity in this tree or not, it was certainly big and old enough to hold a fish owl nest. As I stood on the stump I saw another big poplar, and I raised my binoculars to see fish owl down clinging to the rim of a chimney cavity. A cursory search closer to the tree revealed fish owl pellets nearby as well: no more evidence was needed. I took a GPS point and returned to camp not twenty minutes after I left.

We stayed at the Saiyon territory for two nights but did not hear the fish owls. The fresh feathers at and near the newly discovered nest tree suggested that the pair had perhaps attempted to breed, but we found no evidence of offspring. On May 21, we packed up camp and continued to our northernmost destination, the Maksimovka River. We did not intend to stay there long, only to briefly visit a tributary of the Maksimovka called the Losevka, where Sergey had found a nest tree in 2001, and then return south. The owls had different plans for us.

THE ROAD from our camp at Saiyon traced a terrace above the river valley, following the course of water to its upper reaches. There, precipitous slopes of pine pushed closer and closer until, after we'd crossed into the Maksimovka River drainage, the pressure released and the valley on the far side widened. A long, single-track wooden bridge came into view, extending from one cliff to another, high over the river. The Maksimovka itself was just over a hundred kilometers long and started in a steep, rocky gorge lined by conifers and swamp full of moose, wild boar, and musk deer. The valley remained relatively narrow for most of its flow, then widened abruptly like a trumpet flower around this bridge, where the river broke into multiple channels and flowed another sixteen kilometers east to the Sea of Japan.

We crossed the bridge, then turned off to follow a logging road that shadowed the Maksimovka's north bank. We passed skid trail after skid trail, narrow paths just wide enough for the tree-harvesting equipment, which cut into the forest like vanes of a feather radiating from its shaft. This scene surprised Sergey. The main road was all that had existed when he was last here in 2001—all of this logging pressure was new.

After nearly twenty kilometers, we were closing in on the Losevka River and started looking for a campsite. We found a side road that started enthusiastically but then ended after about fifty meters, when it was swallowed by the Maksimovka River, then emerged unharmed but irrelevant on the far side. The thirty meters of deep, rushing water in between held the splintered remains of a bridge that had by all evidence been there quite recently. This dead end offered us excellent access to water and Sergey thought it was fairly close to the nest tree we were looking for, so this was where we would camp.

After setting up our tents and devouring a quick snack, we went to inspect the Losevka pair's nest tree. Sergey had not visited in five years and was eager to see if it was still occupied. We walked east through deciduous forest plagued by the ravages of high water: understory grasses bent downriver and debris draped unenthusiastically from low branches like faded Christmas garlands. We emerged at a vast, grassy clearing about six football fields long by two wide.

In the center of this expanse, nestled among the bright green grasses of spring and ringed by a forest border of ash and aspen and poplar, stood a single gray house and a dilapidated shed, with the remains of a fence surrounding perhaps half of this complex. A grove of cherry trees bloomed pink just beyond. The main structure was large, built with saddle-notched logs under a gabled roof, and the whole building was covered by an uneven web of patches and repairs. It looked as though it had been there a long time and, as Sergey explained, it had.

This was the last evidence of the village of Ulun-ga, an Old Believer settlement liquidated by the Soviet government in the 1930s. At one point there were at least thirty-five Old Believer settlements north of Amgu alone, five times as many villages as there are in that same space today. The Old Believers had come to Primorye to escape czarist oppression and were not about to bend a pious knee to a devil like Iosif Stalin and his plans for collectivization. In the resulting unrest, some Old Believers were executed while hundreds more were arrested, jailed, or deported.

By the 1950s, all that remained of most Old Believer settlements were open clearings like this one. Eventually, grasses grew thick in these fields, fed by the soils soaked in blood and enriched by the charcoal remains of burned homes. This final house was evidence of the violent past. Sergey said it had been used by the Old Believers as a school, but why it was saved remains unclear. By 2006, it acted as a hunting cabin for Zinkovskiy, a one-eyed hunter who lived in Maksimovka.

We circled the fringe of this field to reach where the small Losevka River flowed into the Maksimovka. This was Sergey's initial point of reference to find the nest tree. As we walked through the forest, we kept stumbling out on skid trails. Sergey was bewildered by this network of logging trails, which threw off his orientation. Our search was complicated by the fact that we did not have GPS coordinates for this nest tree; when Sergey was last here, such technology was not readily available in Russia. He figured he could navigate back to the tree using intuition. Sticky from the rising humidity, we spent the greater part of two hours searching the lush forest, stumbling sweaty among waist-high ferns under a lofty, thick, and dark canopy. At one point we flushed a Eurasian sparrowhawk, a lanky predator that floundered in panic among the branches before reaching the obstruction-free tunnel above the Losevka River, where it disappeared as a gray, horizontal line. Sergey seemed to regularly draw us to the same patch of forest, but there was nothing there resembling a fish owl nest tree. Then we saw the stump.

"Yob tvoyu mat," Sergey swore, using a term too vulgar for me to translate, "they cut it down."

We stood above an enormous stump, staring with the ferns at the clean line of its cut as a crowd might gape at the scene of a hit-and-run. Logging companies in the region routinely harvested large, rotting, commercially useless trees such as poplar and elm to use in bridge construction. It was easier to build a bridge by laying a few huge trees across a stream than a few dozen smaller ones, and hollow sections of old-growth trunks could act as natural culverts, allowing water to flow through. The nest tree was probably part of one of the dozen or so bridges we had crossed to reach this place, maybe even the one that had recently washed away near our campsite. As rivers in coastal Primorye typically flooded every year, and bridges were regularly lost to the insatiable current, demand for large trees was constant. And since most roads and all potential fish owl nest trees were near rivers, these forest giants were obvious targets

for loggers looking to build a quick bridge. This process was systematically removing fish owl nest trees—or potential nest trees—
from the forest, taking an already rare landscape feature and
making it even harder for fish owls to find a place to raise a family.
It took hundreds of years for a tree to become large enough for a
fish owl; what would the owls do if all the big trees were gone?

Without a nest to work with we returned to camp, disappointed. We had intended to sleep here only one night, but it was
clear that if we wanted to learn anything about the fish owls of
the Losevka River, we had to start from scratch.

LATE THE NEXT DAY, I was in my tent, earphones on and testing
my knowledge of local birdsong from a tape of vocalizations I
had recorded during my master's work with songbirds. My fabric dome was suddenly shadowed. I turned off the machine and
realized that Sergey had been shouting and was standing over
me. I unzipped the tent and peered out.

"Jon, I think we're screwed! Don't you hear that?" He looked
absolutely forlorn, with a face red from running and chest waders still dripping with Maksimovka water. He had been on the
river all morning, fastidiously assessing fish owl prey density. I
listened and could make out the rhythmic groan of heavy
machinery—sounds that had been obscured by the birds trilling
in my ears.

"We need to go. Now." I watched as he took down his tent
with surprising ferocity, without folding the poles and leaving
his sleeping bag and pad inside, jamming the whole mess into the
back of his pickup truck. I stared.

"*Move*, for Christ's sake!" he roared. "Do you want to be stuck
here for the next month? That's how long it's going to take us to
dig out. We're being closed off!"

I had no idea what he was talking about, but his uncharacteristic anxiety catalyzed me into action. We hurriedly stripped the campsite and were barreling down the road not five minutes later.

The last half kilometer between us and the fork to the Losevka River was straight, and I understood why Sergey was panicked. Ahead, I could see a bulldozer in the process of piling an ungodly amount of dirt in the middle of the track, blocking us in. Sergey leaned on the horn and flashed his lights. Later, Sergey told me that he had been happily fishing on the river, every once in a while disturbed by the clatter of a diesel engine. Since he knew there was a logging camp around here, the significance of this sound did not register. But then he noticed that the noises seemed to be coming from right where the road forked, and immediately thereafter he recalled that the logging company had the commendable and uncommon habit of blocking access to unused logging roads to prevent use by poachers, who would drive at night shooting deer, wild boar, and even tigers. When he'd realized what was likely happening, he bolted back to camp.

The tractor driver stopped working and stared at us with cigarette dangling and a look of surprise, and three men stepped out of a white, idling Toyota Land Cruiser with similar expressions.

"What the blazes are you doing back there?" the oldest of the men demanded. He was short and in his sixties, with white hair. Then he saw Sergey and exhaled. "Ah, ornithologists! Been a while. How are your owls?"

This was Aleksandr Shulikin, the general director of the local logging company. Sergey had met him in 2001, the last time he'd been on the Maksimovka. Shulikin erected the roadblocks because he and his son Nikolay were hunters themselves, with land nearby, and were interested in keeping deer and boar numbers high. The bulldozer had only just started to fill the road in, so it made a few clearing passes, and we drove to the opposite side of the low barrier, then watched as the machine put its mind to the task. The bulldozer lacerated the dirt track with two perpendicular gashes, each three meters wide and a meter deep, then piled the resultant viscera of loose earth and rock in the space between.

"We don't even have a shovel in the truck," said Sergey, leaning over and dragging on a cigarette while we watched the bulldozer work. "It would have taken us a week to dig out." I noticed that in the years to come, Sergey always kept a shovel or two in his vehicle. When the machine was done, a steep mountain of earth rose about seven meters, an impossible barrier for any vehicle to cross. Had we arrived an hour later, there would have been nothing we could do: the bulldozer would have departed and we would have been stranded.

Despite our near miss, I was impressed: road closures were clearly an effective deterrent to poachers. Anyone looking to hunt here illegally would stop short at this berm, then likely drive on to a more accessible area. This essentially made lands beyond the closure a de facto wildlife refuge. While in theory every logging company had a legal obligation to close a road once they were done harvesting in an area, contradictions in the forest code of the Russian Federation meant that few did.

Suddenly homeless but not yet finished exploring the Losevka River, we drove up the Losevka logging road and found a flat, clear spot to camp right on the riverbank. I went to the river for some water to boil tea and Sergey began preparing lunch. The first thing Sergey removed from the truck was his cooler: a forty-five-liter, light blue box with aluminum trimming that he seemed convinced had magical properties. Earlier in the spring it had done its job admirably, but now that we were seeing warm, summerlike temperatures and concomitant humidity, the cooler was doing little to prevent mold from forming on the perishables we stored within. But Sergey was stubborn in his belief that this supernatural box would allow us to store meats and cheese for long periods of time without refrigeration.

It turned out that we had set our tents fairly close to the logging camp, and the watchman, whom I recognized from our encounter with Shulikin earlier, stopped by on his walk back from the road closure. He was a hefty individual named Pasha, with brown hair and brown eyes under something akin to an engineer's cap. He walked gingerly with knees that had borne his weight for close to six decades and grown weary of the task. We invited him to sit for some food and tea. Pasha was an extremely even-keeled individual, perhaps to a fault, and reminded me of a torporic bear just roused. He told us of the last time he had been in Terney, many years prior. He had taken the helicopter down for a medical evaluation of a chronic condition and while there had been convinced by the intoxicated doctor on duty to have his appendix removed.

"When he stepped out the nurses hissed that I was crazy, that I should get up and leave before he killed me, but I was already there, you know? So he did it, and that's how I got this." He raised his flannel shirt to show me a gargantuan appendix scar. "One less thing I have to worry about."

Sergey meanwhile had been inspecting our food. He removed a long stick of sausage from the cooler, which he held up between two fingers and scrutinized with a wrinkled nose. Pasha looked on skeptically. When Sergey deemed the sausage fit for human consumption and rubbed it with warm water to wash off some of the mold, Pasha voiced his opinion.

"I'm not sure that sausage is safe to eat," protested the man

who'd allowed a drunk doctor to remove his appendix for no medical reason. "It's probably gone bad."

Sergey dismissed him. "It's fine," he said, "we have a cooler,"
and pointed to his blue wonder agape and airing, its silver band
shimmering in the hot afternoon sun.

WE SPENT THAT EVENING and the next morning walking through
the snarled understory of the Losevka River valley. I kept eyeing
Sergey to see if the sausage he ate and I refused was causing him
any trouble, but he offered no cues. I had heard a single fish owl
calling from downriver the night before, closer to the Maksimovka River, and Sergey had flushed a roosting fish owl from
near the river mouth in the morning. So the next day we decided
to strike our camp in the upper reaches of the Losevka and relocate closer to the Maksimovka to focus our efforts there.

We picked an open spot to set our tents right on the Maksimovka River bank, about two kilometers downriver of our previous camp by the destroyed bridge. The scars of campfires past
showed me that this place was used regularly, probably by fishermen from the village of Maksimovka.

We were having an evening snack by our tents before heading out to listen for owls when quite unexpectedly a fish owl duet
rang out from across the river opposite us. This was a fantastic
revelation. Typically, when one of the resident pair dies, the surviving mate will remain at that site calling to attract a new mate,
so we had been worried that our recent detections of only a single bird meant that one of the pair had died. But no—they were
both alive and well. The river was far too deep and rapid here to
negotiate on foot, so we could not get any closer. We sat, listening contentedly. Suddenly Sergey held up a finger and cocked
his head so his right ear was facing downriver.

"Did you hear that?" he whispered.

I replied that all I could make out was the river and the owls hooting across it.

"Not that. Softer and downriver. Another duet!"

Sergey leaped to his feet and was in the Hilux in an instant. The channel prevented us from approaching the birds across the Maksimovka, but owls downstream we had a chance to find.

Mud sprayed behind the truck as we bounded back toward the main logging road; this transitioned to dust and pebble when we reached it. Sergey cut the engine after four hundred meters. I was still a little skeptical that he had heard anything at all, but he assured me that distance from the river and proximity to the source would bring me around.

He was correct. Just after the Losevka pair finished their duet from upriver, a second pair farther down responded with their own. Two pairs at once! These were birds on the edges of their territories, shouting like border guards of rival countries daring each other to cross. Sergey started the engine and we moved closer, stopping another half kilometer later, where the road followed the curve of a small hill. We waited but heard nothing except the now faint duet from upriver. We waited a little longer, and still nothing. Sergey, impatient, played his trump card—the juvenile fish owl shriek. The trees erupted. The pair had been sitting above us in the dense canopy. Like the pair we had agitated at the Tekunzha territory earlier in the trip, they were beside themselves with rage and flew about from tree to tree. They were already excitable from the dueling vocalizations with the Losevka pair, and now an errant fish owl had stolen deep into their camp: an intolerable intrusion.

We stayed there, watching these feathered golems fret above us until it was after dark, then returned to our camp quite pleased by the unexpected turn that day had taken.

THE NEXT MORNING, we drove back to where we had disturbed owls the prior evening and spent a few hours searching the river bottom for a nest without success. In the afternoon, we inflated Sergey's rubber boat and fought the current to cross the Maksimovka, landing opposite where the village of Ulun-ga used to stand and near where the owls had hooted the night before. From our maps we knew the island they had called from was oblong and ran from west to east, with the main channel of the Maksimovka River forming its north and east sides and a lesser tributary forming its west and south sides. The island was about a kilometer and a half long and half as wide. We tested our two-way radios and split up. Sergey would wander the northern half, then park himself on the western slope by dusk to wait for the owls to vocalize.

The eastern half of this island was my purview. I walked straight across the floodplain, which seemed primeval and was breathtaking in its beauty. The trunks of poplars, elms, and pines rose to form a tall canopy, their bases hidden by the green understory and rutted by bubbling streams and pools populated by schools of masu salmon, white-spotted char, and lenok. There was ungulate sign everywhere, mostly of wild boar. I passed droppings and tracks, and their long, split hairs clung to resinous pine trunks. I saw roe deer, a sable, and the carcass of a Ural owl likely killed by a mountain hawk eagle: I found an eagle feather among the owl remains like a macabre calling card. The mountain hawk eagle was an enormous raptor that quietly colonized Primorye from Japan sometime in the 1980s. I followed a small creek to the valley edge on the south side, where I encountered the expected channel abutting a steep slope. It was fairly close to dusk, so I selected a quiet spot on a comfortable log near where the creek flowed into the channel to sit and wait. It was a lovely evening in a spring forest: I sat breathing in cool, aromatic air and listening to the calls of a grey nightjar overhead, a sound like someone briskly chopping a cucumber. I sensed something walking down the channel toward me, the muted slosh of footsteps and the crunch of displaced rocks. I knew it wasn't Sergey; he should already be settled on the slope to the west, listening, as I was. I did not have long to wonder: a moment later the black mass of an enormous male boar sauntered into view, his curving white tusks contrasting against the darkness of his hide. I held my breath and watched. He walked slowly with the water, at one point not more than twenty meters away, then disappeared downstream. I exhaled. While not typically aggressive, wild boar can be dangerous if provoked. Big males like the one that just passed, in fact, have been known to mortally wound tigers with their tusks. When shot at, they can charge rather than flee, sometimes killing their attackers before the hunters can reload. In one particularly gruesome example, John Goodrich once told me of a boar that first killed the hunter who'd shot him and then ate his legs.

I had only just sunk back into the hypnosis of waiting when the radio crackled and I flinched. Sergey was shouting.

"Hold on, here they come!"

"Repeat, please," I queried with confusion.

"Find some shelter, brother! That storm is headed right for you!" he bellowed. I could tell from his voice that he was laughing.

A short while later I heard it, a wave of noise moving through the forest, squeals riding a crest of rustling vegetation and snapping twigs. I stood and pivoted behind a tree for cover just as a tsunami of wild boar broke the vegetation line across the creek and streamed past, half of them piglets. Sergey told me later that a sounder of a dozen boars had come within ten meters of where he was sitting, and he could not resist roaring at them like a bear. The animals stampeded in panic, coincidentally directing their flight exactly toward where Sergey suspected I was likely waiting.

Once the boar passed, I settled again. All was quiet for about thirty minutes as darkness fell, then more static with Sergey whispering.

"Jon. I have something. How quickly can you get over here?"

I turned on my headlamp and bushwhacked for about three hundred meters, following the tributary that I knew led to Sergey's location. Once closer, I could see where he was from the flashlight on the hill, and when I came close enough to see his face, I found him confused.

"I heard a fish owl shriek," he said, "so I was sure I had a nest tree nearby. That's when I contacted you. I crept up and saw the silhouette of an adult fish owl up there." He pointed. "It flew in from the other side of the river, and flew back there when I moved. But there's nothing here. Nothing close to big enough for a nest tree. I thought they only made that shriek noise at the nest . . ."

We crossed the dark river back to camp.

We returned to the island the next day as well, spending hours scouring it for a nest tree, but we had no luck. This place was certainly used by fish owls, but perhaps only for hunting, not nesting. We needed to reassess the function of that particular vocalization, as what we'd thought was true no longer was—the fish owl shriek was not tied exclusively to a nest site. With experience, we would learn that fish owls made the shrieking sound whenever they begged for food—be it at the nest or away from it. In retrospect, I would guess that Sergey had seen and heard a second-year juvenile: a bird large enough for its silhouette to be mistaken for that of an adult but still unable to hunt completely independently. It had been calling to its parents.

It rained that night, and we were running out of time—I had a plane to catch back to the United States in a few weeks, and Sergey had matters at home that needed tending. It seemed clear that the Losevka pair was not nesting this year, and without an active nest to bind them to one place, we had little chance of finding them. We had confirmed they were there and alive, and that was good enough for the time being. We added the Losevka pair and the unknown pair from downriver to our list of potential capture candidates for the next year and decided it was time to return to Amgu. We had one stop left here in the north, the Sherbatovka River, before returning to Terney and other places with amenities such as law enforcement and road signs. The field season was nearly over.

15

Flood

WE REACHED AMGU without incident, the pickup truck wearing a skirt of brown mud flung there from the hidden potholes in the uneven dirt road still saturated from the previous night's rain. We checked on the water level in the Amgu River and saw it had dropped to an acceptable depth in our week-and-a-half absence, and Sergey said he had no concerns crossing it in the Hilux. We paused on the riverbank, watching the shallow water flow serenely over smooth rocks on the river bottom, and charted our course of action. We decided to devote several days to the far side, exploring the Sherbatovka River pair's territory. Conveniently, these fish owls lived not far from one of Vova Volkov's hunting cabins. We knew he was interested in joining us, so we detoured to the Volkov house on the other side of town to find him before crossing the river.

Sergey and I entered through the dark foyer, then moved into the kitchen, where we were met by a bizarre scene that for a moment made me forget why we had gone there. Nearly the entire surface of the kitchen table was concealed by a mound of minced fish being made negligibly smaller by the plump Alla, who was balling and then wrapping the pale meat into tight packages of dough. These were fish *pelmeni*, similar to dumplings or ravioli, which she would boil. I was astounded by the sheer quantity of product, and I asked her where she acquired the fish.

"Vova caught taimen this morning along the coast, by the river mouth," she said matter-of-factly, with fatigue in her voice, her apron and arms painted by flour.

I was impressed. "How many did he catch?" I inquired.

She studied me wearily. "Taime*n*," she repeated, emphasizing the ending in Russian to make sure I understood she had used the singular form. "One fish."

I reevaluated the mound of minced flesh before me. I was skeptical that all this came from a single anything, much less one fish. Alla sensed my doubt and bent over to remove the largest fish head I had ever seen from a plastic bag on the floor. She held it aloft and repeated the words again: "One fish."

Sakhalin taimen are among the largest salmonid fish in the world, growing up to two meters in length and up to fifty kilograms in weight. They are also critically endangered, largely due to overfishing. The fish had attained protected status only a few months before Vova hauled this one into his boat. A nature reserve along the Koppi River, just north of the Samarga River in neighboring Khabarovsk Province, was established in 2010 partially to protect the spawning grounds of taimen.

Vova was home and eager to join Sergey and me on our trip, needing only a moment to gather his necessary belongings into a knapsack. Alla handed him several glass jars full of the fish pelmeni she'd already prepared: our primary source of food for the next few days. I didn't know at the time that Sakhalin taimen were critically endangered, but I would not have eaten it if I had.

That would be like eating a fish owl or an Amur tiger. I doubt that Vova knew it was a protected species either; he was an honorable hunter, and news like endangered species designations can take a while to filter from one side of this enormous country to the other.

Vova's father, an elderly gentleman named Valeriy who had retired from the local border patrol garrison, was in the kitchen as well. He sat quietly on a low stool by the woodstove and kept Alla company while she worked. As I was putting on my boots and still thinking of the taimen, I asked the old man offhandedly if he ever went fishing with Vova off the coast. The old man laughed out loud, slapped his knee, and roared, "I never go out on that water anymore!" Before I could ask for clarification, Sergey and Vova ushered me out the door.

WHEN WE REACHED the Amgu River crossing, Vova explained that there was usually a bridge here, and there had been until about a month ago, but high floodwaters flushed it out to the Sea of Japan like a spring cleaning. The logging company had begun preparations to harvest up the Sherbatovka, a shallow and multichanneled waterway that flowed into the Amgu River a few dozen meters downriver from our crossing, so Vova was sure another bridge would be erected in the near future. Until then we'd have to drive through the water.

The first part of the Sherbatovka road on the far side was in good shape. Sergey noted that we were at the terminus of the old road from Terney, passable only in winter when the river mouths and wetlands froze, and the sole land route to Amgu until the 1990s. Now that you could reach Amgu year-round, inland as we had, the coastal trail had fallen out of favor and was used almost exclusively by loggers, poachers, and Vova to reach his hunting cabin.

After a split in the road, on the far side of a small bridge, we reached the hut. It was a classic Russian hunter's cabin: squat at eight logs tall, with timber-dovetailed corners and a gabled roof open underneath for storage, situated beneath a large spruce in a clearing of overgrown grass. We parked and began unpacking. Sergey had recently conceded that his blue cooler was no longer effective, so he took our fresh supply of meat and cheese and a few cans of beer we had bought in town down to the stream. There, he put them in an aluminum pot, placed this in the shallow water, then anchored it there with a hefty stone to keep our cache from floating away. Vova and I transferred our bedding into the cabin, ducking through the low door that came up to my shoulder.

As with many forest cabins here, the walls were studded with nails hanging bags of rice and salt and anything else edible: a precaution to keep nonperishable supplies at arm's length from the rodents who also called this cabin home. The ceiling was low and black with soot. Once Sergey entered, Vova placed one of the jars of fish pelmeni on the table, opened it, and distributed forks to each of us with a nod. Lunch was served.

The rain had started soon after we left town, a drizzle at first, but soon the droplets fell at a steady pace. After lunch, I put on my rain pants and jacket and we all headed out to inspect the fish owl nest tree, which was about a kilometer farther up the valley, then a short distance across it toward the river. The forest here was largely coniferous. After about thirty minutes of walking, I realized I was saturated below the knee: two months of bushwhacking past *Eleutherococcus*, a fiendish, thorny plant common to these forests, had left my legs pocked with infected, embedded thorns and expensive rain gear leaking like a colander. I glanced at the Russians: they were already soaked through, their cotton-and-polyester camouflage gray and clingy from saturation.

The difference between them and me was that Sergey and Vova had no illusions about the permeability of their clothing. In fact, my Russian collaborators frequently mocked the latest and greatest in lightweight gear I brought with me, something new each season to replace what Primorye's forests had savaged the year before. Such articles of clothing might be suitable for the wide, groomed trails of national parks in North America, but they stood little chance of survival here.

Sergey raised his palm, indicating we were close to the nest tree and should walk quietly; then the colossus came into view among the parting firs. It was a poplar, with the cavity an impressive seventeen meters off the ground—the highest nest I had seen yet. It had been a few years since Sergey had been here, and we had no way of telling if the nest was still occupied. This tree could not easily be free-climbed, which was how Sergey usually verified nest occupancy, as the closest branches were a good ten meters from the ground. Sometimes Sergey used climbing spurs to access a nest, sharp spikes used most often by arborists and linemen to scale trees or telephone poles; but that was not an option here either. The bark of this rotting poplar was thick and loose and did not offer a safe foothold.

We backed off some fifty meters and lingered there in the rain until after dark, hoping to hear a nearby duet or a shriek from the nest cavity. But other than the surround-sound din of raindrops smacking leaves, we heard nothing. With the heavy precipitation, the birds were unlikely to vocalize, and even if they did, we would probably be unable to hear them over the background noise. We returned to the cabin, ate a dinner of fish pelmeni, and went to sleep, with Vova and Sergey crowding onto one of the two beds and me occupying the other.

THE NEXT MORNING, we woke to rain and formulated our plan for the day over a breakfast of cold fish pelmeni and hot instant coffee. We already knew where the nest tree was, so what interested us was learning where the resident pair hunted. Vova would drive the Hilux up the valley and leave Sergey and me a half-dozen kilometers upriver of the cabin. I would cross the river, explore the far side of the valley, and walk downriver until I was approximately opposite Vova's cabin, which I had marked with my GPS. Then, I would cut across the river valley to it. Sergey would follow the main channel and do the same. Vova intended to hike to his second cabin farther up the valley, past where the road ended, and conduct some repairs there.

After being dropped off, I descended a steep slope to the river bottom and crossed the shallow water to the far side of the valley. The main channel of the Sherbatovka never appeared deeper than my waist, and it did not take long to find a stretch I could cross in my hip waders. Not that it mattered too much if river water seeped into my boots—I anticipated a good soaking that day from the rain anyway. Once on the valley's far side, I followed the current of a swampy channel largely overgrown and choked by fallen trees. I perked up: with flowing water and schools of reasonably sized fish, this was a potential fish owl hunting site.

I walked along the bank, scanning the trees for feathers and the ground for pellets. The forest was an interesting mix of primarily deciduous species and periodic dense coniferous thickets. I had just passed one such grove when I began noticing clumps of fur, then a few bones, and then a skull. It was the remains of a roe deer, some bits submerged in the water but most scattered along the channel bank at the base of the valley's slope. I drew closer, seeing the whitewash of bird droppings—a lot of them— and my first thought was that they were from a white-tailed sea eagle, the raptor I'd most expect to scavenge a deer carcass in northern Primorye. There were Steller's sea eagles here too in winter, but they were less common. As I looked up to determine how an eagle could have penetrated this thick canopy, I found myself staring at a mossy, vertical branch pasted with fish owl down. The deer carcass was directly beneath it. Inspecting the ground closer, I saw fish owl feathers mixed among the bones. I harbored no illusions that the owl killed the deer—that would be nearly impossible—but the bird had clearly taken full advantage of the venison food truck that had parked itself downstairs. I photographed the scene, collected a few pellets and a GPS point, then continued on, motivated by the intensifying rain.

When I finally returned to the cabin, it was close to dusk. I was drenched and thankful that Vova was already there; the cabin radiated warmth, the door ajar to allow some of the excess heat from the woodstove to escape. A blackened kettle of boiled water sat on a flat rock next to the stove, ready for tea. Vova didn't have much to report, other than seeing a wild boar. Sergey had yet to return, but the table was set for dinner; there were three forks, the remaining jar of fish pelmeni, and a bottle of mayonnaise. I hung my clothes on nails next to Vova's to dry and we waited. The rain was a wall of thick persistence outside. Vova lit the candle on the table just as Sergey entered, dripping. He reported with concern that water levels were definitely rising in the Sherbatovka: our supply of meat, cheese, and beer in the pot in the stream had been washed away. We scraped the jar clean of the last fish pelmeni. Eating taimen reminded me of the odd response I received from Vova's father, Valeriy, about going out to sea. I asked Vova about it.

"It's really quite something," Vova began, then leaned back, lifting his eyes to the ceiling as one does when seeking to recall a distant but important memory. The cabin was warm and shadowed by soft light from the single candle. Rain drummed evenly on the roof above, sometimes with intensified volleys when the nearby spruce swayed in the wind and shed whatever water had accumulated on its branches. Inside, water droplets hissed as they fell from our drying clothes onto the hot wood-stove. Sergey smiled and reclined on the bed. Apparently he had heard the story before but was not averse to listening again.

In the early 1970s, Valeriy used his fishing boat to take a friend to the village of Maksimovka, which, while difficult to get to by road even today, is only thirty or so kilometers up the coast from Amgu, a nominal distance in a motorboat. Valeriy was al-most back home, well within sight of the village, when his motor died. He tried to restart it but could not; the current drew him farther and farther away from shore. He gripped his single oar in a panicked attempt to paddle back to land, but the current was too strong. The poor man watched helplessly as the coastline grew distant and gradually transitioned to the rolling and silent terror of the open ocean. Valeriy had a handful of snacks left over from the trip, a rifle with a few shells, and a little drinking water. However, his food cache was gone by the second day. He shot at a few passing gulls, exhausting his bullet supply, and killed one, but the current prevented him from reaching its float-ing carcass. On the third day at sea, Valeriy saw a ship. He yelled and waved his oar. The crew saw him and shifted the vessel's trajectory; he thought he was saved. As the large ship pulled up next to him, an amused Russian seaman peered down at this sun-blackened lunatic in a battered rowboat in the middle of the Sea of Japan and asked, "What the hell are you doing out here?"

Hoarse from dehydration, Vova's father replied, "The current brought me out."

"Let the current take you back, then," the laughing sailor re-torted, and with that the ship continued on, abandoning the stunned castaway to what they must have assumed was his death.

On the fourth day, Valeriy awoke docked in Amgu with his wife calling him ashore. A moment later, he discovered himself half out of the boat, still in the middle of the ocean, interacting with an illusion that had almost drowned him. He fought this delirium for countless hours. Five days after Valeriy drifted away from the coast, he was picked up by a Russian vessel in the La Pérouse Strait.

"The La Pérouse Strait?" I nearly leaped from my stool. The strait is about 350 kilometers due east of Amgu.

Vova continued without reaction to my outburst. The ship took Valeriy to Nakhodka, a port in southern Primorye near Vladivostok, where his rescuers recognized the ship that had abandoned Valeriy based on his descriptions of it. Vova did not know what penalty that crew received for abandoning a Soviet citizen on the ocean, but it was certainly severe. Once he was ashore, the authorities listened to Valeriy's story sympathetically, then politely asked for a passport to confirm his identity.

"Passport?" he responded incredulously. "I got in a boat to take my buddy to Maksimovka. What do I need a passport for?"

"Because you're in Nakhodka," the authorities countered, "and you are asking us to let you go to Amgu, the location of a sensitive border patrol garrison. You certainly need to prove your identity to do that."

Given the lines of communication in those days, it took nearly two more weeks for Valeriy's identity to be confirmed and for him to make it home. By then, he had been gone nearly a month. His family had held his funeral, mourned his loss, and begun to heal. When Valeriy reported back for work at the border patrol garrison, his superiors told him angrily that it would have been better for them if he *had* vanished at sea, because his metal boat, undetected for five days as it drifted about in the Sea of Japan, betrayed their incompetence. Their assignment, after all, was to detect and intercept unregistered boats—possibly spies—in the ocean. The central office in Vladivostok had savaged them for this embarrassing failure.

Vova paused and sighed, then concluded.

"My father left home for an afternoon trip up the coast and spent the next month in hell. So no, he doesn't go to sea anymore."

THE RAIN FELL HEAVILY all night. Sergey returned from an outhouse run in the morning, shook the water off his coat, and announced that the odds of us being stranded here were pretty good. The river had risen almost exponentially overnight, and the bridge over the small stream adjacent to the cabin, the one we had crossed two days prior, had been washed away. He lit a cigarette and stood by the door so the smoke would draft out.

"We have a window of opportunity to escape that may have already closed. But I think we should try. Otherwise we are here until the water level drops, which could be another week." He paused. "We need to go now."

I had learned that when Sergey said "We need to go now," we really did. We packed up the Hilux and started back toward town. The river was so overwhelmed by water that it burst its bank and flowed down the road itself for at least a kilometer before returning to its normal course. Three of the bridges along the way had washed out: two of these crossings were not much trouble, but one had all three of us waist deep in the water, tugging and red faced and pushing a log that had jammed there and caused the water to rise higher than the truck could safely cross.

Given these obstacles, when we finally reached the Amgu

River crossing I was not surprised to find it unrecognizable from just a few days before. Then the Hilux had coasted through the clear, shallow, calf-deep water, but the water at present was turbid, probably more than waist deep, and rushed past with considerable urgency. There was no question in my mind that we were too late: we were stranded. There was no way Sergey could drive the truck into this swirling cauldron. But he and Vova continued to consult, arms directing and pointing and hooking as though a game plan were being formed. Then, inexplicably, Vova opened the engine hood while Sergey rummaged around the glove compartment to produce a roll of packing tape. They removed the intake hose from the air filter and taped it to the top of the open hood. They *were* moving forward with a crossing, and they did not want the diesel engine to flood and choke halfway across. Vova, still in his chest waders, walked upriver along the bank some forty meters, then turned into the current and gently sidestepped into it, letting the water push him diagonally the fifty meters across the river, coming out on the far side near where the road picked up again. I exhaled a sigh of relief that he'd made it, and Vova gave Sergey and me the thumbs-up. Incomprehension battered me from all sides. The current was swift and the water was easily a meter and a half deep—it had just about enveloped Vova—and we were still going to try to cross it? This seemed crazier to me than the naleds of the Samarga.

We climbed into the truck. We could not see anything—the engine hood was still open to keep the air intake hose dry—so Sergey rolled down his window and leaned out as far as he could while still holding the wheel. He executed a three-point turn and backed the vehicle up the bank, following Vova's route until the figure on the far side waved for us to stop. Then, flailing his arms in a repeated pattern like a navy flagman, Vova showed us the angle we should take. We entered the water.

The absurd scene unfolded in slow motion; the river coaxed us with it, and water spilled through the door seams. Sergey, still half out of the driver's-side window so he had some idea of where we were going, repeatedly whipped the wheel back and forth in an impotent attempt to assert control, swearing and trying to guide us. The Hilux bounced on the river bottom—meaning we were mostly floating—and at those times the wheel was as effective as a broken rudder. My knuckles were white from gripping the window crank. Water sloshed at my feet. Then the wheels settled and gained traction: we had somehow bypassed the deepest part of the river. The Hilux, streaming water like a hoisted shipwreck, pulled ashore right where Vova had aimed us. Sergey was smiling as though he'd known this would happen, and Vova was laughing as if he were amazed it had. I jumped from the truck, shocked that the crossing hadn't ended in catastrophe, and moved a safe distance away from the river in case it had second thoughts about letting us pass.

The 2006 field season was over. I would make my way south to Vladivostok, debrief there with Sergey Surmach, then board a flight in mid-June to cross the Pacific Ocean via Seoul and Seattle en route to my home in Minnesota. My summer would be busy: I'd been dating a woman named Karen for nearly four years—we'd met in Primorye as fellow Peace Corps volunteers—and we had an August wedding to plan. After that, I would take classes at the University of Minnesota to develop the skills I needed to craft a fish owl conservation strategy. I also needed to scour any literature I could find on raptor captures and consult any relevant specialists in preparation for the next field season. I was only three months into this five-year project and it was already a fascinating journey, one unfolding along the fringes of human civilization and involving new discoveries about a cryptic owl. In these past few months, Sergey and I had found thirteen fish owl territories where we could focus captures. We'd heard pairs vocalizing at most of these sites but, importantly, had found nest trees at four of them. After the first snows fell and the rivers froze next winter, I would return to Primorye and reunite with Sergey to figure out how many of these owls we could catch.

PART THREE

Captures

16

Preparing to Trap

I MET UP WITH SERGEY at the Institute of Biology and Soil Science in Vladivostok, where Surmach worked, in late January 2007. Sergey was his confident self and boasted a fresh haircut, recently shined shoes, and a clean-shaven face. We entered the four-story building of faded brick and Soviet prestige and waited for the elevator. A woman selling baked goods in the unlit atrium gave us a quick glance and asked if we were plumbers. Sergey said no and ordered a pastry. Faux wooden doors then opened to reveal a tight coffin of an elevator, a contraption that took advantage of its captive audience to beg for maintenance by groaning upward along cables of questionable integrity. We progressed down a bare gray hall with footsteps echoing and pulled open a door to crowd into Surmach's small office.

We were there to plan the final details of our upcoming field season: our first attempt to capture fish owls and a critically important stage of this multiyear project. We'd already sketched out where we would target owls over the next few years—the Terney and Amgu areas—and identified more than a dozen potential places to trap. We intended to catch as many birds as possible and put transmitters on them, a process called "tagging," to monitor their movements. This would not be a one-off exercise. Fieldwork is often regular repetition of challenging or unpleasant activities, an application of persistent pressure to a question until the answer finally emerges. Once an owl had a transmitter, we'd need to visit that territory repeatedly for several years, collecting data, and at the end of the project recapture the birds to remove their tags. After the first year or two of data collection, once we had some initial information on owl movements, we'd also survey their habitat to learn if there was anything distinct about where the birds nested or hunted. It didn't matter that we did not yet know the exact locations of such activities—this would come with time and persistence.

We drank tea and ate chocolates as we discussed our plans for the season. The pace this year would be very different from that in 2006. We would work slowly and more methodologically, as our goal was not to find fish owl territories but to hone our capture skills in one region: Terney. We had found the highest concentration of owls here last year, so this was the logical place to start. We needed to familiarize ourselves with the birds at the Serebryanka, Tunsha, and Faata territories and try to find at least one place each pair hunted so that we had a location to trap. Terney was also a convenient location to base our initial efforts, as we had warm beds under a dry roof at the Wildlife Conservation Society's Sikhote-Alin Research Center, within twenty kilometers of all our target sites.

Surmach, who again would not be joining us due to other commitments, talked animatedly about his experiences catching different bird species and the difficulties we would face trying to capture fish owls. He had an endearing habit of whispering curse words instead of uttering them at regular speaking volume. Although he did not swear much, when particularly excited his sentences would plummet sharply and then rise again with the vernacular abruptness of a hunting kestrel.

In the off-season I'd consulted with Pete Bloom, a raptor capture specialist based in California, and reviewed the scientific literature to pinpoint several traps that might be effective with fish owls. There were dozens of options to choose from. People have been catching raptors for hundreds of years, if not millennia. I read about time-tested methods such as the *bal-chatri*, first developed in India, which looked like a lobster trap covered in fine nooses and holding a live bird or rodent inside as bait. A raptor becomes entangled in the nooses when it drops onto the cage trying to snatch the lure. Another method, called a *pit trap*, is a testament to what some people will endure to get a bird in hand. Designed to catch carrion eaters such as vultures or condors, the trap is set up by digging a human-sized hole and dragging a dead cow (or other animal) next to it. Researchers then conceal themselves inside the pit, just a pace or two away from the stinking carcass, sometimes waiting for hours before their target animal arrives to feed. Then they reach out of the darkness to grab the surprised bird by the legs.

Multiple factors come into play when capturing raptors, and we needed to consider this for fish owls. Some species are easier to ensnare than others, but there are also individual differences based on sex, season, age, and physical condition. A younger hawk, for example, is naive and not yet suspicious of traps, while a satiated eagle is harder to catch than a hungry one. I could not find much about fish owl captures in the scientific literature. Most of the few records of these birds being caught in Russia were of owls being killed, including historical records of the

Udege hunting fish owls for meat, and others shot and killed by scientists, destined for museum display cases. There was only one exception. A few years earlier, Sergey had been in Amur Province, nearly a thousand kilometers northwest of Terney and, it had been presumed, outside of fish owl range. He'd found fish owl tracks there and, knowing no one would believe him, built a fall trap and placed it where he'd seen the tracks. Sergey's trap was a crude dome of bent, fresh willow saplings covered by fish netting and held agape by a trip-wired stick on the verge of collapse. It was rudimentary, the kind of thing you'd see in a cartoon, but the owl fell for it. A few days later, Sergey had his bird. He took some photos for proof and let the owl go.

Most of the capture-and-release details I could find about fish owls were from Japan. There, immature fish owls had been trapped using nets, but I could not find any mention of adult captures. We didn't want young birds for this project—juvenile behavior was erratic and not representative of the territorial movements of adults, which was what we needed for our conservation plan. So I sent emails to Japanese fish owl biologists and asked if they had any advice for catching adults. I never heard back. The researchers there were reluctant to share any information about these highly endangered owls, especially details on how to find or catch one. This was possibly due to a history in Japan of overzealous bird-watchers and wildlife photographers inadvertently destroying fish owl nests or otherwise disturbing the birds in their efforts to get a better look. I was an unknown graduate student, not yet established in the fish owl world, so from the perspective of my email recipients I was no more than a stranger cold-calling and asking for their closest-guarded secrets. Given the dearth of information about fish owl captures, and no sense of how wary the owls might be of different traps, Sergey and I would be on our own to learn through trial and error. We decided, rather arbitrarily, that four fish owls would be a reasonable target to gauge capture success in this first year.

The half-dozen transmitters I'd brought with me were critical to the study. These small devices looked like AA batteries capped by thirty-centimeter flexible antennae. The transmitters attached to the owls like backpacks, one loop around each wing and a strap across the keel to hold everything in place. The units emitted a silent radio signal every second, which we could hear using a special receiver. We'd then approximate an owl's location using triangulation, the same principle I had used to find nest trees the previous year when I took compass bearings of owl calls, only instead of orienting to an owl's voice, we'd be homing in on the strength of its radio signal. By amassing location data from a number of owls over several years, we would be able to develop an understanding of what kinds of habitat fish owls preferred and what areas they avoided. This process, called "resource selection," allows biologists to rank the importance of different habitats or other natural features such as prey abundance (collectively called "resources") to better understand the ecological needs of a given species. For example, we know that fish owls are dependent on rivers for food, but can they fish in *any* river? Are there elements unique to the waterways (or even specific stretches) they hunt in, such as channel width, water depth, or substrate? And where do they nest? Is there more to a fish owl nesting site than a big tree, or must the surrounding forest have other characteristics, such as some proportion of conifers, or be a certain distance from a village, before a fish owl will nest there? By tagging a number of owls and looking for repeated patterns of behavior, we would better understand their resource selection. This assessment, a fundamental component of many conservation plans, was the keystone of this project.

We'd identified a number of limiting factors in a field season.

The first was weather. We knew that winter was the best time of year for captures, as this was when the owls were easiest to find and most restricted by where they could hunt. But our experiences on the Samarga showed us that this season was unpredictable. Winter storms might hamper our ability to travel or trap, and the threat of spring was constant, especially by March. Another issue was personnel. Other than Sergey, no one on Surmach's team could afford to spend two months at a time in the woods: they had other jobs or families waiting at home. We anticipated a regular rotation of one or two field assistants each year, all with their own strengths and weaknesses. A final consideration, one that influenced all our decisions, was the budget. Funding for this project was limited to what I could raise from grants, and the technology we were using was expensive. This meant that we could not simply tag every owl we saw; we had to be strategic. For example, depending on how many transmitters we had on hand, after we caught one bird it might make more sense to strike camp and move to another territory than to stay and try to catch that bird's mate. From the perspective of our understanding of fish owl movements, two tagged owls from different territories were better than two owls from the same territory. We started out the 2007 season with a strategy but knew, as with all fieldwork, that these plans would likely change. We needed to be flexible and ready to make big decisions on the move.

SERGEY AND I LEFT VLADIVOSTOK midmorning and, after hours of nothing but darkness, mountains, and forest, arrived in Terney close to midnight that same day. Sergey was behind the wheel of the red Hilux and towing the black Yamaha snowmobile we had used on the Samarga. I was happy to see that in the off-season he had modified the Hilux with a flexible snorkel air intake hose. This adaptation precluded the need for packing tape and open hoods in any future deepwater crossings.

The Sikhote-Alin Research Center in Terney, a three-story wooden structure, was perched on a hill with a breathtaking panoramic view of the village, the Sea of Japan, and the Sikhote-Alin mountains. The center was run by Dale Miquelle of the Wildlife Conservation Society, who had been in Primorye since 1992, longer than any other American I knew of. Dale had given Sergey and me an open invitation to stay at the center whenever we needed.

After a comfortable night, Sergey and I left Terney early the next morning, eager to get started. It was in the mid -20s Celsius, and as we rolled cautiously down the steep, ice-slicked, bumpy road into town, I watched the sun, freshly birthed from the Sea of Japan, highlight columns of white smoke rising from the brick chimneys we passed. We drove west out of town about ten kilometers, following the Serebryanka River to where I'd heard owls vocalizing the previous spring. We parked next to the road and then walked underneath the bare canopies of oak and birch to reach the band of solid ice that was the Serebryanka River. As we moved upon this icy highway, I noted that it was almost completely frozen. Passing only a handful of open patches of flowing water, some as small as a few meters long and wide, I realized that the resident pair of fish owls had few options for where they could hunt. We knew exactly where to place our traps. After exploring the territory, we returned to the truck, where Sergey made a fire and boiled some river water for tea while we talked about our prospects and waited for dusk. The owls rewarded us with a duet. This was going to be easy.

Back in Terney, we began constructing our traps. The first method that Sergey and I wanted to try was called a "noose carpet." A simple trap proven effective at duping a variety of birds of prey, a noose carpet is a rectangle of sturdy, stainless-steel mesh covered by several dozen wide nooses of fishing line that stand erect on the mesh like wide-petaled flowers. Once ready, noose carpets are placed where a bird is expected to land or walk, and when its feet encounter the near-invisible fishing line it instinctively yanks back, thereby pulling the nooses tight and ensnaring itself. A weight with a spring is loosely attached to the noose carpet by rope and offers resistance when the bird attempts to fly away. The knots of the nooses are tied in such a way that if the bird pulls hard enough, they come undone—a precaution to prevent injuring a bird's toes due to constricted circulation. But this also means that a captured owl cannot be left struggling too long in a noose carpet or it will eventually escape.

Although we were eager to start trapping, a blizzard settled on Terney much as one had when I'd waited for the helicopter to take me to Agzu the previous winter. In the end, nearly seventy centimeters of snow accumulated. On the ridge at the research center where we were holed up, the snow drifted above the waist. Captures were not possible in this weather—snow would cover the snares—so Sergey and I hunkered down, making noose carpets, drinking beer, steaming in a banya, and watching the snow fall.

We returned to the Serebryanka River when the weather cleared and were discouraged to find the riverbanks there pristine. Since the storm, there was no evidence that the owls had hunted where we thought they would. Perhaps the deep, fresh snow made landing on the banks inconvenient for the owls, so that they had moved on to another part of their territory. I knew of one fish owl pair in Japan that hunted three kilometers from their nest, and maybe this was what was happening here. Sergey suggested we do as the Udege do: set up a stump. We had heard from the locals in Agzu how the Udege used to hunt fish owls by cutting a tree stump and placing it in shallow water with a metal jaw trap on top. The owls would gravitate to the novel vantage point this new hunting perch offered and land on the deadly spot. We of course were not interested in eating owls, just finding them, so after Sergey used his chain saw to cut five stumps and position them in the shallow river water, I sprinkled each stump surface with snow. Anything that landed there would leave an imprint. When we checked our site two days later, we were thrilled to see fish owl tracks on four of the five stumps. We were ready to trap.

17

A Near Miss

THINGS WERE GOING WELL: within the first week of arriving in Terney we'd found where a pair of fish owls hunted, had prepared traps, and were now driving out to the Serebryanka River to catch some owls. The back seat of the Hilux was neatly lined with prepared noose carpets and the truck bed full of camping gear. Inquisitive loops of nylon found and tugged at passing willow branches as we walked the traps through the forest out to the open river and our capture sites, where we placed smaller noose carpets on stumps and larger ones, about a meter long, on riverbanks where the owls had landed in the past. Each trap was modified to include a trap transmitter, a beacon that would send a radio signal to our receiver when a noose carpet was jostled. If that happened, we would ski to that location from our camp as quickly as possible.

Trap concealment was an important consideration. We didn't know how the owls would react if they flew to their favorite fishing hole and found the scene disturbed. With coyotes or foxes, for example, trappers must boil trap components, use gloves, and be careful not to leave any human scent in an area or the animals won't approach a trap. We were so worried about tipping off the owls to our scheme that, like bandits fleeing a posse, we walked to each trap site in the river water itself so as to leave no footprints in the snow. We were also concerned that if our camp was within sight or earshot of our traps, the owls would be reluctant to hunt there. So we set up our tent far from the river, about a quarter kilometer, and cut ski trails through the tangles of the floodplain leading to each trap, moving logs and clearing branches as needed so that we would not be impeded in our haste.

As the light that first trap day faded, we collected wood and started a fire. The nervousness at camp was palpable: we'd turned a corner in the project. Everything we'd done to this point, the searches for nests and hunting sites, was well within Sergey's bailiwick. He'd been doing this type of thing for a decade and had been a good teacher. But now we were both in new territory: captures were an unknown. Would the owls fall for our tricks? How would a fish owl react when caught? Raptor beaks are sharp and could likely snip fishing line without too much effort. Would an owl understand this and free itself immediately, or would it panic and entangle itself further?

Radio waves invisible to us swirled about in the winter night, and static from the receiver was a source of tension. Flashes of interference popped and hissed while Sergey and I, unaccustomed to the noise, flinched in response. We expected the beacon to sound any minute, and we sat ready. It stayed silent. Eventually we became too cold and retreated to the embrace of our down sleeping bags in our tent, where Sergey and I alternated three-hour shifts all night to monitor the receiver. I took first watch, lying still and clutching the device to my chest to keep the batteries from draining in the cold, trying to appreciate the strange music this radio played. Sleep did not come easily even when it was my turn to rest. The temperature approached the −30s Celsius with only a thin layer of polyester between us and the outside air. Frozen exhalations within the tent rained fine slivers of ice at the slightest shift of position.

This went on for four nights, and nothing visited our capture sites. We'd check our noose carpets every morning, fiddle with them, and adjust our placements. We heard the owls hooting every night. Why were they not coming to our traps? We'd expected captures to be challenging, but I had not anticipated the additional stressors of constant cold and irregular sleep. There was little we could do about captures during the day, and we didn't want to disturb our target owls by tromping around their forests, so in order to feel productive Sergey and I spent our days looking for fish owl sign in a nearby territory before returning to the Serebryanka at night. There was a triangle of lush riparian forest wedged between the Tunsha River, the Faata River, and their confluence some ten kilometers northeast of our trapping site. Sergey and I had heard a pair calling near a logging camp the previous spring. Walking through the bright, mixed forest and inspecting open water along the Faata River for tracks made us feel productive: our trapping efforts might be stagnant, but we could at least investigate future capture sites. I was experienced enough looking for fish owls that Sergey and I would split up and agree upon a time, usually closer to dusk, to meet back at the truck. We'd return to our camp to huddle in the freezing tent and wait for our owls in silence, like suitors agonizing over a phone that never rings.

On our second day of searches along the Faata River, I came upon a short stretch of open water. Here, where the river was no more than four meters wide and no more than twenty centimeters deep, I found fish owl tracks. I was thrilled: the river edge was hemmed by a shelf of flat ice and snow generously strewn with the characteristic K impressions of fish owl tracks both faded and fresh. This was clearly an important hunting site. I smiled with relief as I took photographs of the scene and recorded the location with my GPS. We had made some progress! This would be a future trap site.

When I reconnected with Sergey a few hours later and shared the news, we compared notes. He'd met a man named Anatoliy living alone in a cabin a mere half kilometer from where I had found the fish owl tracks.

"He seems like a nice guy," Sergey started, then hesitated. "A little . . . strange. He has a crazy look in his eyes, but I think he's harmless. He said we could stay with him if we wanted to."

A heated cabin would beat winter camping, but I was wary. The forests of the Russian Far East are sprinkled with recluses, and some of them are there for unsavory reasons: criminals evading the law, people hiding from criminals, and criminals avoiding other criminals. Meeting a person in the woods was usually a bad thing. This was true even a hundred years ago, when Vladimir Arsenyev observed of the forest that "it is the human encounters . . . that are the nastiest."

SERGEY WAS ON DUTY around one o'clock in the morning on February 24 when the beeping pulse of a jostled trap electrified the tent. One of our transmitters had been activated—the downriver noose carpet farthest from camp. We burst from the tent, struggling in the darkness to push into hip waders stiff from the deep freeze, and flung ourselves into the forest on skis, our surroundings illuminated only by headlamps. Sergey disappeared ahead of me. Although we had prepared our trails beforehand, they still wound among trees, over logs, and through brooks, and I did not share Sergey's nimbleness on these slippery planks. The forest was quiet but for my heavy breathing and the friction of skis; the strobe-lit trunks moved past with agonizing sloth. The whole trip took only a few minutes, but it seemed longer. When I reached the river, Sergey was in the water, looking at signs of a struggle on the bank. I saw fish owl tracks and a mangled noose carpet with broken nooses. We were too late.

I looked closer at the scene. We'd used a small log as a weight, which I'd concealed in the snow so the owls would not see it, and this was likely the flaw that caused the trap to fail. The snow had hardened around the log like a snow anchor, so when the owl tried to fly away, the weight held firmly in place instead of dragging on the ground to impede flight. This resistance allowed the owl to pull the nooses tight until the knots released. The bird could not have been trapped for very long, just the time it took us to reach the river, but we had no idea what influence the stress of that brief detainment had caused. It had taken almost a week for an owl to even show up—now that it was aware of danger, how long would it be before it came back? We decided to temporarily halt capture attempts at the Serebryanka and refocus on the Faata. There, at least, we had owls who weren't expecting traps and, potentially, a warm place to sleep. We closed our traps and packed up camp, hitched the snowmobile trailer to the Hilux, and headed to Anatoliy's cabin, hoping his invitation still stood.

18

The Hermit

WE REACHED ANATOLIY'S CABIN by returning to the main road and tracing its icy flatness along the Tunsha River valley. Despite the ice, the road was in better condition in winter than most other times of the year because the snow had filled in the potholes and made its surface level. After about ten minutes, we turned onto a logging road that led us across the floodplain and through groves of old-growth pine mixed with large poplars, elms, and chosenias: the telltale signs of good fish owl habitat. Within minutes we passed the confluence of the Tunsha and Faata Rivers, then the forest peeled back to reveal a clearing occupied by a single hut, a smokehouse, and a dilapidated and unusable pagoda overlooking the Tunsha.

Anatoliy was indeed a strange man. At age fifty-seven, he had lived alone in the woods for a decade, in a cabin that had once been part of a hydroelectric station on the Tunsha River that powered Terney during the Second World War. Apparently, this base had been operational until the late 1980s as a Soviet youth camp. There were a few crumbling concrete pylons protruding from the river like worn boulders, some rusty bits of machinery, and the two-room caretaker's cabin that Anatoliy currently occupied as his home. I assumed he was squatting.

Anatoliy was of average height and build, balding but with sideburns creeping aggressively to midcheek and long hair pulled into a thin ponytail. There was something almost elvish or gnomelike about him, particularly when he wore his peaked winter hat. Anatoliy possessed a ready smile and warm laugh that instantly assured me he was a gentle, welcoming individual. When we shook hands, I noticed he was missing most of one pinkie.

The cabin's exterior had not been attended to in recent years, but a few sections shielded from the elements suggested that the wooden boards had once been painted green. The chimney was in poor condition, with several of the topmost bricks loose or missing. Beyond an atrium to help buffer the cold, the door opened to a kitchen with plaster walls stained yellow as though by nicotine and a ceiling smudged by soot. A large brick woodstove, cracked and with crumbling corners, dominated the room; the space was warm and aromatic from burning wood. A narrow table stood across from the stove and underneath a window, its flower-patterned tablecloth cluttered with stacked dishes, a kerosene lamp, and boxes of sugar and tea bags. The window was shielded by thick plastic to keep out the cold. Beyond the table in the far corner was a short mattress on a metal-spring bed under a second, similarly enclosed window, and in the space between the bed and the far side of the stove was a doorframe leading to the second room. Anatoliy restricted himself mostly to the first room in winter and hung a blanket in the doorframe to contain the warm air there. But in anticipation of our arrival, Anatoliy had pulled the curtain back. Beyond it there were two beds, one on either side of the room, and a desk in between stacked with boxes of canned food.

It is difficult to say what effect the weight of solitude had had on Anatoliy's psyche, at least in relation to how much emotional baggage he brought to the forest with him to begin with, but the man certainly had quirks. For example, on my first morning there he asked if gnomes had tickled my feet in the night as they sometimes did his. I replied that they had not. Over breakfast I learned a little more about him, but he remained vague about why exactly he was living alone in the forest in the ruins of an abandoned hydroelectric station. For someone in his position, he seemed surprisingly ill adapted for winter survival. The only tracks emanating from the cabin were two snowy trails: one leading to the outhouse and the other to the river, where he collected water and sometimes fished from a hole hacked in the thick ice. He had fashioned a pair of skis out of boards, but they were heavy and cumbersome and, as such, not very useful. In the autumn months he caught pink salmon along the river, which he smoked and sold to acquaintances who sometimes visited from Terney. In the warmer months, he occasionally joined a firewood-collecting crew that provided him with enough wood for the winter and a little extra money for food. For a few years he had tried growing some vegetables in a garden, but he could not keep the wild boar from ravaging his crops. Anatoliy offered to cook for us for the duration of our stay as long as we provided the food.

Although we didn't know why Anatoliy had isolated himself from the world to begin with, he confided that he lingered in the Tunsha River valley because of an eighth-century Balhae-era temple he'd discovered while exploring the top of the closest mountain. Sometimes at night he saw lights from there, he claimed, and he said if you stood at the temple and a friend stood at the next peak, you could clearly hear each other and also teleport small objects. Anatoliy didn't know what the spirit of the mountain wanted him to do, but he knew it was somehow connected to the temple. So he remained in the valley below, patiently waiting for his life's purpose to reveal itself.

REJUVENATED BY A NEW LOCATION and fresh start, Sergey and I immediately began scouting for trapping locations. We were back in our element. We skied the three hundred meters up the frozen Tunsha River to its confluence with the Faata River, which we then shadowed through the forest, as much of the river itself was shallow and flowing. As in Amgu, there was possibly a radon spring nearby to keep the water just above freezing. Another three hundred meters later, we reached the curve where I had found owl tracks the week before. There were even fresher tracks, and we jubilantly placed a number of snared stumps there and in a few other locations farther downstream that we thought looked convenient for fish owls. I felt that we were regaining our momentum after the stumble at Serebryanka.

However, after three days our traps remained untouched. We monitored trap transmitters at night—with Anatoliy taking shifts as well to give us a little extra sleep—and during the day we searched for additional hunting areas not only of the Faata owls but also of the Tunsha pair, which were occupying a territory abutting the Faata pair's to the south, downriver of Anatoliy's cabin. This was the pair that John Goodrich had heard the year before.

The Tunsha River had some of the densest riparian understory I had encountered; I battled impenetrable tangles hunched over and with eyes squinted in case a wayward branch chose to stab at them. Eventually, I realized that I could cover more ground by walking rather than on skis that regularly snagged underfoot. Despite the physical difficulty of these hikes, the walks were cathartic. Self-doubt had started to tug at my mind almost as much as the dense snarls of branches did my clothing; so the silence, fresh air, physical exertion, and excitement of searching for and finding owl sign reminded me that even without captures, this work was progressing. After a few days we had identified two hunting areas used by the Tunsha birds, and one of them was ideal for capture: a broad bend in the river between pools where the water flowed just over the pebbly substrate.

At seven-thirty one morning, after another uneasy night enduring the taunts and heckles of radio wave static, I turned off the receiver and rolled over for some sleep. Not long after, I heard Anatoliy announce to Sergey in the next room that he intended to make *blinchiki*, or small blini, for breakfast. One of Anatoliy's idiosyncrasies was to repeat a single word periodically and indefinitely. For the next hour, as Anatoliy beat the eggs and mixed the flour and heated the pan, all I heard from the next room was a monotone mantra of "blinchiki . . . blinchiki . . . blinchiki . . ." repeated every minute or so. Eventually I got up and shuffled to the table, where I poured myself a cup of boiled water and mixed in some instant coffee.

"What are you making, Anatoliy?" Sergey said, looking at me with a deadpan expression.

"Blinchiki," came the oblivious and cheery response.

When I finished my coffee, and my stomach was full and warm from blini, I strapped on my skis and shuffled up to the Faata River to investigate our traps and see if perhaps an owl had landed nearby. The walk north along the Tunsha was truly gorgeous: the river was lined by rocky outcroppings, and its deep pools were interspersed by shallow riffles. Its beauty helped distract me from the difficulties of failed captures. It had been nearly two weeks of sleep-poor nights, and we had nothing but a single escaped fish owl at Serebryanka to show for it. I looked down at myself: I'd lost some weight, from both the physical exertion and the stress; I was using a length of rope as a belt for my now baggy pants. My beard was becoming unwieldy, my clothes were filthy, and my exposed skin was tan from all the hours I spent wandering the river and absorbing the sun's reflection off the snow.

As I turned the final curve of the Faata River before our trapping site, I caught a flash of brown rising from the river. It was a fish owl flying low and away from me. I quickly reached the capture site, crushed to once again find the scene of a struggle and broken nooses. I had turned the receiver off at seven-thirty—about dawn—meaning that this owl had been caught after that, sometime in the last hour and a half. While I had been trying to sleep, listening to Anatoliy chant "blinchiki," and asking myself what we were doing wrong, there had been a fish owl fighting against the trap. Eventually it had freed itself.

We ate a silent, introspective lunch back at the cabin. Anatoliy tried to lift our spirits by suggesting that the owls could sense our anxiety: if only we changed our attitudes and relaxed, the owls would want to be trapped and our problem would be solved. We drank tea in a prolonged silence.

Sergey had begun to doubt the effectiveness of a noose carpet method. While I did not blame him, my perspective was that the trap was sound and worth sticking with for the time being: all of our problems had been the result of amateurism. With each failure, we tweaked our methodology to ensure the problem would not be repeated. Regardless, in addition to the noose carpets, Sergey decided to construct a pair of fall traps and place them in

two locations: one on the Faata and one on the Tunsha. This was
the trap style Sergey had used to successfully capture a fish owl
in Amur Province. Our desperation was mounting, so I agreed.
Sergey cut a few willows from the riverbank, and once the domed
frames were ready he covered each with fishing nets that Anatoliy had in his storeroom. We staked frozen, store-bought
marine fish to the pebbly river bottom so that they would
wiggle in the ankle-deep current and act as live lures, then
propped the frame above them with a stick. We used fishing line
to tether the fish to the stick, which would buckle when something moved the lures and cause the frame to fall, trapping an
owl underneath in the shallow water. When Sergey offered this
as an idea, I was unconvinced that a bird as cautious as a fish
owl would succumb to a trick as obvious as this one.

We were running low on some nonessential food items such
as flour and ketchup, so in early March, after nearly two weeks
at Anatoliy's, we used this as an excuse for a break. Sergey and
I drove the twenty-odd kilometers into Terney to resupply. After
visiting a few stores, we drove up the hill to John Goodrich's
house and heated his banya, which we had free rein to stoke even
if he was not home. Snow started falling as we bathed, a steady,
quiet massing that threatened to rival the storm that had halted
our work in February. We dried ourselves and got back in the
truck. The main road out of town was already deep with snow,
but a few logging trucks had driven ahead of us and created a
drivable track. However, by the time we pulled off the main road
and onto the smaller one that led toward the Tunsha River and
Anatoliy's cabin, we were pushing the Hilux through knee-deep
accumulation, darkness, and the whiteout of a full-on blizzard.

19

Stranded on the Tunsha River

T HERE'S A SAYING IN RUSSIA I am fond of: "The more souped-up your truck, the farther you'll have to go for a tractor when you get it stuck." Sergey's Hilux was hearty, and we assumed we could make it back to the Tunsha River despite the blizzard, but we were wrong. About two kilometers after turning off the main road, only just over halfway to Anatoliy's cabin, the truck simply couldn't go on. The snow was too deep and too heavy for us to keep plowing forward. We'd already shoveled the Hilux free a few times and were wet with sweat and swirling snow. We had a number of items in the vehicle that needed to reach the cabin. Sergey, shouting over the wind, suggested that I walk ahead and bring back the snowmobile while he stayed behind trying to coax the Hilux a little farther.

There had been several serious snowstorms in March, and the snow was waist deep in the forest. I followed the road—a barely visible line between the truck and the warmth and dryness of the cabin. If I could keep to the compressed tracks left by the Hilux when we drove into Terney earlier that day, I wouldn't sink too far into the snow and could move efficiently. But with my haste and the confusion of the blizzard, I largely stumbled the kilometer and a half to the cabin, my hood cinched tight against the storm's constant onslaught, my legs sinking deep in the fresh accumulation, and my headlamp largely useless, like car lights in a dense fog. Eventually I reached the cabin, breathing hard. Anatoliy was outside in his coat and hat, concerned. He had seen my approaching headlamp and was dumbfounded that we had come back at all.

"Why didn't you just stay in Terney? It's warm there, and you can't trap in this weather anyway."

When we were in Terney, I had been convinced that we needed to get back to trap—but Anatoliy was right: we should have stayed away. Once on the forest road driving the snowmobile, I was having an impossible time keeping it on the road. The snow underneath was uneven, and I could not seem to keep the heavy machine on track. If I slowed down, it sank into the snow and got stuck, so I tried to keep up my speed, careening in one direction and then the other, in a constant struggle to keep from smashing into the trees lining the road. I weaved and thrashed like a marlin on the line nearly the whole way back to the marooned truck. By the time I reached Sergey, I was sweaty and fuming from my inability to properly steer a simple machine like a snowmobile. Sergey was bewildered.

"What were you doing?" he asked with genuine confusion, staring at me. "I'd see the snowmobile headlights, but then they'd disappear and reappear. Were you flashing the lights?"

Sergey laughed when I explained, amused by my inexperience, and said I needed to ride in the posting position on that kind of snow. I shrugged, not knowing the Russian word and too irritable to ask for clarification.

We loaded our supplies onto the Yamaha, and I asked Sergey
if he was worried about leaving the Hilux in the middle of the
road: someone might find and strip it. He wasn't. There were two
kilometers of impassable snow between the main road and the
vehicle—no one was going to come across the truck. While we
probably should have stayed in Terney, we were glad to have
fresh supplies in the cabin. It was clear that we would be stranded
at Anatoliy's cabin for the foreseeable future. Sergey took control
of the snowmobile, driving us quickly and efficiently through
the blizzard, shaking his head and grinning at my serpentine
track, which was quickly disappearing under the continuing
snowfall.

THE FALL TRAPS did not pan out. Either the resident fish owls
were not interested in the frozen marine fish we offered as lures
or the birds were unwilling to walk under the suspicious netted
domes to investigate them. At about two o'clock one morning, a
few days after the blizzard ended, Sergey and I sped three kilometers on the snowmobile in response to a beeping trap transmitter, only to discover a false alarm: ice had caused the net to
sag and this tugged on the string that activated the beacon.
Sergey, tired and frustrated and cold, kicked at the frame, breaking it, then threw the remains into the forest. Thus concluded the
fall trap experiment.

The capture learning curve was steep. There were multiple
nuances specific to each trap and to each capture site. Since late
February, we'd had a few very near misses. When we started out
the season, we thought that four owl captures seemed like a reasonable target, but I was ready to backtrack on that goal with
the realization that simply learning how to safely and efficiently
catch these birds would be success enough for me for this year. If

we had one or two captures to show for it at the end of the season, after all these failures, I would be satisfied. We were well past the midway point of the field season; if the weather held, we'd have three, possibly four, weeks left before the capture window closed. After that, spring would bring unstable ice, rising waters, and unsuitable conditions to trap fish owls.

The pattern of no owls, poor sleep, second-guessing, and general stagnation continued on for more than a week. I felt trapped, more so knowing that we really were trapped. Even if we wanted to throw up our hands, leave, and start fresh as we had when we left Serebryanka, we could not: our truck was still stuck in the snow a kilometer and a half away. I tried changing my outlook. We'd still made some progress this year, even if we hadn't caught any owls. It had been arrogant of me to think we could stroll up to some of the least-studied birds in Northeast Asia and assume they'd hand us their secrets.

IT WAS RIGHT AROUND THIS TIME, when I'd come to terms with our failures, that we caught our first owl. Anatoliy slapped me on the shoulder and told me he knew it all along—all I had needed to do was change my attitude. But in reality, we'd improved our trap. Up until this capture, we'd placed our noose carpets along the riverbank in areas we hoped the owls would land, which was inefficient. Our modification, something novel enough that we were able to later publish a description of it in a scientific journal, coaxed the owls to land where we wanted them to. We created a prey enclosure: an open-top mesh box about a meter long and thirteen centimeters tall, constructed from material left over from our noose carpets. We placed the box in shallow water no more than ten centimeters deep, sprinkled the bottom with pebbles so that from above it looked like any other stretch of river, and then filled it with as many fish as we could catch—usually fifteen or twenty salmon smolt. Then we set a single noose carpet on the closest part of the riverbank. The owl would see the fish, approach for a closer look, and get caught.

Masu salmon, the species most common in these rivers at this time of year, are among the smallest of all salmon. Full-sized individuals reach about half a meter in length and weigh about two kilograms, or more than half the weight of an adult fish owl. The masu have the most constricted range of any Pacific salmon, largely confined to the Sea of Japan, around the island of Sakhalin, and in western Kamchatka. Like many salmon, juvenile masu spend several years in freshwater systems before migrating to the sea, and the coastal rivers of Primorye are full of these pencil-length fish. As a result, this abundant species is a critical resource for fish owls in winter. Masu are also an important food source for local villagers, who can catch scores of them in a leisurely day of ice fishing. There is a misconception among locals that the small masu found in winter—which they call *pestrushka*— are a different species entirely from the larger fish—called *sima*— that come in summer to spawn. This complicates management of this species, as the same person who recognizes the commercial and ecological importance of sima may view the pestrushka as a common species that can be exploited.

The second night after we arranged this trap configuration, the male fish owl of the Faata River pair approached the enclosure and ate half the salmon inside before stumbling onto the noose carpet on the bank and engaging the trap transmitter. We were eating dinner by kerosene lantern light, as the hydroelectric plant no longer generated electricity, when it sounded. Despite nothing but false alarms so far, we treated every trigger with dead seriousness. Sergey and I stared for a second at the receiver and its regular, confident beeps, then locked eyes and flew out the door in a tumult of down jackets, hip waders, and uninhibited urgency.

We approached the trap, a few hundred meters away, on skis. Up ahead I saw Sergey's spotlight reveal a fish owl sitting on the bank, watching us. Like one of Jim Henson's darker creations, this was a goblin bird with mottled brown feathers puffed out, back hunched, and ear tufts erect and menacing. I'd seen other owl species adopt this posture in order to look bigger and more threatening to an aggressor, and it was working: this was a creature braced for battle. I was taken aback, as I still am every time I see one of these birds, by how enormous it was. The beast stood immobile, glaring at us with yellow eyes in the winter dark and illuminated unevenly by Sergey's light as our pace quickened. Everything was silent except for the rhythmic friction of skis on snow and our gasps of exhaustion. The urgency to reach the owl before it freed itself was palpable.

My heart stopped as the fish owl pivoted and took to the air in retreat, but the weight of the noose carpet held and drew the bird softly back to ground. The huge owl moved away from us with awkward bounds along the broad, snowy bank, dragging the noose carpet with it, until finally, when we were only meters away, the raptor spun onto its back on the river's edge. It lay there facing us, talons extended and agape, ready to shred any flesh within striking distance.

In the off-season, I'd trained in raptor handling at The Raptor Center at the University of Minnesota and had learned that hesitation with a defensive raptor doesn't do anyone any good. I swooped my arm in a fluid motion the moment I was within reach, scooping the bird up by its extended legs. Upside down and confused, the owl relaxed its wings, and I used my free arm to tuck them first against its body and then the body against me as though holding a swaddled newborn child. The owl was ours.

20

An Owl in Hand

WE STOOD in the shallow current, adjacent to the bank, with neoprene hip waders insulating our feet from the cold water. Sergey removed a pair of scissors from his backpack and, still breathing heavily, cut the ensnared nooses free of the bird's talons. The sky was clear and moonless. Illuminated by headlamps, with the river water murmuring and gently rushing past, I stared into the enormous yellow eyes of this magnificent bird. How was the fish owl going to behave in hand? Some raptors are docile, while others, like falcons, twitch and fight the whole time when restrained. Bald eagles stretch their long necks to snap intimidating beaks at their captor's jugular vein, as if aware that the right snip would reduce their abductor to a panicking volcano of blood. I'd found no written accounts of handling a wild adult fish owl, and even Surmach hadn't held an adult before.

It was frigid out, so we carefully carried the captured owl back to the warmth of the cabin, where Anatoliy cleared the desk for us in the back room. Here, we could collect necessary measurements, draw blood, and give the owl identifying leg bands without losing finger dexterity to the cold outside. The owl, we found, was remarkably calm in the hand. It lay still and stunned as we poked and prodded it, offering almost no resistance. Birds as large as this have few natural predators, and I suspect this experience was as novel to it as it was to us. To be safe, we wrapped the owl in a simple restraint vest, custom-made for fish owls by a volunteer at The Raptor Center. The fish owl weighed 2.75 kilograms—almost three times the average weight of a male great horned owl—had a wing length of 51.2 centimeters and a tail length of 30.5 centimeters. Female fish owls are larger than males, a pattern seen in most raptors, but records of fish owl weights were scarce, so it was hard for us to say with certainty which we'd caught. In fact, this was the first record of a fish owl weight from the Russian mainland, and from the island subspecies we could find weight records from only four males (range: 3.2–3.5 kg) and five females (range: 3.7–4.6 kg). We did not know if one subspecies was inherently larger than the other. Given that our bird was lighter than all published records, and had adult plumage so we knew it was not a juvenile, we suspected we had caught the resident male. We did not yet know that fish owls could easily be sexed by the proportion of white in their tail feathers.

Next came the transmitter. Following established protocol of tag attachment to a large raptor, we tucked straps over and under each wing so that the lipstick-sized transmitter sat squarely in the center of the bird's back, like a backpack, with a lateral strap crossing the keel to keep everything in place and a long antenna contouring down the body toward the tail. I first attached the harness loosely, then, holding the bird aloft by his legs, released pressure from his wings and allowed him to flap them. This process permitted the transmitter and harness material to settle naturally amid the owl's dense plumage. I then tested the fit and repeated the process until the transmitter and harness sat just right. If too loose, the transmitter would flop around awkwardly and impede flight or hunting; and if too tight, the keel strap would squeeze the owl as if in a corset as it gained weight. We were almost at the end of winter, certainly a lean period, and this fish owl was probably the lightest he'd be all year. He would gain mass over spring, summer, and into autumn, as rivers melted and more food became available to him. We needed to take this weight gain into account when fitting the harness.

We had to decide what we were going to call this owl and any others we caught for this project. We'd been so focused on captures that we had not given names any thought. There's debate within the larger research community regarding what to call study subjects, with some scientists arguing that naming encourages a familiarity that can lead to biased results. For example, some investigators might be disinclined to think a lion named Braveheart might engage in infanticide. There was, however, regional precedent for naming: the forests around us were filled with VHF-collared tigers with names like Olga, Volodya, and Galya. We ultimately settled on a more traditional approach. Since the birds we'd be capturing were residents of stable territories, we'd refer to them by their territory and their sex. This, then, was the Faata male.

We double-checked his radio frequency, confirmed that we'd properly recorded his leg band identifiers, and carried him through the crunching snow to the clearing behind Anatoliy's house. Sergey placed the quiet owl on the ground facing away from us, then stepped back. Confused, the Faata male sat still for a moment before realizing he was free, then lifted from the ground with rapid wing strokes and made for the river. I turned on the receiver once again to assure myself that the steady, strong beat was still there. After more than a year of planning, and after weeks of failure, the telemetry project had finally begun.

Sergey and I shook hands in mutual congratulation, then returned to the warmth of the cabin, elated. We had been saving some vodka to celebrate a capture, and I dusted it off and portioned off some shots. Anatoliy rubbed his hands together, smiling, and cut some bread and sausage. Our host was giddy. Sergey and I had been moody of late, and Anatoliy was reveling in this celebratory air. He was not much of a drinker, but with so few opportunities to imbibe he would not let the moment pass. We drank, ate, and savored the victory. When I went to bed that night, it was the first deep, uninterrupted sleep I had known in weeks.

THE NEXT MORNING, we refocused our attention on capturing the owls downriver, who we called the Tunsha pair. There was a small hunting cabin constructed of larch logs two kilometers from Anatoliy's cabin and seven hundred meters from our trapping site on the Tunsha, and we relocated there by snowmobile for a few nights. We had discovered the Tunsha pair's nest lower on the river a few days prior, eight meters up a broken-top poplar that stood straight and branchless like a tower among a fortress of tangles, from which an incubating female fish owl regarded us coldly. This meant that only the male was available for capture: as long as the female had an egg to warm, she was not going far, not while it was still so cold out. The first night, after finding some fish owl tracks on the riverbank, we placed the prey enclosure brimming with salmon smolt and a few Dolly Varden trout there without an accompanying noose carpet, just to see if the

Tunsha male would find it. He did, almost immediately, and re-moved all of the fish. The next night we placed the noose carpet on the bank, added more fish to the prey enclosure, and hid out of sight around a bend in the river. We did not wait long. He ar-rived at dusk, happy to find more fish, and moved without hesi-tation into our trap. Just like the Faata male, this owl flung himself onto his back on the riverbank in defense as we barreled toward him out of the darkness, his talons gleaming in Sergey's spotlight. These outstretched legs meant he was easier to grab, and just like that we'd captured our second fish owl. Behavior-ally, this bird was similar to the Faata male: docile and stunned into inaction. He weighed 3.15 kilograms, more than our last capture, and we might have even thought this was a female if not for having just seen the female sitting on the nest. We pro-cessed him quickly, attached a transmitter and leg bands, and released him about an hour later. We chose not to spend another night in the small, cramped hunter's cabin and returned to Ana-toliy's that same night instead, triumphant.

IN THE DAYS FOLLOWING the captures of these neighboring male fish owls, we used our directional antenna to record the locations of our first study animals. The Faata male still roosted where he had prior to capture, and both pairs continued to duet. These were strong indications that the capture experience had not been too traumatic for them, and they had returned to their regular routines, which relieved us. We were still interested in capturing the female of the Faata pair, who did not seem to be on a nest. We rebaited our prey enclosure at the Faata site, retied our nooses, and waited at dusk in the forest nearby. Again, within an hour of sunset we had our bird. The prey enclosure was the piece to the capture puzzle we'd been missing. We were gaining in both confidence and experience.

This fish owl was larger than the previous two we had caught and at 3.35 kilograms was about 20 percent heavier than her mate, although her wing and tail measurements were similar. She was sixty-eight centimeters from head to tail, slightly larger than the Tunsha male. Her behavior, though, was a notable departure from that of our previous captures. Whereas our first two birds—both males—had been compliant, this female was not going to suffer these indignities without protest. She drew blood from Sergey's finger with a darting nip of the beak when he moved in to measure her bill and struggled unceasingly under my restraining grip while we worked. Was this a characteristic difference between the sexes? She did not pause upon release as her mate had; hers was an immediate, hurried, and purposed exodus.

We had completed all the trapping we could expect based out of this location, and on March 22, we packed up. We had been stranded at Anatoliy's cabin for seventeen days, unable to leave due to our snowbound truck. We left the majority of our food behind for Anatoliy, secured the rest of our gear to the snowmobile sled, and had Anatoliy drive us on the snowmobile out to the still-stranded Hilux in the middle of the forest road. It had sat there on a white plain of snow, disturbed only by the tracks of passing roe deer and red fox. It took us nearly three hours of shoveling and pushing and swearing to make it the two kilometers back to the main road. We said our goodbyes to Anatoliy, who returned to his cabin on the snowmobile. Sergey would collect it and its trailer from him in a few weeks, after the snow had further settled or melted entirely and we could again reach the cabin with the Hilux.

We drove into Terney for an overnight break of beer and a

banya at John's house, then turned our eyes back to the Serebryanka River. We were calmer and more confident. The addition of
the prey enclosure, little more than a box full of fish, meant that
we could set one in the river, have a normal night's sleep, and
relax until the fish owl found it. We'd check the site every day for
evidence of an owl visit, tracks or fish blood along the adjacent
bank, then we'd set the actual trap, the noose carpet, that night.
We'd crouch out of sight nearby with a receiver to alert us to a
snared owl, and we'd catch the bird and be home by bedtime.

We placed an enclosure on the Serebryanka River toward
the end of March with nearly a dozen live fish. They were all
gone the next morning, with the snow nearby scattered with fish
owl tracks. I set the noose carpet on the bank while Sergey bored
a hole in the ice and started dipping his hook to replenish the
bait. We'd trap that night. After a few hours of unsuccessful fishing, I started watching the clock anxiously. We had a site ready
for capture, an owl that was almost certain to walk into it in a
few hours, but we could not catch a single fish. Out of desperation we began turning over river rocks and collected about a
dozen lethargic, hibernating frogs. Fish owls seemed to prey
upon frogs almost exclusively in spring, so we suspected that
they would be attractive lures now too. We put the frogs in the
prey enclosure, where they tucked themselves into the corners,
looking like smooth, dark stones. We double-checked that the
noose carpet was ready, that the snares stood erect and the knots
slid freely, then backed away around a bend in the river to wait
for darkness.

At 7:45 p.m., the trap transmitter squeaked in my hand, and
we barreled along the riverbank toward the trap. False alarm.
An owl had been there, we could see its tracks, but it had approached the prey enclosure from the side and had only bumped
into the transmitter and engaged it. It had not yet stepped on the

noose carpet and had almost certainly flown away as we approached. We settled in for a long night. We had not been expecting this to be a prolonged wait, so we were ill prepared. We didn't have sleeping bags or heavy coats to block the cold and wind, just a backpack with our capture gear. We huddled silently near the river, camouflaged in the growing dark against the steep bank. We did not know how the fish owl would react to the earlier disturbance . . . would it even be back that night? At 10:30 p.m., after nearly three hours of waiting, the transmitter beeped once again. Sergey and I were up and running, our headlamps guiding us through the dark. Like the other owls, this one lay on its back on the compact snow along the river with talons outstretched as we approached. A quick scoop from Sergey and it was in hand. The riverbank there was narrow, too much so to work comfortably, so we carried the captured owl back to where we had waited and processed it there. Based on its weight—3.15 kilograms—we decided that this was the resident male. We took measurements, drew blood, and fitted the transmitter harness.

As I took over restraining the owl for Sergey to fit leg bands, a deer ked emerged from the owl's breast feathers. This was a flat-bodied parasitic insect about the size of a dime, with long, stout legs. Named for the mammals it often parasitizes, deer keds land on a prospective host, then work through the thick hair (or feathers) to lie flush against the skin, surviving in this microcosm of blood and body heat even in cold winters. I'd seen plenty of these insects over the years, but it had not occurred to me that they might live on owls. It must have decided that the bird was a sinking ship and was entertaining other options.

"Hey," I said to Sergey, looking at the insect with curiosity. "There's a deer ked."

Sergey, focused on crimping the metal of a leg band, grunted distractedly in response. The fly started moving my way. I was unable to counter its slow approach—I held the owl's legs with one hand and its wings closed with the other. If I let go, the owl might hurt itself or put a talon through Sergey's hand.

"Hey," I said again with rising alarm as the fly crawled from the owl to my arm, then up to my shoulder to reach my bare neck. By this point I was bellowing. I felt the insect find and then burrow deep into my beard, where it nestled against my jaw. There was nothing I could do but swear in Russian with as much color as I could muster and implore a now laughing Sergey to take control of the owl. When he did, I plucked the deer ked from my face and flicked it as far away as I could into the snow.

21

Radio Silence

FTER OUR SIGNIFICANT STRUGGLES starting out the season, I was surprised by how quickly everything fell into place at the end. Three of our four owls were caught in only five nights, fortuitous timing as daytime temperatures were often above freezing. The next storm that moved in shed rain instead of snow, heralding the end of captures for the year. In addition to the increased difficulty of travel during the thaw, the river water became murky with spring melt, and the owls could no longer see the lures swimming in our prey enclosures.

These past months had been remarkably stressful. Over the years I'd taken part in many other wildlife captures, everything from checking snare lines set for tigers and lynx to pulling hundreds of birds from mist nets. But in those circumstances, capture protocols were established and based on years if not decades of prior knowledge. I'd also always been a field assistant or volunteer, and with that lack of accountability came peace. If something went wrong—for example, if a tiger broke a tooth or a hawk plucked a rare songbird from a mist net—I was not at fault. The responsibilities of this project, however, most importantly the lives of these endangered owls, lay squarely with me. A hastily set snare could conceivably cause an owl to lose a toe. A trap too close to riverside shrubs might result in a broken wing as the snared bird tried to escape. Once the bird was in hand, a whole suite of things could go wrong, and the release had to be perfect. These were the thoughts that sparked in my mind incessantly throughout the field season, stressors that manifested themselves physically in weight loss and mentally in lack of sleep.

There was some relief knowing, then, that we'd pushed captures as far as we could that year and that this phase of the work was over. As winter moved into spring, we in turn transitioned to monitoring. We spent our nights in the comfort of Terney, eating warm meals at normal hours and steaming in John's banya with regularity. We leisurely drove the roads of the Serebryanka, Tunsha, and Faata River valleys at all hours of the day and night, collecting movement data from each of our tagged birds by triangulating their locations. We stopped the truck periodically along the roads running parallel to the fish owl territories, dialed the receiver to that particular owl's frequency, and then slowly waved a large metal antenna that looked like a deer rack in the air to determine the direction of the transmitter's strongest signal. We were learning, however, that this practice, common in wildlife studies, was almost as much an art as it was a science. The signal from a bird sitting near the valley edge, for example, might echo off the nearby cliffs, masking the owl's true position. The resulting location would be imprecise—plus or minus several hundred meters—and not of much use for our goal of understanding exactly where an owl might be. Or if an owl was on a riverbank hunting, as opposed to sitting high in a tree, the signal was far weaker (and appeared to be farther away).

I felt self-conscious waving what looked like outsider art as loggers and fishermen slowed their vehicles to watch as they passed. But the residents of Terney were accustomed to seeing scientists track tigers with such devices, so our actions likely were not viewed as being as strange as they might be elsewhere in Primorye. Indeed, tigers were all people thought these antennae were good for, and the few people who saw us told their friends and family. We were such a noteworthy presence along the roads those next weeks, with our dowsing rods in search of owls instead of water, that rumors began swirling in Terney that tigers had moved into the Tunsha River valley in great numbers and any fishermen headed that way should take warning. We used the antennae in the forest as well, where I gained new appreciation for the deer and moose of these forests: I thought of them often as I fought through the understory with my antler-like antenna, snagging it here and catching it there, and was amazed that any ungulate could evade tigers and hunters by running along these river bottoms with something like *this* affixed to their skulls.

We were new to this work and hoped these early data points would reveal important locations for these owls. They did. We ended up with hundreds of newly acquired locations, which we plugged into our GPS units before wandering the forests and rivers of our fish owl territories, homing in on places the owls seemed to be spending the most time and becoming more familiar with the landscape these owls called home. We found hunting spots along the rivers as well as roosts where the owls spent their days resting. At the Tunsha territory, we hammered together a ladder out of lanky willow trunks, which we carried across the river valley to the nest tree. There, we found a single white egg, about 20 percent larger than a chicken's. For a bird as exotic as a fish owl, the egg seemed disappointingly plain.

AS THE FOREST TURNED from the austere grays of winter to the optimistic greens of spring, Sergey and I shared a final meal; then I made my way to Vladivostok in mid-April, where Surmach met me at the bus station. I spent a few days with him describing the season and planning for the next one. We had lined up a few field assistants in Terney to collect movement data from tagged owls in my absence, and good help was not easy to find. The equipment we used could conceivably track tigers as well, so we needed people we could trust. And since the work required a lot of driving at unpredictable hours, it was important that field assistants also had unrestricted access to a vehicle. In a remote village such as Terney, where few people owned cars, these criteria shrank the candidate pool to only a few individuals, and not all of them were excited to be up all hours of the night, walking through a dark forest.

Surmach and I also began discussing plans for future captures, a conversation that played out over months as I returned to the United States. I intended to be back in Russia in February 2008 and, with owls from three pairs already caught in the Terney area, focus our efforts around Amgu. In St. Paul, I took courses at the University of Minnesota in landscape ecology, the regulation of wildlife, and forest management. I needed not just to learn where owls were going but also to interpret what they were doing there and then form this information into a conservation plan that was realistic for Primorye's forests and its industries.

I received monthly updates from Sergey and field assistants dutifully collecting movement data from the owls. Not all the information was positive. In autumn 2007, Sergey responded to a report from a Terney hunter bragging about shooting and killing a huge owl. He was able to track down the person, a teenager, who although young had already developed a reputation in town as a poacher. In fact, the first thing he said to Sergey when they met was that he had bear gallbladders at a good price. Sergey pivoted the conversation to owls, but the boy pleaded ignorance. Sergey was persistent and convinced him that our interests were scientific, not punitive: we just needed to know if it was a fish owl, and if so, was it one of ours? The boy admitted the kill and led Sergey to an owl carcass in the Serebryanka River valley, not far south of both the Serebryanka and Tunsha territories, scattered by time and scavengers. Sergey recovered a wing, a leg, a shot-ridden skull, and an assortment of feathers. It was a fish owl. The leg lacked a band, and the boy, who had no reason to conceal information at this point, said he would have remembered seeing one had it been there when he killed it. Sergey asked why he had shot the owl, and the poacher said it had been opportunistic: he'd wanted fresh meat to bait his sable traps and happened upon this bird. I was disgusted. Instead of wringing the neck of a chicken in his yard, the boy had shot and killed an endangered species for a few scraps of meat. He hadn't known fish owls were endangered until Sergey told him, but this new information did not seem to resonate one way or the other: free meat was free meat, and sable skins were up to $10 each.

If this was not one of our owls, where was it from? There were only two fish owls without leg bands that we knew of in the Terney area: the Serebryanka female and the Tunsha female. Was this dead owl one of them? This news was confusing and depressing, but there was not much I could do from the other side of the world. My angst only increased in December, still in Minnesota and a few months before I was set to return to Russia, when the story got worse. Despite repeated efforts to locate our owls, field assistants reported that the transmitters had gone silent. This type of technology was reliable—these units should last for years—and if it was a problem with the transmitters, it seemed unlikely that all transmitters would fail at the same time. The logical explanation, the one that lingered in the back of my mind as I tried to ignore it, was that all four fish owls were dead. When I arrived in Russia in February 2008, my top priority was to resolve this mystery.

I JOINED THE TEAM of Sergey and field assistants Shurik (from the 2006 Samarga expedition) and Anatoliy Yanchenko (new this season), and our first move was to patrol the roads by our fish owl territories near Terney to check signals and listen for owl calls. Yanchenko, hired by Surmach to help us with captures just for the first few weeks of this season, was a bald and cynical fifty-six-year-old falconer. He'd spent twenty-four years of his life in a Chukotka coal mine, an unquestionably gloomy combination of place and vocation that may have indelibly stained him with pessimism and risk aversion. I liked Yanchenko, and I heard he was good at catching raptors, but he could be a dour companion.

Back in the forests outside of Terney, my receiver coughed empty static at all the places I'd heard strong owl signals the spring before. My heart sank: the owls really were gone. Toward dusk I lingered at the Tunsha territory, hoping against hope that I would miraculously hear them call, but I did not have great expectations. I was sick with worry: the research project was collapsing, and I might be complicit in the deaths of four endangered birds.

These thoughts dissipated instantly in the early dusk when, standing along the Tunsha road, the resident pair began to duet. It was a forceful sound that rolled through the winter forest in deep, earthy waves. I knew that fish owls could be heard only if you were listening at exactly the right time and under perfect conditions—the field assistants had simply missed them. The calls came from far across the river valley, at the base of the mountains, where I knew their nest tree to be. I listened for a few minutes, a smile on my face in the growing dark of this winter evening, as the owls announced to all who would listen that they were alive. Then, remembering the silent signals, I pulled my receiver from my coat and turned it on. Even with the owls hooting, there was nothing but static. The owls were not dead—not these two, anyway—but the project was still at risk. I needed to know why the transmitters had stopped working.

We spent the next few days patrolling the Faata and Serebryanka territories, looking and listening for evidence of life. We heard the pair calling at the Serebryanka territory but similarly found no signal at a distance of only a few hundred meters from the vocalizing owls. The transmitters were powerful, and we should have been able to hear the signal for up to several kilometers. This left only the Faata territory as questionable, so Yanchenko and I drove out to Anatoliy's cabin at the confluence of the Faata and Tunsha Rivers to see if he had any news.

Anatoliy welcomed us. He knew that February and March was the fish owl season and had been expecting me to return. Anatoliy's cabin was tidy inside and even boasted a fresh coat of white paint on the walls and ceiling. There had been a modest pink salmon run up the Tunsha River that autumn, and Anatoliy had been busy: a rich and sticky aroma wafted from the smokehouse, and dozens of splayed carcasses hung red and drying under the sun-facing eaves. I noticed that the battered pagoda that had perched on the cliff above the Tunsha River was gone. It had been felled and washed away, he said, in last summer's typhoon.

Over tea, Anatoliy reported that he had heard the Faata owls vocalizing regularly all autumn and winter, sometimes as close as the rocky outcropping on the river opposite the cabin, where

I had found some feathers the previous winter. On a few occasions, a fish owl had even called from the cabin roof itself. Anatoliy laughed as he recalled this event: the bird had emitted a sudden and thunderous sound that seemed to come from everywhere and propelled him from sleep, suddenly upright and alert.

This reassuring news, that there had been no prolonged absence of owls, suggested that there had not been any pair turnover. The birds we had caught last year should be the same ones we were hearing. So had the units failed? Also, whose carcass had Sergey recovered in autumn 2007? All territories known to us seemed to be occupied. Either all four tagged birds had disappeared and been replaced by new birds in just a few short months, which seemed improbable given the birds' long life span and territorial behavior and the fact that it takes a young owl three years to reach sexual maturity. If we were hearing new owls here, that meant one (or both) of the old pair had died or otherwise disappeared and been instantly replaced by a new adult. For this to be true, there would have to be a large population of unpaired fish owls nearby, waiting in the wings for these territories to free up. This type of scenario was possible in parts of Hokkaido, Japan, where aggressive conservation efforts were recovering fish owl populations, and in some places there were more breeding-ready birds than there were breeding sites. However, our surveys of the Terney area found no evidence of such a reserve population of breeders. The other possible scenario, that all of the backpack units had failed near simultaneously, seemed equally unlikely. The only way to know for sure what was happening was to recapture one or more owls from these territories. Faata was the logical place to start, as both the male and the female here were tagged, so catching either one would give us some answers. A pressing concern, however, was how easy it would be to catch one of these birds again. Some animals become "trap shy"—that is, they develop wariness after an initial capture and are difficult to trick a second time. Amur tigers, for example, typically avoid the general area of a previous capture, even if it's been years since they were caught there. Would fish owls be trap shy?

22

The Owl and the Pigeon

YANCHENKO used a *ðho-gaza* as his go-to trap, the work-horse of the raptor capture world, and I was excited to see it in practice. This is a net trap comprising a wispy, barely visible black nylon net about two meters by two meters in size, placed between a lure of some kind and the expected approach path of the target bird of prey. Sometimes the lure is a large predator, such as a great horned owl, with the goal of eliciting a defensive attack from a territorial raptor pair. In other cases the lure is prey, such as a small rodent or a pigeon, a tactic often used to trap migrating raptors looking for a quick snack on the go. The net is suspended between two poles with loops at each of the net's four corners, hung on thin and malleable wire hooks attached to the poles. The precariousness of this attachment means that the net will release and wrap around anything that hits it at speed, such as a large raptor a moment from striking its prey. A length of rope with a weight at one end is secured to one of the two lower corners of the net, so once entangled, the netted bird cannot wander too far.

We needed bait, so Yanchenko caught two rock pigeons in Terney by simply sauntering into a barn and grabbing them. "They never expect you to actually do that," he explained, "so they are pretty easy to catch." When he pulled back the red tarp covering the bed of his Hilux to reveal a small wire cage and a bag of birdseed, I saw that he had come prepared. This was not his first pigeon kidnap caper.

Back at Anatoliy's cabin, Yanchenko and I skied up the river to the capture site from the previous winter, bringing back memories of the tense unpleasantness and eventual elation of our first capture attempts. Yanchenko carried one of the pigeons with him, tucked complacently under his arm. Although fish owls are aquatic prey specialists, Yanchenko reasoned that they would not pass up an easy kill regardless of what it was, especially during the lean winter months. We found what looked like a fish owl perch on the exposed root of a downed tree next to the water near where we had trapped last season. Yanchenko paced off about twenty meters, then tied a swiveled leather lead to the leg of the pigeon and used a stake to hold it to the ground, where he sprinkled birdseed. The pigeon could walk around, but not very far. We paused to watch a northern shrike pursue an unidentified songbird through the canopy above us, then hung the dhogaza between the perch and the pigeon. The bird observed us with mild curiosity and suspicion before wandering about and pecking at the seed. I attached a trap transmitter to the end of the net and we returned to the cabin to wait. If something jostled the net, we would know immediately.

Yanchenko and Anatoliy got acquainted over tea while the receiver, on low volume, stood on the table interrupting our conversation with hummed static. Anatoliy, no less eccentric than the year before, declared that the nearby mountain was hollow and inhabited by men in white robes. All one needed to do was dig down twelve meters to reach this enclave, where they guarded a cavernous underground reservoir that was the source of the living water Anatoliy collected from a spring halfway up the mountain. There had once been a staircase leading to this reservoir from the temple on the hill, he said, but this entrance had been blocked for centuries. I studied Yanchenko's face for a reaction while we listened, but whatever he was thinking was masked by a veil of dispassion behind large and deep-set hazel eyes.

"Twelve meters isn't that deep. Why don't you just dig down there?" Yanchenko finally queried in his deep, monotone voice. His expression didn't change, and I could not tell if he was just filling an uncomfortable silence, poking fun at Anatoliy, or asking a serious question.

"Not deep?" Anatoliy retorted. "Dig twelve meters? Are you kidding?"

Just then the trap transmitter engaged. It was only fifteen minutes after dusk. I thought this was too easy and probably a false alarm, but Yanchenko and I rushed outside, kicked into our skis, and hustled upriver. There, a dark form lay entangled in the dho-gaza on the snow, wrapped tight like a cigar, after having hit the net at top speed. It was a fish owl and, by his leg bands, the Faata male. The pigeon, unharmed, stood stock-still as far away from the owl as its length of rope would allow, watching silently. I held the raptor while Yanchenko untangled it, and just as it had been last year, the bird was docile. He had also gained some weight. At 3 kilograms, he weighed 250 grams more than last winter. At first I thought the transmitter was gone, but as I buried my fingers into the dense plumage I could feel it there, close to his skin. After pushing feathers aside to get a better look, I understood immediately why we were having trouble acquiring a signal: the transmitter was scarred with beak scratches and the antenna was completely gone, ripped from the unit at the base. It had taken him nine months, but the Faata male had found the device's weakness. The transmitter was useless to him and to us. We cut the harness loose. We had spare transmitters with us, but these were the same models as the one the owl had destroyed; attaching another would only result in the same problem. Frustrated and with no other alternative, we let the bird go while we planned our next move.

Just as some birds are more likely to fall for certain traps, different species react differently to transmitters. Some raptors, like great horned owls, tend to snip at the harness material to cut the device from their bodies as soon as possible, while other birds seem to pay the extra burden no mind. In a 2015 study of more than a hundred tagged black kites in Spain, for example, only one of the birds removed its harness. It seemed we knew how fish owls responded: they attacked their transmitter antenna. How could we monitor fish owl movements if they were breaking the devices? This development was a significant setback.

After we released the Faata male, I performed a quick test to see how far the transmitter could be detected without its antenna. I tied the damaged transmitter to a tree on the edge of Anatoliy's clearing, turned on the receiver, and then moved away slowly until the beeping ceased. I had pulled back about fifty meters—this was the maximum distance I could expect to hear a fish owl's broken transmitter. Unfortunately, fish owls rarely allowed a human to approach so close, and if I was within fifty meters of a fish owl, the odds were I would already see it. I could only assume that the devices on the Faata female, the Serebryanka male, and the Tunsha male had all failed for the same reason.

Luckily I had a solution—at least a partial one. Even before I learned that the owls had disabled the transmitter, I knew I could not deploy such units with fish owls in the Amgu area. Transmitters require someone to be physically present to record bearings and triangulate fish owl locations. The Amgu region was simply too remote for me or the team to visit with any regularity. Instead, I had scraped together a number of small grants to purchase three GPS data loggers. These units sat on an owl's back using the same type of harness system as the transmitters, but instead of emitting a radio signal, they would collect several GPS locations per day, lasted up to six months, and were rechargeable. These devices were not without disadvantages, however. First, each one cost approximately ten times what its radio transmitter counterpart did: nearly $2,000 each. Second, these units were data loggers, meaning that they only collected and stored data. In order to retrieve the archived information, we had to recapture the owls to download it. This was potentially a serious problem; if one of our tagged owls died, disappeared, or was trap shy, the data would be lost.

YANCHENKO could not stay with us long: he had a wife and a goshawk to care for at home near Vladivostok. So after helping to resolve the transmitter mystery, he left me with a dho-gaza and climbed into his truck to drive south. We were planning more remote captures and could not rely on warm beds in Terney or in Anatoliy's cabin, so Kolya Gorlach arrived in Terney behind the wheel of a GAZ-66, a huge green truck that looked as though it belonged in a military column. This was where we would be living the rest of the field season.

Kolya was tall and lanky and had worked as a driver and cook for Surmach's research team for more than ten years by

that point. He was surly, but in a harmless, endearing way: easy
to rile up and impressively indifferent about basic sanitation and
personal comfort. In his youth, Kolya had occasionally found
himself in police custody on "hooliganism" charges, and he was
heavily tattooed. He had the words *We Leveled* across one foot
and *Siberia* on the other, in recognition of the years he spent
clearing forest for the ambitious Baikal-Amur Mainline railroad
project in the 1970s. He had also been briefly employed as a delivery driver for a brewery in the 1980s during Mikhail Gorbachev's anti-alcohol campaign, a time when beer was a precious
and controlled commodity. He'd leave the factory driving a truck,
he said, and by the time he reached the store or bar where the
delivery was to be made, he felt like the grand marshal of a pa-
rade, tailed by a pack of thirsty Soviets wanting the rare chance
to wet their palates with cold lager. Some cars would even U-turn
to follow him; they didn't know where he was going or how far
the destination, only that he had beer and they wanted some. He
recalled once even being driven off the road and shot at by high-
waymen looking to commandeer his kegs.

The GAZ-66 had a cramped cab with two seats separated by
the engine block—climbing into it felt like shrinking into the
cockpit of a jet fighter. Behind the cab was a large, two-room
living compartment. The smaller room was an eating area with a
table and benches that could sleep two. The larger room had an
iron woodstove by the back door and benches that ran down either side under three portholes of thick and grimy glass. These
benches were sufficiently wide to sleep a person each, but if needed
boards could be laid across the intermediary space to create a
larger sleeping platform for up to four people. Although the vehicle looked as if it were from the 1960s, I was surprised to see from
the registration plate that it had been built in 1994: it had not aged
well. The interior panels were cracked and yellowed, and the

truck was scarred by Kolya's temporary fixes that, with neglect and no further complications, had quietly become permanent. A button on the front wall of the living quarters sounded a buzzer to alert the driver that those in the back wished to stop, but it had not operated for some years, or Kolya had disabled it. In times of dire need, the best one could do was whack repeatedly against the front wall, hoping to be heard over the engine's roar.

Driving the GAZ-66, we moved to the nearby Serebryanka territory to recapture the Serebryanka male and remove his broken transmitter. We set up camp near where Sergey and I had stayed the winter before. As at all new campsites, the first step was to pull everything out of the back of the truck to make the space inside livable. While Kolya set up the propane stove outside to boil water, Sergey handed down boxes of food, supplies, and backpacks full of gear, skis, and firewood, which Shurik and I stacked out of the elements under the immobile GAZ-66. Once the internal area was clear, it was converted to a sleeping space. Sergey and I occupied the smaller room closer to the cab, while Shurik and Kolya shared the larger space in back. The GAZ-66 was well insulated, and the small woodstove filled the confined space quickly with its heat. We'd often sit in short sleeves at night before bed, irrespective of the temperature outside. But the winter cold laid siege throughout the night as we slept. As the stove cooled, tendrils of frost tested cracks and seams to eventually penetrate the truck's defenses. By morning, ice often clung to the interior walls. Lying down in summerlike conditions and waking hours later in deep winter presented a unique set of sleeping challenges. If I started the night in my winter sleeping bag—rated to –26 degrees Celsius—I'd suffocate. And my three-season bag—rated to –6 degrees Celsius—was woefully insufficient by the time morning came around. So I learned to sleep sandwiched between both, starting the night sleeping on my winter one and covered by the other like a down comforter. In the early hours of the morning, woken by the cold, I'd flip over and pull the warmer bag on top of me.

Shurik slept closest to the woodstove, a position that brought advantages and disadvantages. His spot was the warmest—no question—and as the shortest person in the crew, he was also least likely to set his sleeping bag on fire if he inadvertently stretched out too far in the middle of the night. But someone had to get the stove heated again in the morning. At the start of the season, Sergey had strategically issued Shurik the sleeping bag with the least insulation, meaning he would be the coldest the earliest. As a result, Shurik would usually be the one forced to brace the morning frost to light a new fire. Each day started with the GAZ-66 creaking and rocking gently on its axles as Shurik hastily fumbled with the stove. Cursing and with cold hands, he packed it with wood kindling and a scrap of birch bark to coax a hurried flame. Before sinking back into the relative warmth of his bag, he'd also place a kettle on it. Then we'd wait, sometimes talking and sometimes not, our voices muffled from inside our bags. The air would eventually warm, and the boiling kettle was usually a sign that it was safe to emerge. I'd stick my face out to test the air temperature, like a rabbit sniffing for predators from its burrow, and if satisfied, I'd call to Shurik to pass the kettle up to me. I'd put it on the small table next to me, and the rest of the crew would then rouse and pile into the forward compartment for tea or coffee, and we'd get on with the day.

SHURIK HAD SKILLS that I was hoping to exploit at this territory. Specifically, I had been itching to show someone with adequate scampering skills a few trees I suspected might be the Serebry-anka nest. Most of the candidate trees I had found in 2006 were

timeworn poplars with no branches within reach and thick layers of decaying bark threatening to slip off at any moment—that
is, trees not particularly safe to climb. Therefore, when I pointed
Shurik to my leading contender for nest tree, he walked around
the massive target in assessment, then selected a tall, scalable,
and adjacent aspen. He slid out of his rubber boots and inched
his way fourteen meters toward the sky in his socks. From there,
Shurik was able to confirm that we had indeed found the Serebryanka nest tree, a broken-top depression fifteen meters up the
colossal poplar.

Within a few days, a fish owl visited one of our prey enclosures. We set our traps, and the next night we had it in hand. We
were mystified by the discovery that this bird, based on weight
and molt, was both male and adult but was not the owl we had
captured at this territory the year before. Had there been a male
turnover? We'd heard a duet, so we knew the birds were paired.
Given what we'd observed about fish owls, it was unlikely that
this was a new pair entirely. There simply weren't enough fish
owls around for even a seemingly prime territory such as this to
be filled so quickly if last year's pair disappeared. Where, then,
was last year's Serebryanka male?

The following day I approached the nest tree, moving as silently as I could through the snow and branches. Leaning against
a tree to stabilize my binoculars, I inspected the roost tree Tolya
and I had found in 2006. There, I could see the shape of a fish
owl blending among the branches and long pine needles. This
was a strong indication of nesting: this must be the male we recently caught, guarding the female, who was likely out of sight in
the nearby tree cavity. The owl had seen me coming, knew the
threat I posed, and was on high alert with ear tufts erect. He
flushed from the pine, pushing a low, single hoot from his throat
as a warning to his mate that an indefensible danger was ap-

proaching. As he flew off, through my binoculars I could see the glimmer of his leg band: it was definitely the male we'd just caught. A moment later another fish owl flushed, this time from the nest tree itself, and I saw the yellow of its color band. This was the owl we'd captured last year—the one we'd thought then was a male: it had been a female after all.

The fact that we were flubbing something as fundamental as this bird's sex highlighted how little we really knew about fish owls. Given that by this point we had more experience with fish owls than anyone else in Russia, this was a remarkable admission. It also had implications for our project and the birds we were targeting. When we'd caught this owl last year, we suspected that the female of the pair was nesting. If true, that meant she must have left the nest for a quick bite when we grabbed her. Had that hour off the nest, as we'd measured her and attached a transmitter, caused her clutch to freeze? Was that why she was nesting again this year? We would need to be much more certain in the future about which owl we had in hand—weight alone was clearly an insufficient indicator of sex.

The bird was still less than a hundred meters away but flying off fast, so I quickly turned on the receiver and could hear a signal from her transmitter, but just barely. The signal stayed weak but present even as this bird disappeared, and then I realized the signal was not strongest from the direction she had flown in. Confused, I walked in a wide arc around the nest tree, noting with growing understanding that no matter where I was, the faint transmitter signal seemed to be emanating squarely from it. She had probably removed her harness, possibly by snipping it off, and the transmitter lay useless in the nest. Not wanting the owl to stay away from her clutch too long in the cold because of me—a second year in a row—I returned to camp and shared the news. There was no point in staying at Serebryanka to trap this winter: this broken harness had come off, and we did not have enough GPS data loggers to devote one to this territory. We needed them all for Amgu.

We moved to the nearby Tunsha territory for reconnaissance, where Sergey and I approached the nest tree to see if the pair, which we'd heard calling, was breeding. The nest tree was less than eight hundred meters due east from the road as the crow flies, located on a low river terrace some thirty meters from the main channel of the Tunsha River and opposite a wide talus slope that was holy to Chinese inhabitants of this region a hundred years ago. Experience here had demonstrated that a direct approach to the tree was ill-advised due to the obstacle course–like sequence of impenetrable thickets, logs, thorny plants, and channel crossings that stood in the way. It was faster and less irksome to loop south, then approach along the hindrance-free ice of the main channel. By the time we were within a few hundred meters of our target, both Sergey and I were soaked by the wet, sloppy precipitation that alternated between snow and rain. We were less than a hundred meters from the nest tree when I spied a flutter of vanishing movement up ahead—presumably the Tunsha male. We crept within fifty meters of the tree and I raised my binoculars to see tail feathers protruding horizontally from the vertical line of the nest tree's trunk. It was almost comical: there was a fish owl on the nest, incubating, and the cavity itself was too small to accommodate her enormity. We did not want to advance any closer; should she flush, the exposed egg might freeze. We started to back off quietly, pleased at the discovery.

She lit from the nest unexpectedly. I instinctively raised my camera to snap a half-dozen shots of her massive form as she flew downstream among the branches of the river-bottom canopy. I squinted at the small camera screen to see if any of my shots were in focus: they were. My eyes fixed on the exposed legs of this fleeing owl, and my brain quivered as I stared at it. I was looking at the leg band of the Faata female. I stammered something to Sergey, who came over. His eyes narrowed, then widened, and his mouth opened in silent amazement. The Faata female, whom we'd caught on the adjacent Faata territory the previous year, was incubating a nest on the Tunsha territory. We returned to camp, lost in thought. Where was the Tunsha female, the one that had been sitting on this nest last year? Was she the bird who had been shot by the poacher? That would make sense: the carcass was unbanded and only a few kilometers downstream from the Tunsha territory. But what had prompted the Faata female to switch mates?

To confirm the territory abandonment theory, we drove the Hilux to the Faata territory that evening, where we heard the male calling alone. The female had left him. Was this common behavior among fish owls or an anomaly? I talked to Anatoliy, who had told us he'd heard the pair vocalizing earlier that winter, but it was clear that he did not discriminate between the hoots of a single fish owl and a duet. In fact, he did not acknowledge that the duet was even possible: it was so coordinated that he refused to believe that it was two birds acting together. Sometimes a bird hoots twice, sometimes four times, he said. This meant that when he told us he'd heard the Faata owls calling regularly all year, which was why we'd thought the Faata and the Tunsha territories were still occupied, he had not necessarily been hearing both the male and the female at each site.

I wished we had more time in Terney to recapture some of these owls, but we hadn't planned to work here at all this year. We'd been forced into this distraction by the transmitter mystery, which was solved. We shifted focus to the Amgu region. There, we had multiple sites where we wanted to trap owls and three GPS data loggers ready to deploy.

ABOUT FIVE HOURS after leaving Terney, our small caravan of GAZ-66 and Hilux arrived at the Sha-Mi River site after midnight, some sixteen kilometers shy of Amgu. The last time I was here, Sergey had shown me where radon gas seeped into and warmed the river channel. The change in only two years was striking: Shulikin, head of the Amgu logging company and the dominant employer in town, had engaged in local enrichment by developing the site. He'd erected three cabins there; the first was a large, single-room structure adjacent to the hot spring, a building with a full-sized woodstove, a table with benches, and an elevated sleeping platform that would comfortably sleep three sober people or five drunken ones if in a pile. We parked the GAZ-66 next to it. The two smaller cabins housed the hot springs themselves. Shulikin had used an excavator to gouge the riverbank where the gases seeped into the water, and these spaces had been lined with timbers and capped by roofs and log walls.

One of the hot-spring cabins was occupied when we arrived, and as we set up camp its occupant emerged. Amgu is a small town and Sergey had visited often, and he recognized the man as a neighbor of Vova Volkov's. Vova was the man who had helped us cross the flooded Amgu River in 2006. The radon bather was a local hunter with a hunting lease farther up the Sha-Mi River, and Sergey had helped him fix his truck once. We walked over to say hello. The hunter said he'd just been upriver on his hunting lands; he'd spent the afternoon laying out bales of hay to sustain the deer that lived in those forests. I found it interesting that although he'd be eager to shoot these same animals when hunting season came, he did not want them to suffer before then. He asked Sergey if we needed any meat, saying he could bring some by in a few days if we were still around. This was often how we fed ourselves on these northern forays: people took care of one another here. We'd bring huge sacks of staples such as flour, sugar, pasta, rice, cheese, and onions with us, then fish in the rivers for trout or rely on locals to supply us with meat.

23

Leap of Faith

OUR TRAP SITE was within a hundred meters of camp, just out of sight around a small bend in the river. There was a deep pool where the river turned, followed by a shallow riffle, a perfect spot for an owl to wait in ambush for fish entering or exiting the pool. In fact, the river edge was covered with fish owl tracks. There was not sufficient space here for a dho-gaza, there were too many riverside shrubs, so we set out a few prey enclosures and returned to the warmth of the GAZ-66 for dinner. We were not sure how long it would take for the owls to find our traps, so we were pleased to have the Sha-Mi female in hand by 8:30 p.m. that same night. Given the trouble that Sergey and I had last year, I could not believe how smoothly captures were going: a little experience was going a long way. We brought the captured owl into the cabin and took advantage of the large table and warm, spacious area to take measurements and put on a leg band. Kolya started our generator outside and plugged in a cord to power a single bare bulb that he snaked inside and then hooked to the wall above the table. This was the third female fish owl that Sergey and I had handled, and we were learning that female fish owls are feistier than males. At one point Shurik, recording the molt of her primary feathers, loosened his grip on her body. Just as I was warning him to apply pressure again, she burst free, instantly smashing the light bulb with her powerful wing and plunging the room into darkness. I was in a pitch-black cabin with three people and a loose fish owl. Luckily, the sudden loss of light disoriented her as much as it did us, and I was able to almost immediately restrain her again before Sergey and Shurik turned on their headlamps. This was just her first attempt to struggle free: by the end of that capture session, the Sha-Mi female had drawn blood from both Sergey and Shurik.

It was almost –30 degrees Celsius outside, and the poor bird had become soaked from the capture process. She'd flown into the shallow water rather than onto the bank as we approached her in the snare, so after some discussion we decided to hold her overnight to dry in a cardboard box. We would give her the GPS data logger in the morning, along with some fish so she would not spend the day hungry. We celebrated with a few shots of vodka and were settling in for a quiet evening when a knock rattled the metal door of the GAZ-66. We had not heard a car or seen a flashlight, and we were far from Amgu. Sergey opened the door to reveal two young men standing in the snow, probably in their twenties, squinting from the sudden exposure to the brightness of the truck's interior. They had been on their way to the hot spring from Amgu when their car broke down about a kilometer shy. They had walked the rest of the way, freezing but knowing they would be able to spend the night in the cabin, and when they saw the GAZ-66 they could not resist investigating. They seemed friendly, and when the first asked if they could enter, Sergey obliged. They climbed in and put a two-liter bottle of 95 percent ethanol on the table.

"You guys want to drink?" the first said, smiling in a way that told me they had been swigging from the bottle on the cold and dark walk to the hot spring. We cut the ethanol with some water and drank a fair bit of it. I noted with some curiosity that Shurik refused refills after only a shot or two; I'd never seen him turn down alcohol. But I was in a celebratory mood and distracted by our successes. The men asked what we were doing in a truck next to the Sha-Mi River. They assumed, as most people did, that we were poachers. Sergey, always vague about our specific agenda, replied that we were ornithologists from Vladivostok looking for rare birds. He then asked them if they'd ever seen a fish owl, or the "owls that ask for a fur coat." I'd never heard this before, but the mnemonic made sense: the four-note duet could be interpreted in Russian as *SHU-bu HA-chuu*, or "I want a fur coat." These boys just grinned; they had no idea what Sergey was talking about. We did not offer the information that we were catching fish owls at Sha-Mi, nor did we disclose that we had one in a box in the truck with us.

When we woke at dawn to release the Sha-Mi female, there was no sign of our guests from the night before. They must have bathed in radon, then moved on. We carefully fit a GPS data logger to the owl, a unit programmed to record four locations a day, meaning we could expect to get three months of battery life out of it. Sergey would come back in summer and try to recapture her and recharge her data logger. We fed the somber bird four fish and released her. She did not fly at first, probably traumatized from her night in a box, but eventually she took to the air and disappeared.

The release made me uneasy. That was some very expensive hardware flying downstream on the back of a wild bird, enough money to hire a field assistant for two months or buy all the food and then some for this year's expedition. Given our meager budget, it was risky to use an expensive technology that was still relatively untested. With our original transmitters we at least had some peace of mind: we could check whenever we wanted to know if the device was working or not. Here, we had to trust that this thing the size of a cigarette lighter was working, properly programmed, and able to communicate with satellites twenty thousand kilometers above us in space. Then we had to believe the data would be safely stored in this tiny plastic box for a year and the owl carrying it would survive this period for us to catch it again. It was a leap of faith.

I could not understand the severity of my headache that morning. I noticed Sergey had one too.

"We didn't drink that much," he moaned, rolling an unlit cigarette absently between his fingers. "Why does my head hurt this badly?"

"It wasn't ethanol for drinking," Shurik revealed, "couldn't you taste it? It was lower-grade stuff—for cleaning."

"You knew it was bad and you let us drink it?" Sergey fumed. I certainly hadn't noticed; all that stuff tasted like poison to me.

Shurik shrugged. "I figured you knew and didn't care."

After a short soak in the radon hot spring—long soaks intuitively seemed like a bad idea—we packed up and moved east to the Kudya River, a small tributary of the Amgu River closer to the coast. Our spring 2006 crossing of the Amgu had been harrowing, but this time its surface was as hard as concrete and we passed over it easily. We then moved through a thin band of riparian forest and out into a clearing about a kilometer long and 150 meters wide: a space dominated by grasses hidden under snow and the occasional conspicuous shrub or birch. To the north of this oblong field was open larch woodland, and to the south was a line of old-growth riparian forest that clung to the Kudya River like a wet shirt. Sergey and I had heard fish owls vocalizing from this general area in 2006, but we had not had time to explore the area then. Now, we were not sure what we would find.

WE SELECTED A SUITABLE FLAT SPOT near the Kudya River and left Kolya with the vehicles to set up camp while Sergey, Shurik, and I set out in different directions on skis to explore. We were fresh off a morale-boosting capture—the first GPS data logger on an owl in Russia—and were excited to explore a new site. As the crow flies, we were only six kilometers from the Sha-Mi River, but the landscape here was notably different. The Kudya was more of a stream than a river, with shallow, interweaving channels constricted tightly on both sides by groves of willows about as thick around as ski poles. I had no idea how fish owls, as big as they were, could possibly hunt in these claustrophobic jumbles. I had so much trouble fighting through the understory that eventually I just walked in the shallow river water in my neoprene hip waders, skis slung over my shoulder. A few hours later we met back at camp, where Kolya had a fire going, with boiled water ready for tea, and was making lunch. As everyone compared notes, it quickly became apparent that we'd all had productive outings: Sergey and I both found hunting locations along the river and, more important, Shurik found the nest tree. It was an old-growth chosenia only a few hundred meters downstream of camp, on our side of the Kudya River. He'd spied a weathered down feather along the lip to the cavity so did not think the owls were nesting this year. The day could not have gone better.

We were ready to trap, but given the congested nature of the river's channels, we did not feel comfortable setting up noose carpets or dho-gazas; both of these traps require an obstacle-free space for the owls to struggle in, or the net might get tangled somewhere and the trap could become dangerous for the bird. So we suspended mist nets above the river channels that the fish owls almost certainly used as travel corridors to reach their hunting locations. A mist net looks superficially similar to a dho-gaza in that it is constructed of thin black nylon and is suspended between poles, but it differs in that it does not break away and does not use a lure; it is hung perpendicularly along a bird's route of travel. Mist nets are a standard bird-trapping tool by which a bird strikes the unseen wall of thin netting and drops to suspend in one of several "pockets" of loose netting material, which closes behind the weight of the hanging bird. As with our previous traps, we added a trap transmitter so we would know when something had hit it.

The indiscriminate nature of mist nets meant we caught and released a lot of things that were not fish owls in the next twenty-four hours, including several brown dippers, a male Mandarin duck resplendent in his breeding plumage, a northern goshawk, and a collared scops owl—a small bird similar to a screech owl of North America with grayish-brown plumage and striking blood-orange eyes. As we settled into our nocturnal routine, the trap transmitter triggered again. Shurik and I jumped from the warm truck and, hurrying through the dark toward the net, could tell from quite a distance that our quarry was a duck, based on the distressed quacks we heard. We found a mallard hen, quiet since our lights fell upon it, upside down and staring at us from one of the mist net's pockets. Another false alarm. Shurik moved toward the duck and I cursorily swiped my flashlight across the remaining stretch of net, where my beam settled on a brown form in one of the upper pockets on the opposite side of the net. We had caught a fish owl as well. I deduced that the female mallard had made such a racket that she had acted as a lure to pique the interest of one of the Kudya pair. Shurik, having never been confronted with a fish owl in a trap before, was beside himself with conflicting emotions of elation and trepidation. He had only ever seen these owls in hand, after Sergey or I brought restrained birds back to camp. Now, he'd have to help extract one from a net.

The owl had hit the trap right where we were hoping it would not, just above a waist-deep pool in the river. There was no way around it: we'd have to wade into this ice-cold water, well above our hip waders, to free the bird. I had Shurik disentangle and release the mallard while I approached the owl, the breath-stopping water filling my boots and settling at about my belt. Shurik then joined me in the river as the released mallard shot downstream. I was trying to understand if our bird was a male or a female—I did not want to repeat the mistake of Serebryanka—and based on behavior, I thought it was a female. She was fierce, as other females had been, recoiling at our touch and snipping at us with her beak and needle-sharp talons. Eventually we disentangled her and dismantled the net so nothing else would get caught in it that night. We took the owl back to the GAZ-66.

Based on how long Shurik and I were absent from camp, Sergey suspected we might have an owl and had cleared space in the back of the truck for us to work. Shurik and I changed out of our wet pants while Sergey wrapped the bird in a restraint and took it inside. Shurik had considerable experience working with birds in the hand, and contrary to my initial guess, he deemed this owl to be a male by manipulating its cloaca, the multipurpose orifice used by birds to excrete waste and copulate. I knew that some birds, such as ducks and grouse, could be sexed this way, but I was unaware that the technique worked on owls. In fact, other than weights, which had already proved inconsistent for fish owls, the only method I knew to accurately sex a raptor lacking sex-specific plumage was to sexually stimulate it. If the bird ejaculated, it was a male; if not, it was a female. We outfitted this owl with the second of our three GPS data loggers, took some measurements, and drew blood samples. As we worked, we could hear the other bird of the pair above us in the trees, hooting. It had followed us back to camp, knowing we had its mate.

The captured bird was large, weighing in at 3.8 kilograms. This gave me pause about the bird's sex. All the males we'd caught came in lighter than the published weights of the island subspecies (3.2–3.5 kg), yet this owl exceeded them and fell within the range of a female there (3.7–4.6 kg). With so much still unknown about the full weight range of fish owls, especially of the mainland subspecies, Shurik's insistence swayed me: male, it was. We stayed at Kudya for an extra day to make sure the pair was vocalizing normally, then packed up to move on to Saiyon. We'd be back here in a month to recapture this owl and download his movement data.

WE STOPPED at the Amgu gas station on our way north to the Saiyon territory, where I had discovered my first fish owl nest tree. This was the only place to refuel between Terney and Svetlaya, a distance of nearly five hundred kilometers. Like many other mundane tasks, the simple act of filling up a gas tank can be a challenge in the Russian Far East. Sometimes there's no fuel, and other times, like now, they simply refused service. You want fuel, the woman behind the counter barked at Sergey, you need to talk to Shulikin at the logging company. To his credit, Sergey had had the foresight to pack an extra hundred liters of fuel, so we were able to dip into our personal supply and continue on to the Saiyon territory without delay.

Not many outsiders came north to Saiyon. On occasion, people from as far as Terney, Dalnegorsk, or even Kavalerovo would make the pilgrimage, having heard of the therapeutic value of the radon-infused hot spring. They'd spend a few days to a week here, soaking in the water and relaxing in nature. The vacationers usually came in summer, the opposite of my schedule, so I almost never saw anyone else here. But they left their mark. The last time I'd been to Saiyon, almost exactly two years prior, an Orthodox cross had loomed over the dug-out pit of water and a small log cabin had stood a few paces away. The cross was still there, but the roof and two walls of the cabin were gone, cannibalized by visitors desperate for a fire among the slim pickings of the surrounding Saiyon swamp. The two surviving cabin walls leaned unnaturally, and where they converged a snowdrift occupied the space the woodstove once had. As we set up camp, Kolya seemed almost unaware that the hut was ruined and walked into it where the door used to be to place a metal folding table next to one of the remaining walls, upon which he laid a gasoline-heated burner to prepare our meals while we were based there. If nothing else, the cabin's hull could act as a giant windscreen.

We strapped on our skis and set off to explore. Sergey and Shurik headed south to the river to find where the owls fished, and I pushed north into the willows to check on the Saiyon pair's nest tree. It should have been close by, but I was having trouble orienting myself. Something was amiss upon my approach through the mess of riparian shrubs—where was the tree? As I removed my skis to cross a large snow-covered log, I suddenly realized that I'd found it. I followed the log down to a splinted stump; it had been felled in a storm. These decaying forest giants, already a rare resource for fish owls, were at the end stages of life and could not suffer bouts of wind and ice with the same resilience they had in their youth. After the several hundred years it takes a tree to grow large enough to fit a fish owl, a nest cavity might be suitable for only a few seasons.

Shurik discovered something valuable: a reliable fish owl hunting spot along the river. It was a modest swath of shallow water washing against a low, pebbly rise. A large tree branch, perfect as a fish owl perch, hung over it. Shurik reported that the banks were littered with owl tracks both new and old. I decided to try my luck at seeing these owls themselves, suiting up in a body-length layer of down, which I concealed under a soft and quiet white fleece shell. Although I looked like a giant marsh-mallow, when sitting immobile and hidden among the twiggy understory waiting for dusk and fish owls, I would be warm and near invisible.

Just after dark, a fish owl flew noiselessly upriver and landed on a perch above the fishing hole, no more than twenty or twenty-five meters from me. I sat hypnotized. The bird remained there for a few minutes, still as the surrounding night, and then dropped with a soft plunk into the shallow water. It had caught something. A shriek from another owl nearby startled me; I had not noticed its arrival. The bird in the water responded with a hiss, then moved onto land, hunched over like a feathered troll, gripping a fish in its beak. The second owl landed a dozen meters away. It advanced toward the other on foot, chattering, with wings held aloft and flapping vigorously, seemingly both at-tracted to and apprehensive of this thing come ashore. These shadows drew closer and then, just before touching, stopped. The first owl extended its beak, offering the fish, which the sec-ond accepted and swallowed whole before flying up to a nearby tree.

The shrieking, wing flapping, and feeding was a ritual of

courtship behavior: this was the male feeding the female to assure her of his hunting prowess and his ability to nourish her while she sat on the nest, incubating eggs or keeping her brood warm, reliant on him for food. I was already in my third year studying these birds, and this was the first time I had directly observed foraging or any kind of behavioral interaction between adult birds. The only reason I'd been able to view this small glimpse of fish owl life was that I'd gleaned experience in these years: I knew exactly where to sit, and I'd waited in the cold for an hour dressed as the Stay Puft Marshmallow Man.

CAPTURES SEEMED ABSOLUTELY STRAIGHTFORWARD at Saiyon: we had a wide bank where we could easily set a noose carpet or a dho-gaza, and both birds of the pair clearly visited this site. We had only one GPS data logger left, and it did not matter too much which of the pair we caught. Soon, however, our options dwindled to one: Sergey investigated an old nest tree not far from the riverbank and could see the female sitting firm. I must have seen her on one of her last nights out of the nest. We caught the Saiyon male on our first attempt and attached the last data logger. We'd done all the work we could here, so we packed up the GAZ-66 and spent a few weeks exploring other potential fish owl territories near Amgu, scouting possible future capture sites since we had no more data loggers on hand. We tried to reach the Sherbatovka River territory, where Sergey and I had stayed in Vova Volkov's cabin in 2006, but the logging company had erected a series of enormous earthen berms across the road leading there. They were designed to prevent poacher access but acted as a deterrent to fish owl researchers too.

In one place we woke to the fresh tracks of a male tiger that had walked just a few meters past the edge of our camp overnight. The presence of a massive cat caused Kolya significant angst; he stopped drinking evening tea for the rest of the field season to avoid potentially fatal midnight bathroom runs. In another place we captured a Tengmalm's owl in a mist net. This is the same species as the boreal owl of North America, a diminutive predator of small mammals, birds, and insects. With chocolate-brown plumage and a large, flat-topped head strewn with tears of silver, the Tengmalm's owl recalls a severe-looking cupcake. But we found no new fish owls.

We still needed to kill some time before returning to Kudya to recapture our GPS-tagged bird and download data, so we looped back to Saiyon to flush the sitting female and check the nest. She flew off a short distance, maybe seventy-five meters, and sat in the crown of a tree, glowering at us. The nest cavity was low enough that it was easily accessible using a ladder of thin willows that Sergey and Shurik had constructed and concealed nearby. Inside the nest were an egg and a recently hatched chick. The bird was only a few days old, still blind, and covered in a bright white down. The chick sensed my presence after its mother's hasty departure and hissed softly, mistakenly thinking I could meet its needs of warmth and food. I took a few photographs and descended the ladder. I did not want the chick to be alone too long given the number of crows and hawks in the area. After Sergey and Shurik headed back to the GAZ-66, I lingered about fifty meters away to ensure the nest was not raided before the female returned. I hid next to a log and under a bush and waited, with the intention of rushing out should a curious crow land near the nest. I could still see the female owl in the distance, enormous and immobile. After about twenty minutes, neither of us had moved. Why had she not yet returned to her chick? Surely she had forgotten about me. I lifted my binoculars slowly to my eyes and found myself meeting her direct stare at ten times magnification. She had not come back because I had not left. I stood and moved quietly away.

WE RETURNED to the Kudya River with the goal of capturing the tagged owl there, downloading a month of his movement data, and recharging his data logger before driving south to Terney. We camped at the same place we had earlier in the season, a site with good access to water and close to the nest tree that Shurik had found in February. A visit to the nest tree showed the cavity had been cleaned but was unoccupied. Fish owls sometimes rotate between nest trees in different years—they are certainly aware that a nest tree can topple without notice, so they have a reserve—and we set out in search of another. Luckily, we did not have to look very long. Shurik and I found it not more than five hundred meters from our camp on the far side of the river. Shurik clambered up a limber tree and reported eye contact with the female sitting tight in a broken-top cavity twelve meters up an enormous elm. This was good news. This meant that the pair was nesting and, more important for our short-term needs, that our target owl (the Kudya male, with the data logger) was the only bird available for capture.

On our second trap night we caught a fish owl in one of our traps, but the bird did not stay long enough for us to grab him. He left behind some down feathers and the fish he had taken from the prey enclosure. We spent a week at Kudya, but this was the only instance when we almost caught one. Winter breathed some last gasps, and the naleds and resultant ice dams, my nemeses from the Samarga, returned to render our prey enclosures useless. The slushy ice caused water levels to rise overnight, flood the enclosures, and allow our lure fish to swim free. We started hearing frogs in the early spring forest, which made us suspect that the resident owls had shifted to a new prey base and weren't even cruising the rivers for fish. Unable to use prey enclosures, we had to rely exclusively on strategically placed mist nets, and it seemed that we were catching everything except fish owls. In one evening alone we pulled four brown dippers, three male Mandarin ducks, a solitary snipe, and a male scaly-sided merganser from our nets.

The mergansers are interesting birds. Most of the global population of these ragged-looking fish eaters breed in Primorye, and like fish owls, they are reliant on fish-rich rivers for food and on cavities in riparian trees to nest. Once, Surmach had even found a tree with a fish owl nest in one cavity and a merganser nest in another. Given this overlap, as rivers melted in early spring we'd often see scaly-sided mergansers at our fish owl sites, birds freshly arrived from their wintering grounds in southern China.

WE WERE AT KUDYA LONGER than expected, and Sergey and Shurik ran out of cigarettes. Nicotine withdrawal only augmented the already tense atmosphere caused by the lack of owl captures. Shurik spent most of the morning swearing as he rooted around in pockets and drawers and under car seats for a single, precious forgotten cigarette. Sergey handled his withdrawal with a little more dignity by obsessively crunching hard candies. A simple and short drive into Amgu would have resolved this crisis, but such a submission would signal victory for the addiction that Sergey did not like to admit he had. By evening, however, he had a change of heart and a plan in mind.

"Shurik wants to go to the Amgu River to map the locations of rocky shoals along the banks." Sergey spoke with purpose, as though this made sense. "We can compare these over time to see how the river is shifting. I will drive him to the river, and since we're out we will also go to the store. Need anything?"

This was a fairly complicated plan that rationalized use of the vehicle and would conveniently result in the acquisition of cigarettes. Masterful.

STILL UNABLE TO CAPTURE the target owl, we decided to bring some excitement into our lives by flushing the Kudya female from the nest to see how many eggs she was sitting on. The weather was much warmer now, so her brief absence from the nest wouldn't be dangerous for her clutch. We approached quietly and I became distracted by some pellets under a nearby roost, which consisted mostly of fish and frog bones. Only one of the seven pellets contained mammalian remains. By the time I looked up, Shurik had already scaled the trunk halfway to the nest and the bird flushed. I raised my camera with enough time to snap off a few frames. Shurik called down, announcing that the nest contained two eggs.

The reproductive rate of fish owls intrigued me, as it did Surmach. There was some evidence that fish owl broods, or the number of chicks that hatched from a clutch of eggs, used to be larger. In the 1960s, the naturalist Boris Shibnev reported two or three chicks at sites along the Bikin River, and Yuriy Pukinskiy, a decade later in the same place, regularly reported nests with two chicks. But the majority of nests that Surmach and I knew about had only one chick. That the Kudya nest had two eggs was interesting, and I looked forward to coming back next year to see how many juveniles were found.

As I reviewed my photographs of the female flying off the nest, I was shocked to see leg bands. This was the bird we had been trying to catch, the bird we had thought was the Kudya male. But it was in fact a female, and she had been hiding in plain sight. I was flabbergasted by how poor our record was of sexing these birds. After this season, when I compared photographs of the tail feathers of all the fish owls we'd caught, it became clear that females had far more white in their tails than males did. In this case, our sex determination had been based on Shurik's examination of the bird's cloaca, although I'd thought that behaviorally the aggressive bird had acted more like a female.

Given this confusing revelation, after eight days of fruitless capture attempts we decided to back off the Kudya territory in defeat. The last thing we wanted to do was cause a nest to fail by recapturing and overstressing an incubating female. My only regret was not flushing her from the nest right when we arrived in early April. This would have saved us a fair bit of time, effort, and frustration. The GPS unit on her back would collect locations until at least late May. Sergey had already been planning to return to the Amgu area at the end of that month, after I had left Russia, to recapture the Sha-Mi and Saiyon birds, and he added Kudya to the list. An outstanding mystery was where the Kudya male spent his nights. We knew he was there because we heard him calling with his mate, but we had no idea where he hunted. From what we could tell, it was not along the Kudya River.

24

The Currency of Fish

WITH NO MORE DATA LOGGERS and thus no reason to catch more owls, the season was over. The team dissipated south. I went with them as far as Terney, lingering there to wrap up loose ends and explore fish owl territories before continuing on to Vladivostok, the airport, and then Minnesota. At home I took more courses at the university, including one called Forest Planning and Management, where I learned about different types of logging and how to adjust timber harvest practices to lessen impacts on wildlife. I worked as a collections manager at the university's Bell Museum, cataloging freshwater bivalve mussels and reorganizing the large fish collection, a job that covered my university tuition and paid me a living wage. In theory, to work at the museum I needed to be present during the spring semester, but I was always in Russia then. The fish collection curator, Andrew Simons, was sympathetic to my schedule and allowed me to work off the time in the summer months, after I'd returned from the field. One of my tasks, as I spent July and August in a university basement, was replacing the formaldehyde used to preserve specimens with ethanol. Some of the fish were nearly a hundred years old and quite large, such as lake trout. I considered myself an ornithologist, but even in Minnesota, I noted, my currency was fish. Only instead of catching spry masu salmon smolt in a down jacket and neoprene hip waders to feed fish owls, here I wore safety goggles and a respirator to net hundred-year-old trout from vats of formaldehyde.

In autumn, I heard from Surmach. Sergey had returned to Sha-Mi, Kudya, and Saiyon as planned and successfully recaptured all our owls. Their data had been downloaded, the units recharged, and the owls released again to collect more data. At Kudya, despite quickly recapturing the Kudya female, considerable flooding had stranded him on the wrong side of the Amgu River for several weeks. This wasn't his first spring flood; Sergey was accustomed to the inconvenience. He set up his tent, kept his eye on water levels, and used the unexpected free time to assess fish owl prey density as often as possible. With his friend marooned, Vova would row across the swollen river periodically from the village to bring Sergey cigarettes and other supplies. When the waters receded and the data made its way via email to me, I immediately understood that the effort had been worth it. The information from the fish owl's back revealed an important hunting location several kilometers from the nest tree, on the Amgu River itself. This was probably why we had not caught the male that season: he had been fishing in a completely different area from where we'd set our traps. Without this GPS data we never would have thought to look for a hunting spot so far from the nest tree, knowledge that expanded my view of what habitats were important for fish owls. I'd thought that nesting and fishing sites were closely tied, but if this pattern held with other owls, just finding and protecting a nest site would not be enough to conserve the species.

The data from other owls also brought insights. Based on their GPS locations, which had accuracies to a dozen meters or better, these birds seemed almost tethered to their respective rivers, as though an invisible lead kept them from straying too far. For example, instead of quickly crossing the low ridge to reach the Amgu River from the narrow Sha-Mi valley, the tagged female always preferred to go around. And the Saiyon male, occupying a valley that was at places a kilometer across, clung to the waterway so precisely that if I only had his GPS points to work with, I could sketch the river's course with reasonable accuracy. Between this information and the hunting data from the Kudya female, I was starting to better understand fish owl habitat needs. A conservation strategy was beginning to take shape.

MORE PEOPLE in the public were taking notice of our fish owl work. An article about the project appeared in the local Terney newspaper in spring 2008, and on Christmas Eve, I closed myself in a bedroom at my brother-in-law's house in a Milwaukee suburb to talk to a reporter from *The New York Times* about fish owls. With a finger in one ear to muffle the sounds of excited children in the background, I told her about tracking, field conditions, and fish owl vocalizations. I was just a graduate student, and all this attention was flattering, but more important, press like this was good advertising for the project that helped me secure more of the grants I was applying for. I raised enough funding for five new GPS data loggers for the next season. These units, each one costing hundreds of dollars more than the older versions, had larger batteries and would collect data for up to a year, nearly four times longer than the data loggers we'd used in

2008. This meant more efficient data collection and fewer repeat captures of fish owls.

An issue in past seasons that I sought to improve upon was our capture methodology. The previous two seasons largely saw my Russian colleagues and me crouching camouflaged against riverbanks in the dark, flinching at the sounds of cracking ice or creaking branches, enduring the cold as we waited in ambush for owls that might or might not arrive at our traps. So between the 2008 and 2009 seasons, we schemed of ways to make the capture process less unpleasant for us. I bought a sturdy winter tent that would act as a blind, and Tolya, the mustached cameraman, sewed a thick felt insulation cover for it. We experimented with wireless infrared camera technology—the types of things people buy as security cameras for stores—so we would not have to be exposed to the elements while we waited for the owls to trip our traps.

I smiled when I thought of how the next field season would go: we'd sit in the relative warmth of an insulated blind, tucked into lofty down mummy bags with hands gripping mugs of hot tea, watching our trap sites in real time on a flickering, mono-chrome screen. When an owl flew in to inspect our bait, we'd know immediately and be ready. No more guessing about the nature of strange sounds in the dark and no more questions about how much cold my extremities could take before I needed to start worrying about frostbite. I had no idea how inconvenient these conveniences would turn out to be.

I RETURNED TO PRIMORYE in mid-January 2009, just a few weeks after an aggressive winter storm dumped two meters of snow in just two days. The precipitation then transitioned to heavy rain hurtling earthbound like an artillery barrage. The assault was so forceful that droplets penetrated the snow to the ground before the storm abated and a deep freeze set in. The village itself was wholly unprepared for these attacks. Streets remained unplowed, no one went to work, and able-bodied neighbors tried to dig out stranded pensioners. After several days like this, the logging company in Plastun sent a fleet of trucks sixty kilometers north to Terney without request or notice, where they cleared all streets and then returned south without waiting for thanks. By the time I reached Terney ten days later, the town reminded me of the western front: roads were a network of connected trenches lined by towering walls of snow.

The storm had caused trouble not only for Terney; more significant, it had been catastrophic to local ungulate populations. The inability of deer and boar to move freely caused exhaustion and mass starvation. To make things worse, it exposed a darkness in some residents of Terney County. Many deer had been forced out onto plowed roads, the only passable travel corridors, where they were vulnerable to attack. Even people who did not normally hunt began patrolling these thoroughfares as though intoxicated by the ease of slaughter. They ran the fatigued animals down and killed them with everything from guns to knives to shovels. There was neither sport nor honor in the wave of carnage they rode. County Wildlife Inspector Roman Kozhichev, in a sobering opinion piece in the local newspaper, asked residents to wipe the blood from their collective brows and return to sanity before the forests were purged of life.

I arrived in Terney a week ahead of the team to assess the capture landscape for the year. I started by scouting our territories: I went to the Faata River first, where I wanted to visit Anatoliy—I didn't even know if he was still there—to lay the groundwork for trapping out of his cabin. I caught a ride the sixteen kilometers out that way, put on my skis, and pushed into the woods. After months away, my return to the forest was welcome. I was truly comfortable here, alone among the trees, breathing in the cold air and passing familiar landmarks. Woodpeckers and nuthatches paused to watch me pass, and I scanned the snow cover to see which mammals had walked by. I had enough experience with winter forests that I could identify track freshness: marks made overnight or in the dawn hours had a sharp delicacy to them, details lost when the morning sun breached the ridgeline, flooded the valley, and softened the snow. This was about as far from the streetlights, asphalt, and predictability of Minnesota as I could be, both geographically and in spirit. I felt at home in the United States, but I was at home here too.

After I crossed the valley through widely spaced poplars, elms, and pines, I came out at the Faata River north of Anatoliy's cabin about a kilometer later. I saw a figure downriver, high on a rocky outcropping, and raised my binoculars to see Anatoliy looking back at me through his own field glasses. He smiled and waved with a free hand. The frozen river led me to him, and we entered his cabin through a door decorated with worn fish owl feathers and shed snakeskins. He had been expecting me, he said.

I joined Anatoliy for a few cups of tea and asked if he had any news of the Faata owls. He had seen and heard them regularly, but when I prodded him, he could not be sure if he'd heard solo calls or duets. I sought permission to trap out of his cabin and asked what supplies he needed. He was happy for our company and asked for very little: some eggs, fresh bread, and flour. That settled, I listened while he confided that the Egyptians used levitation to construct their pyramids. He also spoke at length about Atlantis and energy and specific vibrations. When it was time to return to the road to meet my ride back into Terney, I put on my skis, and Anatoliy gave me a hunk of deer meat and a pink salmon. I followed an old logging trail for about a kilometer and a half to the main road, a route that looped through the forest and was intersected by the labored tracks of red deer, sika deer, roe deer, and red fox. In one place I saw the trough of a single boar where it had plowed through the deep snow. I was met on the road by Zhenya Gizhko, the same man who'd met me at the dock after my trip to the Samarga. He asked if I'd been visiting Anatoliy.

"You know him?" I asked, intrigued.

"Not personally but I know *of* him. He lived in Terney awhile. He was involved in some business deal with some scary people in Vladivostok. The deal went bad, and he's been hiding in the forest for, like, ten years."

Now I knew what had driven Anatoliy to the Tunsha.

I spent the next few evenings listening for owls. I heard a duet at the Serebryanka territory, and at Tunsha I found owl tracks on the riverbank and feathers by the nest. This meant at least one owl was alive there. After my quick assessment of our target territories, I felt that we would be in a good position to recapture our fish owls at the Serebryanka and Faata territories and give them GPS data loggers. I was less certain about the Tunsha birds, and since this was the most difficult to access of all Terney sites, it always seemed to fall at the bottom of my list of priorities.

I returned to Terney to wait for Andrey Katkov, who had been involved in fish owl fieldwork since my departure from Russia last spring and had helped Sergey recapture some of our GPS-tagged owls. Andrey had developed a new fish owl trap based on the prey enclosure, and he was eager to try it out. New captures were imminent.

25

Enter Katkov

IN HIS FIFTIES and bearded, Andrey Katkov was stout with the paunch of a Roman hedonist. He showed up twelve hours late to Terney; he'd driven the domik off the road on Whale Rib Pass and spent the night there cold and at an uncomfortable angle. Eventually, he flagged down a truck with a winch. I knew Katkov had been a police officer and was a seasoned parachutist—experiences that suggested discipline and stability—so I dismissed his rocky arrival as an anomaly.

I'd come to learn, however, that Katkov viewed careening off an icy road as an unavoidable inconvenience inherent to driving. He engaged in this activity with surprising calmness and frequency, and a disregard for safety that was a liability in the field. We had enough trouble dealing with natural obstacles in our work, such as blizzards and floods; we didn't need self-manufactured problems as well. Katkov also had a challenging personality: given his near-pathological need to talk and the close field quarters, it was hard to feel at peace around him.

Perhaps most catastrophic, Katkov was a champion snorer. Everyone on the field crew snored, but he was a virtuoso. Whereas the rhythmic pattern of gasps and exhalations produced by an average snorer might eventually be acclimated to by co-sleepers, Katkov liked to keep those within earshot in a heightened state of agitation with an astonishing range of pops, whistles, shrieks, and groans. Sleep was already a rare commodity in our work, and restful slumber within any proximity of this man was almost impossible. Taken together, these traits made Katkov a difficult person to spend time in the field with. I was about to endure seven weeks in his close company.

KATKOV WOLFED DOWN SOME BREAKFAST in the kitchen of the Sikhote-Alin Research Center that first morning, stretching out and pressing his back against the warm wall shared with the furnace room as a cat might to take advantage of its radiating heat. We reviewed the video equipment he'd brought. The setup included four wireless infrared cameras, a receiver, and a small video monitor. Each of these items required its own twelve-volt car battery for power, which he also brought, as well as a small generator, twenty liters of gasoline to recharge the twelve-volt batteries, and a handheld camcorder to record the capture process. We had considerably more gear than in past seasons, and most of it was also inordinately heavy: between the generator and the car batteries alone, we were looking at more than 150 kilograms.

The weight didn't worry me too much, at least not at first, especially since we had planned to begin the trapping season out of Anatoliy's cabin and we'd been able to drive there in the past. However, my recent reconnaissance showed that the waist-deep snow and unplowed road precluded such conveniences. We left the domik in Terney and then arranged a ride out that way on the main road, getting as close as eight hundred meters across the valley to Anatoliy's cabin. This didn't seem very far, and by this point I could move quite efficiently on the hunter skis. Katkov and I would have to take multiple trips across the valley to haul all of our gear there, so when we unloaded the truck we dragged everything into the forest out of sight of the road. We strapped on our skis, grabbed what we could carry, and got walking. I breathed in the cold air. At first the skis sank deep into the snow under the weight of our loads, but on subsequent trips we glided on the packed ruts.

My initial excitement declined over the next three hours, as it took eight trips for us to move everything from one side of the valley to the other. Katkov and I eventually found our own paces and walked separately, crossing paths only occasionally and using those encounters to take breaks, wipe the sweat from our necks, curse, and question why we hadn't thought about bringing a sled. The heaviest items, the car batteries and the gasoline cans, were not designed for long-distance hauling. Their thin hand straps dug into my fingers, leaving them hooked and raw from the constant weight. After dark and finally done, we collapsed in Anatoliy's warm and waiting hut. He had made blinchiki in honor of our arrival.

The next day, after a lazy morning of instant coffee and leftover blini, Anatoliy showed us to his fishing hole. It was a round opening in the river ice about the circumference of a basketball, located among the reinforced concrete ruins of the hydroelectric dam. He kept it ice free by chipping at it regularly with a hatchet. Katkov was eager to fish, so he prepared his tackle and dropped his line baited with frozen salmon eggs while I returned to the cabin to work on our strategy for camera placement. By midafternoon he'd caught dozens of fish, which we carefully carried upstream about seven hundred meters and placed in two prey enclosures in areas we knew had been visited by the Faata male in the past. It took us a good part of the next day to haul, set up, and check all our cameras and batteries at these sites. We then scouted for a location approximately equidistant between trap locations for our blind, which would house the receiver and monitor, a place close enough to each wireless camera to receive the signal. Everything worked. Wireless signals were strong. We settled into the blind that night for a final equipment test with every belief that things would go well. Wrapped in our sleeping bags, capped with heavy wool hats, and clutching mugs of sugary tea poured from a thermos, our mood was jovial. I had had enough experience with fieldwork to recognize that we were still in the honeymoon phase of both field season and relationship; the novelty of long nights in a subzero tent had not yet shifted to fatigue, and personal idiosyncrasies, which would inevitably be amplified in this tight, cold space, were at this stage easily ignored.

Despite expectations, our equipment test was a failure. Assuming recreational-grade technologies would work in the forest at –30 degrees Celsius had been naive. Sergey and the team had initially tested this gear in the warmer autumn months, when clear images appeared on the monitor both day and night. Here in the winter, the image quality was good during the day, but in the extreme cold that settled on the forest after dusk, the equipment failed entirely. The screen darkened to black in concert with the falling nighttime temperature. The entire system was unusable. To make matters worse, our generator had a faulty ignition coil. This meant that even if the video-monitoring system had worked as planned, we would have been unable to recharge our twelve-volt batteries. Adding insult to injury, we still had to haul all this useless stuff back to the road a week later, when we were done working out of the Faata.

We fared better with the camcorder, which we were lucky to have on hand. In fact, we ended up relying on it for the remainder of the field season: we attached a twenty-meter video cable to it and powered the device with one of the twelve-volt batteries we had no other use for. This provided us with live feed from a single capture site from the blind.

I distracted myself from these frustrations by puzzling over Anatoliy's past. Over dinner one night, Katkov picked up on, then later relayed, some things that Anatoliy said about his time overseas that I had missed. Apparently, Anatoliy had worked as an informant for the KGB for a period in the early 1970s as a sailor in the Soviet merchant marines. It was not uncommon for Soviet citizens to be asked to inform on their peers, especially those traveling abroad. In fact, one estimate suggested that by the Soviet Union's collapse in 1991, up to five million people could be considered informants. It was not clear to me if this had been Anatoliy's function or if he'd served some more structured role in espionage. When I asked him specifically about it the next day, he brushed me off with a smile, saying, "That was in the past." This was the same answer he gave when I asked how he'd lost the pinkie on his left hand, as he absently rubbed the truncated nub.

On our fourth night on the Faata River, after two nights of calling alone at dusk, the Faata male finally discovered one of our prey enclosures and consumed about half the fish there. We immediately set our trap, an ingenious construction designed by Katkov and Sergey and based on the prey enclosure. Simply put, the trap consisted of a snare of monofilament fishing line set on the prey enclosure's rim, with trip wires that released the snare when a fish owl plunged into the enclosure. At 7:20 p.m. the next night, the Faata male was, for the third time in as many years, in our hands. We outfitted him with the first of our new GPS data loggers—I had five of them—units that would record a location every eleven hours for about a year. I was confident this new model would work; we'd field-tested the technology the year before on smaller versions, and it had performed splendidly. The larger battery meant we wouldn't need to bother this bird again until the following winter, which was less stress for all involved. Of course, he had to survive until the next winter for us to find him again.

For the time being, our work on the Faata River was done, and not a moment too soon. I had not been able to acclimate myself to Katkov's snoring. The moment I'd adjust to one rhythm at night, he'd roll over and switch to something jarringly different, and I was eager for a restful sleep in Terney. After the Faata male's release, the mood in Anatoliy's hut was mixed. Katkov and I were still high on the capture rush, but Anatoliy was sullen. Perhaps this was because it was clear his guests would soon be leaving and his only company would again be the gnomes that tickled his feet and the silent mountain. I had noticed that Anatoliy tended to amp up the crazy when he sensed our departure. He talked long, loud, and with urgency on a variety of topics all united by a central theme: the Ancients had possessed a certain mystical knowledge lost over the centuries, but their secrets could be unlocked by properly interpreting the true meaning of specific objects, such as playing cards, Russian icons, and triangles. I'd realized that my responses to Anatoliy's musings were dependent on how the work was going. During the difficult periods of previous capture seasons, I bristled when he blamed the lack of success on our negative auras or when he asked us for help digging down to the cave containing the white-robed men. But on the heels of this very successful capture and release, I indulged him. His beliefs were deeply held, yet his opportunities to share these thoughts with anyone were few. I was sorry to be

leaving him alone in the forest. The next day, we used our satellite phone to arrange for a car to meet us on the main road, and
Katkov and I once again kicked into our skis and traversed the
Tunsha River valley multiple times and for hours, hauling the
broken generator, unused car batteries, and other items to its far
side. We'd work out of Terney while we attempted captures at
the Serebryanka site.

26

Capture on the Serebryanka

OUT OF ALL OUR OWL SITES, the Serebryanka River valley was where I was most comfortable. Given its proximity to Terney, over the years I'd kayaked the river, hiked along its fringes to the coast, and tracked tigers and bears on the slopes overlooking the valley. So, following our clockwork capture at the Faata territory, I felt a little betrayed when we couldn't seem to catch any fish for our lures at Serebryanka. I spent three frustrating days wandering the frozen river in my bright red jacket and neoprene hip waders with an ice auger over my shoulder and rod in hand. After many ice holes drilled, multiple hours wasted, and not a single nibble, it became clear that more was at play here than my admitted incompetence as an ice fisherman. I began asking around Terney why the fish were not biting, and the general consensus was that the Serebryanka became the river equivalent of a ghost town this time of year, possibly due to short-distance fish migrations. Katkov and I decided that the best course of action would be to return to

Anatoliy's reliable fishing hole on the Tunsha River. We would ski the eight hundred meters from the road empty-handed along our well-worn trail, hustle back with a spilling bucket of river water and live fish, and then quickly drive to the Serebryanka trap site to release the lures into our prey enclosure there.

Each trip yielded upward of forty fish, and Anatoliy enjoyed our unexpected company as we sat there for hours jiggling lines. But this exercise required a lot of time driving between sites, and Katkov filled our commutes with loud music. He was particularly fond of a mix tape of Russian songs dominated by wolf-related themes, which we listened to exclusively for the first week. Eventually I tired of this and began to poke around the glove compartment for other options, but there were few. It turned out that growling, protracted howls and lyrics like "You may think I'm a dog, but really I'm a wolf" become tolerable when the alternatives are dance remixes of the Carpenters' love ballads.

Except for the tension of car rides, most of my time was spent in a kind of daily meditation and workout routine. By spending hours skiing across river valleys and hauling buckets of water filled with fish, my body was responding. I was in the best physical shape I'd been in in years, and mentally I was doing well too. Past field seasons had been stressful, but I was familiar with conditions at the field sites now, knew the birds, and was comfortable with our trapping methodology. There was a calmness to the process; all I needed was patience and fish, and the rest would take care of itself. There was a sense of purpose to this work: fish owls were a species that needed a voice, and by teasing out their secrets, we were giving them one.

Eventually, after two days of no fish owl sign at all at Serebryanka, tracks showed that one had hunted less than a meter from the prey enclosure. It did not fish from it, however, as a severe overnight frost immobilized our prey enclosure under ice, preventing access to our visible, wriggling enticements. We predicted the owl would return the next night to investigate again, so we set up our camera and wrapped it in thick, cotton wadding with an air-activated, disposable hand warmer folded in among the layers, in hopes that this modification might keep the mechanism from freezing. We then strung a twenty-meter cable from the camcorder to a video monitor inside our concealed blind. We had a rudimentary remote control that allowed us to zoom but not pan; for our purposes this was sufficient. We could watch an owl approach, then zoom in to view its leg bands to identify our prospective target.

The wait in the tent was frustrating for both of us, as Katkov constantly sought to engage in whispered conversation while I repeatedly implored him to stay quiet. Luckily, we were soon distracted into a rapt silence. After only a short wait, a dark form appeared in the corner of the monitor, landing in the snow high on the riverbank. Its arrival was awkward, almost like a stage-shy actor thrust into the spotlight by an unseen hand. The fish owl sat still for a moment, assessing the scene and composing itself, then pushed through the billowy snow to the flat ice edge and the prey enclosure. I zoomed in: I could see by the leg band that it was the Serebryanka male. After another period of quiet deliberation, he stared intently at the fish with a craned neck and the posture of a tiger preparing to pounce. He then leaped, feet-first, with wings extended above his head as an osprey might dive, jumping a mere pace away into water deep enough to cover only his feet. The delivery was comical, like watching the pre-jump routine of a high diver who then steps into a kiddie pool. I'd expected something more viscerally powerful from the world's largest owl. I'd seen a fish owl hunt before, at Saiyon last year when the male caught a fish and then fed the female, but that observation was more abstract, as the owls then were largely in shadow. This, in comparison, was like going from a black-and-white screen to a high-definition television. The owl was in clear focus, illuminated by our infrared camera.

He was in the enclosure. His wings were still held aloft and flapping slowly for a moment before being tucked back in against his body. I could see why Katkov's snare method would be effective with these birds: the trap did not activate until the owl had fully committed to the kill and, in doing so, cleanly offered both legs to the snare. The fish owl stood in the enclosure for a moment, his feet hidden in the shallow water, and again looked around as if making sure he was not being watched. Then he raised a foot to reveal talons gripping a writhing salmon. He lowered his head and transferred the fish to his beak, killing it with a few strategic nips to the head. He then slowly swallowed the whole fish with a jerking motion and head tipped skyward. The owl peered at the water flowing around his feet, curious, and pounced again in the same manner as before. This time he walked ashore with his new prize and consumed the fish with his back to us before pivoting again to face the river.

We watched, enthralled, as the Serebryanka male spent nearly six hours lingering at our prey enclosure. We were comfortable in the tent, Katkov had a large thermos full of hot tea, and the river noise prevented the owl from hearing us as we shifted positions or whispered commentary about what we were seeing. It occurred to me that at that very moment, scenes like this were playing out all across Northeast Asia. From Primorye to Magadan—two thousand kilometers north—and even in Japan, a sparse scattering of owls were hunched by frozen riversides. These burly masses of feathers and talons braced themselves against the cold, still and focused on the water, waiting for a shimmer or a ripple to betray the presence of a fish. I felt as if I were sharing a secret with them. By two in the morning, all the fish were gone. Even after he had cleaned out the enclosure, the owl remained on the bank for more than an hour, watching the rectangle of steel mesh and wood intently, as if wondering when the magic fish box would again begin producing snacks. We would set our trap the next night.

TO PREPARE THE CAPTURE SITE, we had to acquire more fish at the Tunsha fishing hole, switch out the twelve-volt battery that powered the monitor for a fresh one, make it back to the Serebryanka site before dusk to set the trap, and wait in the blind for the fish owl to return. A trifle on paper but an ordeal in reality.

The first thing we did was drive from Terney to the Tunsha River valley, ski across to Anatoliy's cabin and catch some fish, then haul them back to the Serebryanka capture site. By this point it was early afternoon, and we were still on schedule. On the way back to Terney from the Serebryanka, however, the domik slowed to a stop. We'd run out of gas six kilometers shy of the village. I knew that Sergey was on his way toward Terney with the GAZ-66, stopping only to pick up Katkov and me on the way to more pressing captures in Amgu. This was our night: if we missed the opportunity, we might not get it again.

Katkov stayed with the truck, hoping to flag down someone with a funnel, hose, and enough spare gasoline to transfer some from their tank to ours, while I started hitchhiking toward Terney. None of the few vehicles that passed me stopped, which was a bit of a surprise. I was accustomed to hitchhiking here; in the warmer months I tended to dress deceptively similar to a Terney fisherman, and logging truckers were especially eager for the prospective company of a local to tell them which fish were biting where. Most were genuinely disappointed to learn my pursuits were feathered rather than finned.

I carried the intensely heavy car battery we needed to power the video camera as I walked all the way to Terney and then up the hill to the Sikhote-Alin Research Center. This took several hours, and it was only when I got there that I realized I could have left the old battery at the domik and picked up a fresh one from my supply in Terney; there had been no reason at all to carry a car battery for six kilometers. I had assumed I'd get a ride and had not been thinking clearly.

Time was short; we had perhaps an hour until dusk. I selected a new battery and threw some capture gear into a duffel bag. Next, I needed a gas canister and a ride to the gas station, which was another six kilometers on the other side of town, before heading back to the stranded domik. After several attempts I reached someone on the phone, a young man named Genna. He'd spent a brief period working for the Siberian Tiger Project and had once helped me look for fish owls, and at present he worked for the Terney County Forestry Department. Clearly amused by the frantic urgency in my voice, he agreed to help. He sped out to the gas station for the fuel I needed, then doubled back to collect me en route to the domik.

We reached Katkov just at the threat of dusk. While he turned the truck around, I shook Genna's hand and told him I owed him a beer as thanks and money for the fuel. He waved me off with a grin, saying he was glad to be part of the adventure. Katkov and I were back on the river, setting up the snare, when the owl pair began hooting from the direction of the nest tree. We were cutting it very close. Once the birds stopped calling, which could be any moment, the male would almost certainly fly to the prey enclosure to see if more fish had appeared. Knowing that I could make mistakes under pressure, I double- and triple-checked my knots and the snare placement and asked Katkov to check as well. Everything looked good. We ran through the snow to hide in the nearby blind.

Panting and bristling with adrenaline, we crouched in the tent as the owls continued to call in the distance. They hooted about once every sixty seconds, and as a minute of silence drew out to two and then to five, we knew the countdown was on. The male had begun the evening hunt. We listened for the telltale whooshing of an approaching fish owl. This time, I didn't need to remind Katkov to stay silent: like me, he had worked hard for this moment.

I tensed as the male appeared on our grainy monitor. Since I had not heard the sound of wings, I guessed he'd glided in over the river. My heart thumped in my ears. The bird barely paused and, just after landing on the bank, launched into the prey enclosure. Only twenty meters away, we heard the swish of the rubber band releasing and tightening the snare, but on-screen the bird recoiled to the riverbank and sat there, looking around, as though he had been startled but not trapped. Had he been, I expected the owl to immediately turn his attention to the line around his feet and pick at it with his beak. But this owl just looked at the prey enclosure. We were stunned into inaction. Then Katkov pointed at the monitor, hissing at the dark cord quite clear against the white snow leading to the owl's feet: he had been snared! With a flurry of tent zippers and spraying snow we ran to the river, and as the male tried to fly away, we watched the rubber spring coax him back to ground. The Serebryanka male was ours, and just like that, we had two data loggers collecting information for us.

SERGEY, KOLYA, AND SHURIK ARRIVED in Terney late the next day. However, despite recent and significant repairs to the GAZ-66, including a new engine and entirely rebuilt living quarters, after reaching us, the GAZ-66 had three major repair problems, one after the other, in the following twenty-four-hour period. This delayed our departure. My naivete around vehicles and their repair meant that I could not fully comprehend the breadth of the problems, but I could gauge their severity based on the effort it took to remedy them. The first problem was quickly resolved with some tinkering, the second was held at bay by a length of wire, but the third required a new part not found within a 150-kilometer radius of Terney. It was also a holiday weekend—International Women's Day—so most stores were closed.

International Women's Day was always on March 8 and had been a major national holiday of prime importance in Russia since 1917. It was international in the sense that it was observed globally, but with the greatest vigor in Russia, former Soviet states, and communist countries such as Cuba. Men spend this holiday, often just called "the Eighth of March" in Russia, heaping flowers, chocolates, and opulent praise upon the women in their lives. Declarations of appreciation can be so hyperbolic that they don't translate well culturally, as evidenced by a recent exchange at the University of Wisconsin. There, Russian students visiting on International Women's Day wished their female American counterparts success in childbirth and thanked them for their patience with the sterner sex. The women, deeply offended and unsure of how to respond, nearly reported the Russians for sexual harassment.

Given that everyone's attention in Terney would now be on women, without cannibalizing another GAZ-66 somewhere in town it was unlikely that we would leave anytime soon. While Kolya, Sergey, and Shurik worked on fixing the GAZ-66 or tracking down parts, Katkov and I drove out to the Tunsha territory to see if the resident pair were breeding that year. It was snowing heavily when we left the domik in the ditch Katkov slid it into, then called a parking spot, and we started skiing across the valley toward the nest tree. The wind was wild and the snow falling heavy and wet, adding additional stress to one of my already cracked skis, which snapped about halfway across the river valley. We continued on, Katkov waiting patiently as I lagged behind, laboring through the snow with skis slung over my shoulder. We found the nest tree apparently unused: either the Tunsha pair were not breeding this year or they had found a nest elsewhere. The weather worsened on our hike back to the road. As we drove to Terney in the whiteout conditions of a blizzard, listening to the Carpenters lament lost love at ear-bleeding volume, I asked Katkov if he had any songs about wolves.

27

Awful Devils Such as Us

SERGEY CALLED a friend of his in Dalnegorsk, who found the needed GAZ-66 part and sent it north on the next passenger bus. Drivers commonly made a little money on the side by acting as postal couriers between towns—it was much faster and more reliable than the Russian mail. When we finally left Terney, we were a few days behind schedule and it was already the second week of March: spring could come at any time. The only glitch with the GAZ-66 on the way to Amgu was on the icy Kema Pass, when the horn inexplicably began blaring in the darkness and would not turn off until Kolya, irate and swearing, pulled over and disconnected some wire.

Our goal for this leg of the season was to recapture three GPS-tagged fish owls in the Amgu area (Sha-Mi, Kudya, Saiyon), the birds Sergey and Katkov had caught last spring when I was still in Minnesota. We needed to download the information from their backs and outfit them with the three remaining new data loggers to start collecting a final year's worth of movements.

As we rode past the Amgu dump into town, two white-tailed sea eagles lit from the half-eaten carcass of a dog recently exposed from under the snow by the coastal winds. The eagles flung themselves into the air, surprised, with heavy wings and sagging talons, before accruing enough momentum to veer out of our way and circle back to defend their treasure from the descending crows. With every trip to Amgu, I have been taken aback by the ruggedness of this frontier town. We passed bearded men in home-sewn coats chopping wood and smoking filterless cigarettes, and women in felt boots and cinched shawls who stood back off the road to watch as we passed. In almost every yard, amid the debris of a culture apprehensive about throwing anything away, hunting dogs barked and fishing nets hung from the walls of haphazardly constructed sheds.

We camped near the hot spring on the edge of the Sha-Mi River west of Amgu, in the same place where we'd captured the resident female the previous year. We had to recapture this bird to retrieve data from her data logger and capture the male. After setting prey enclosures with fresh fish, we fanned out in the river bottom to search for the Sha-Mi nest tree. It took Shurik less than an hour to find it.

Female fish owls sitting on the nest always appear calmer to me than they should be. These birds spend a fair bit of time avoiding humans at all costs, so I would think panic would be a suitable response to direct eye contact with awful devils such as us, those who catch and poke and hold. When confronted, however, fish owls seem rather casual about the whole affair. At the Kudya territory last year, Shurik scaled a neighboring tree and found himself at eye level with the resident incubating female, whom we had tagged about a month earlier. She looked at him for a moment and then, deciding she had better things to do, cast her gaze aside. Now, as we stood at the base of the old and massive Japanese poplar, gaping at the fissure above containing our prize, the female sat immobile and hidden. Her presence was betrayed only by her ragged ear tufts, peeking out over the lip of the tree cavity and jostling in the breeze. We'd found the nest, but the female, whom we desperately wanted to catch, was incubating a clutch. She was off-limits for capture.

Back in the GAZ-66, we talked about our prior experiences at Sha-Mi. This territory had long been an enigma for us; Sergey and I had spent days in 2006 chasing the resident pair around the Sha-Mi and Amgu River bottoms, trying unsuccessfully to find their nest tree. Sergey was here years earlier with Shurik and a Japanese fish owl biologist named Takeshi Takenaka, before I started studying fish owls, and they were given a similar runaround by the birds. Sergey told a story of that expedition, where Shurik free-climbed an old broken-top Japanese poplar. He and Sergey had been fairly certain it was the nest tree. When Shurik reached the dark cavity some ten meters above the ground, he yelled down with confusion that he'd found "hair" and dropped some for Sergey to inspect. As Sergey held the clump of what was obviously Asiatic black bear fur, and began to understand that Shurik was poking his head toward a hibernating bear, Shurik reported warm air wafting out of the cavity. Sergey roared for Shurik to scale down as quickly as possible, hoping that the bear had not been roused.

Asiatic black bears are similar in size to American black bears but look rougher around the edges. They have shaggy black fur, a broad stroke of white across the upper breast, and perky round ears that make them look as if they're wearing Mickey Mouse Club hats. They may look cute, but they're dangerous. They are more aggressive than brown bears—their larger cousins and the other ursids of Primorye—and more likely to attack humans. While not endangered, they are prized on the

Asian black market for their paws and gallbladders, which are ostensibly used to treat everything from liver disease to hemorrhoids. When poachers come across a tree like Shurik's poplar and think a bear may be inside, they chop a small hole by the base, thrust something flammable inside, then wait with guns ready for the confused bear to crawl out of the top to escape the smoke.

The evening after we discovered the Sha-Mi female on the nest, I struggled into my marshmallow outfit and quietly moved to within about twenty meters of the nest tree. I concealed myself there with a microphone to record the duet I was sure would come at dusk; I had never had the opportunity to record fish owl vocalizations in such proximity. It was 6:15 p.m. About a half hour later, aching from immobility and feeling impatient, I saw the male swoop in. He landed on a broad, vertical branch of a neighboring tree, within sight of the cavity. The incubating female made a sound like a sneeze. I had only ever heard this vocalization when there was a predator nearby, like a crow or a fox, and realized she was warning the male about me. She could not see me from her nest, but she had heard me approach more than thirty minutes before and had not forgotten. The duet began with the male hunching over, his white throat patch bulging, and deep notes forced out into the frigid evening air. The female responded, on cue, with her calls muffled from inside the nest cavity. This went on dutifully for nearly a half hour, with a bout almost every minute, until the female curtailed the duet atypically twice in a row, and after the second of these she flew from the cavity to land in a tree some twenty-five meters from the nest. The male flew over to join her; it was dark and I could see them only by their silhouettes against the sky. They faced each other on this large, horizontal branch, and after one more duet, he mounted her briefly with flapping wings before coasting off.

They'd copulated. Before returning to the nest, the female clapped her bill a few times: an aggressive behavior that was probably directed at me, the lurking voyeur. Once she was back in the nest the pair resumed their duets, which continued for another fifteen minutes. Both the male and female were hidden from view, she by the lip of the cavity and he by the darkness.

IN ADDITION TO the Sha-Mi male, whom we caught on our first night trying, we used GPS knowledge gathered from the Kudya female to capture all three of the Kudya birds—the male, the female, and their year-old chick—in the span of an hour. In the off-season, the GPS data had revealed a hunting location two kilometers away from where we'd focused our efforts the year before, and Sergey and I had done some reconnaissance while based at Sha-Mi. We found that we could get quite close to this place by vehicle. In fact, we discovered scores of fish owl tracks and drops of fish blood on islands of ice only fifty meters upriver of the bridge over the Amgu River toward the Volkov cabin. We relocated there once done at Sha-Mi, setting up camp at the end of a fisherman's trail that led to the river, opposite a steep slope of birch and oak that abutted the water on the far side. We set a few prey enclosures and waited for dusk.

The speed with which our lures were discovered was a surprise—just minutes after dark—and even more unexpected was the unobstructed view we had of fish owl hunting behavior right from camp. And not just of one bird but of the entire family: the resident pair and their year-old offspring, who resembled the adults in plumage but had a darker face mask. There was no evidence of a second juvenile, although I recalled that Shurik had found two eggs in the nest the previous year. What had happened to the second egg? I was eager to return to Saiyon next to see if that nest, where I'd found a just-hatched chick and an egg last year, had produced two fledglings.

The chosen hunting spot for this family was, remarkably, right near us and the bridge. There, with a background chorus of baying village dogs, rumbling logging trucks, and ocean static, the Kudya family began their evening hunt. The female glided in first, low over the river, then rose to perch on the branch of a birch that overhung the water. The silhouette of her mate passed without a pause and he perched some fifty meters downriver, right by the bridge. Last, the juvenile landed screeching and impatient next to its mother. For a few moments they all sat motionless, presumably assessing the situation, their forms fading into the background of snow and tree as dusk became night. Both adults dropped to the icy bank of the Amgu River at almost the same time, then walked toward the water's edge, where they watched for fish. The juvenile, a year old and almost as big as an adult, fluttered down to its mother's side. Its begging was ignored there, so it flapped downriver to its father, who passed along a fish from the recently discovered prey enclosure. The family hunted actively for the first hour or so following dusk. Once satiated, they all sat on the banks above their chosen fishing holes and scanned the water lazily for fish.

One thing that surprised me, besides the unprecedented views of hunting and familial interactions, was that the owls did not care too much that we were there. Certainly they knew: the GAZ-66 and our crackling campfire were hard to miss. Kolya even walked down to stand in the middle of the Sherbatovka bridge for a better view, where he watched the male dive twice into the water from his tree perch. Was it because we were so close to the village that these owls were more accustomed to humans than most? We set our traps the next day, capturing all three in the span of an hour. The adults were given data loggers, but we only took measurements and blood from the juvenile and tagged it with leg bands. This young bird would be dispersing from its natal territory sometime over the next year and we did not want to put a data logger on an owl we would not be able to find later.

28

Katkov in Exile

WE MOVED NORTH to Saiyon, with one data logger left, where we were delighted to find that here, as at Kudya, the pair seemed to hunt in different places, which would make captures easier. The discovery that a year-old juvenile hunted with them was also exciting. Presumably, this was the chick I had photographed on the nest the year before. There was no sign of a second juvenile. We set one prey enclosure only a hundred or so meters from camp, where a river channel remained open due to the influx of warm water from the Saiyon radon hot spring, and a second prey enclosure about seven hundred meters downstream, by the nest tree. We hoped to catch the male first; he had one of our old data loggers. We could recharge it after downloading the data and then have a unit on hand for the female as well.

We made camp at the hot spring itself. The nearby cabin, a structure that had been mostly destroyed when we arrived the winter before, had been repaired sometime in the interim months with new walls and a roof of larch logs. Some unknown person cared enough to constantly restore this building, but most visitors to the hot spring seemed to view it as a convenient source of firewood. By the time we arrived in late March, the cabin was unlivable: the door, the window frames, and some logs from one of the walls had already been pilfered. The waters at Saiyon were not as warm as the hot spring at the Sha-Mi territory and thus presented a tepid place to soak after a sweaty day of work. Leeches were regular bathing companions in the clear water, swimming above the small stones on the pool's floor. This was a little unsettling, but the leeches tended to stay in their corner of the two-by-two-meter pit and we in ours.

The five of us had been living in the GAZ-66 for nearly two weeks, with Sergey and me sleeping in the forward compartment and Katkov, Shurik, and Kolya nestled like hibernating bears on the platform in back. Katkov, who snored aggressively, slept between the other two. They'd maintained this arrangement seemingly without incident so far, but over a breakfast of the previous night's dinner, a blurry-eyed Shurik announced he was out of patience. Not only did he have to endure operatic explosions a mere twenty centimeters from his face, but Katkov also tossed heavily and flailed his arms in his sleep. Even if Shurik could ignore the cacophony of noise, he could not escape the irregular battering. Even Kolya, who could probably sleep soundly on a rock pile during a hailstorm, agreed.

Katkov dismissed these attacks. "If you guys have trouble sleeping, maybe you should see a therapist. Your psychological problems have nothing to do with me."

Shurik sputtered obscenities, slapped the table with his palm, and asked Sergey for intervention. It was agreed that from then on we would have one person spend nights in the blind by the lower trapping site to better monitor that location and to free up some space in the GAZ-66 for sleeping. We took a vote. For the foreseeable future, that person would be Katkov.

WE CAUGHT AND RELEASED the Saiyon male quickly, freeing up his old data logger for the female, but a blizzard hit in late March, a disorienting frenzy of snow and wind that shook the GAZ-66 and buried our woodpile and the Hilux in snowdrifts. We could not trap under these conditions so took refuge in the truck. Katkov, stinging from his recent social rejection, stayed in his tent and made appearances only at mealtimes. The blizzard was not the only storm; I also suffered from significant bowel distress. Everyone else seemed fine, so the source was probably not the food Kolya had prepared. I tried to recall any risky behaviors of late and quickly generated a lengthy list. First, we were drinking and cooking with radon water, as no one wanted to walk the hundred meters to haul buckets of fresh water from the river in a blizzard. It was not clear how my sensitive Western gut might react to the extra radiation. Second, I had eaten a medallion of sausage that had fallen and then rolled on the disgusting floor of the GAZ-66. Third, I had used my knife to open the belly of a dead frog I found, then—fourth and fifth—washed neither my hands nor the knife before—sixth and seventh—cutting and eating some bread. And all of this since morning: no wonder I was sick.

My discomfort was a source of tremendous amusement for the rest of the snowbound team, who sat reclined in the back of the GAZ-66 playing cards, drinking tea, and eating cookies. They'd snicker as I hastily pulled on my snow pants, leaped off the truck, and ran across the frozen swamp to my cathole in the bushes. There, I accumulated a coat of heavy snow atop my miserable and crouched form.

By midafternoon the following day, both storms had passed. I walked the seven-hundred-meter trail to the lower trap site, where Katkov had been exiled. With our traps for the Saiyon female ready to be set, it made most sense to have two people monitoring each site from dusk until dawn. Neither Shurik nor Sergey thought he could endure twelve hours a day of close co-habitation with Katkov, so I volunteered. While he could be intense—his sleeping habits were erratic, and he insisted on talking almost constantly—I liked Katkov and appreciated his genuine interest in the work. Inside, the tent was a cave of odors and disarray. Katkov had engaged in some impressive wallow-ing during his eviction from sleeping in the GAZ-66. He had erected the tent on the snow surface itself instead of digging down to the hard ground first, and so with time and the occa-sional use of a butane heater, the tent floor had settled unevenly. Everything inside—the viewing monitor, the twelve-volt battery to power it, Katkov's sleeping bag, and his thermos—was perched on the lip of a wide depression in the middle: a sinkhole that threatened to envelop the tent entirely. There was probably a forty-centimeter difference in height between the floor of the tent along its fringe and the floor at its center. There was stand-ing water at the bottom.

"How do you sleep in here?" I asked, astounded.

Katkov shrugged. "I curl around the edge."

The tent was surprisingly comfortable for sitting: with the hole in the middle it was more like sitting on a bench with our booted feet slopping in the puddle. We set the snare on the prey enclosure near dusk and began our wait. The plan was to work in four-hour shifts, one person watching the screen for owls while the other person rested. Katkov, delighted to have a cap-tive audience, admitted that he was not having a great time in the field. He had accepted his banishment to the tent without complaint, but it was wearing on him and had started to turn to paranoia. For example, he accused Shurik of hiding or discarding his belongings. And the night before, he had believed Sergey was throwing snowballs at the tent to torment him, until he realized it was merely the wind in the storm loosening snow from the tree boughs above, which hit the tent in clumps. Once, when he saw the red glow of the infrared camera outside at night, he forgot it was there and thought Sergey was sneaking up on him, filming to make sure he was not sleeping. Katkov continued in this fashion, forsaking his sleep to lean in close and exhale a stream of consciousness, and as the hours wore on it became a tireless river of noise. He fueled his monologue with sausage and cheese, then belched zeppelins of aroma into that confined space. When my shift ended without an owl sighting, I wrapped around the sinkhole rim to sleep while Katkov took over watch, but I found it was nearly impossible to relax in that position. When I emerged from the tent the next morning, I helped him move it and dig out the snow underneath so that the base would be level.

THE NEXT NIGHT, Katkov recounted the first time he had ever seen a fish owl. "When Surmach described these birds to me," he said, hissing loudly, so he wasn't really whispering, "I formed a mental image of a majestic creature living in only the most immaculate of environments: roosting in a snow-covered pine, then dropping into the clear water of a mountain stream to grip an enormous salmon." He paused and laughed. "Want to know the first time I saw one? I was driving with Sergey to Amgu last spring to recapture the Kudya female. It was almost midnight, and it was absolutely pouring rain. As the road took that last big turn at the base of the Amgu Pass, the headlights illuminated a fish owl. It was sitting on the side of the road on a discarded truck tire, its feathers flat from the pouring rain, and it was choking down a frog! Not what I was expecting, I can tell you that. Not very regal!"

A few hours later, I was in my sleeping bag when Katkov kicked at me from across the tent and yelled that we had caught something. I burst from the tent and stumbled toward our snare, where I found the juvenile fish owl flapping on the riverbank. I grabbed it and brought the confused bird back to our blind, where Katkov was setting up a folding table outside. This owl had grown considerably since I had last seen it—this was the same bird we found on the nest last April at only a few days old: downy, blind, and unreservedly helpless. It was no longer so vulnerable. I'd learned to discriminate between the plumages of adult fish owls and those of adolescents and was pointing out the darker face mask of the juvenile to Katkov when the bird took advantage of the opportunity to sink its sharp beak deep into the tip of my finger with a viselike grip, drawing blood and leaving a nasty gash. I washed my wound and, lacking a Band-Aid, wrapped it in gauze and secured it with duct tape. We took measurements of the young owl, gave it a leg band, and let it go.

With two of the three owls at Saiyon captured, the male and the juvenile, odds were good that we might inadvertently catch one of these again if we left the snares out while trying to get the female. To avoid this, we modified both traps with hand-release triggers, meaning that owls could hunt freely in the prey enclosures and would not be caught unless we yanked on a wire to manually release the snare. Shurik and Sergey remained at the upper blind while I returned to Katkov's domain at the lower trap.

29

The Monotony of Failure

THE NIGHTS DRAGGED ON, a deep winter stillness perfo-rated by occasional firecracker-like pops: ice expanding in tree cracks as air temperatures plummeted after sun-set. The adult female fish owl was like a ghost. We heard her vocalize with her mate almost every night, but she appeared on-screen only once, when she hit our snare but pulled the knot free before we reached her: the only fish owl ever to do so. After that, nothing. She must have maintained a hunting location we had not identified. Based on our experience with the Kudya owls, it could have been kilometers away.

We had been living in the forest for nearly a month, repeat-ing the same actions day after day with little new progress. Tired from our overnight shifts in the blind, Katkov and I would load the heavy twelve-volt camera and video monitor batteries into backpacks and haul them to the GAZ-66 for charging. Maybe we'd spend the day repairing traps or wandering the forest for fish owl sign and then return the batteries to the lower blind in time for dusk and to check trap components, then huddle in the tent until morning.

THE BANDED JUVENILE, a regular visitor to the lower trap, became a source of light among the surrounding monotony and field season fatigue. Specifically, I was captivated by its hunting behavior and looked forward to its arrival outside our blind almost every night. Few people in Russia have seen adult fish owls at the nest or hunting, but the observations of the juvenile were even more unique: these were the first detailed views of a young fish owl learning to hunt on its own. The bird would typically arrive soon after dark. We'd watch it wade in the shallows, illuminated by the invisible infrared lights of our camera, as it moved with a slow, cautious swagger. The fish owl paused often to focus on the water and then leap in practiced attack. Interestingly, it only periodically removed fish from the nearby enclosure, as if it knew the fish box was ephemeral and that it needed to learn how to capture prey for itself. Occasionally, it would rake at the pebbly substrate at the water's edge with its talons, then stare intently at the resulting pit. At first this behavior baffled me, but later, when I discovered hibernating frogs just buried among the gravel of shallow rivers, I realized that the young fish owl was digging with the hope of dislodging a frog.

The graveyard shifts with Katkov were draining. We were bound to each other for twelve hours at a time in a stagnant tent with little forward progress. One night, as Katkov and I sat in our winter jackets and hats, covered loosely by sleeping bags and illuminated by the gray light of the monitor, he told me about his urine fetish. He described his photo collection of erotic and novelty urinals: latrines shaped like vaginas, gaping mouths, or Hitler, that sort of thing. Then he spoke about his love of urinating on, or from, beautiful landmarks. I recalled then how we once, on a drive, paused to watch the setting sun gild a cliff face, and Katkov remarked that he'd love to pee off it. That seemingly random comment fit into the now-larger puzzle of the man I knew. The explorer Arsenyev wrote that Chinese hunters in Primorye at the turn of the twentieth century ascended peaks to become closer to the gods; Katkov, on the other hand, climbed them to void his bladder. Eventually I'd had enough.

"Look, Katkov," I started, "maybe the female is not coming in because we are talking so much. I think we should stay quiet for a while."

Katkov did not agree: "There's no way the fish owls can hear us. We're whispering and the river is loud."

"All the same," I countered, "we want to do what's best for the birds."

He conceded—he really did want what was best for the owls—but was not happy about it. Every five to ten minutes he would blurt out a thought before I reminded him of our agreement and he quieted.

The next evening, I approached the blind and was surprised to see that Katkov had erected a thick wall of snow between the river and the tent. He was clearly bored, so I did not pay it much attention and entered the blind, prepared for another night of waiting. As we sat inside and Katkov began filling my head with trivialities, I waited impatiently for the juvenile to appear so I could use it as an excuse for quiet. The second the bird moved on-screen, I hushed and pointed.

"No worries," Katkov said, beaming in the monitor's glow. "I built a sound barrier."

Suddenly the wall of snow made terrifying sense.

"I'm pretty sure they can still hear . . . ," I protested weakly.

"Nope!" Katkov was still smiling. "Watch."

He slapped his hands together as hard as he could. The fish owl on the screen, in reality only thirty meters away, did not flinch. In the low light of the tent, Katkov mistook my grimace for a smile and clenched a fist in victory. All was lost.

REGARDLESS OF THE DELIGHTS I took from the juvenile owl, the lack of progress was frustrating for all on the team. To release some pressure, we took a day's break from Saiyon to drive twenty kilometers north to the Maksimovka River, famous to fishermen for its white-spotted char, taimen, and lenok and famous to us for its high fish owl density. This was where Sergey and I were almost stranded by loggers a few years earlier and had heard two pairs of fish owls duetting from a single spot. Sergey, Shurik, Katkov, and I piled into the Hilux, while Kolya, the only one of us indifferent to inactivity, stayed behind to watch camp.

The road to the Maksimovka River had been closed all winter due to the earlier snowstorm that buried most of Terney County, protecting the wildlife of the Maksimovka River basin from poaching. Yes, the snows were still a considerable difficulty for local ungulates, and I did see several frozen carcasses of starved deer, but until recently these animals did not have to worry about the threat of humans. This changed when a local official decided he wanted to go fishing and paid someone to plow the forty kilometers of road from Amgu to the Maksimovka River bridge for him. He fished near the bridge for a few hours, then went home. This opened the poaching floodgates, and we drove in silence past banks of white snow splashed red with the blood of deer and wild boar.

When I was last on the Maksimovka River, in 2006, all that remained of the village of Ulun-ga was a small schoolhouse that

Zinkovskiy, the one-eyed hunter, had converted to a cabin. In 2008, he and other hunters from the village of Maksimovka, men who controlled the legal rights to hunt along the river, had grown tired of poachers from Amgu driving north and killing deer and boar on their lands. The Maksimovka River basin is enormous— nearly 1,500 square kilometers—and it was impossible for the half-dozen hunters to defend it without help. So they posted sentries along the lonely roads: handfuls of nails and crudely soldered spikes hidden in the dirt to puncture tires. The Maksimovka hunters knew where to drive around these hazards, but unwanted guests did not. It is a vulnerable feeling to be stranded along the Maksimovka River, a place where winds howl through the funneled valley, bears are more common than people, and help is on the other side of a mountain range. Visitors from Amgu—some poachers but also undoubtedly innocent fishermen and mushroom or berry pickers as well—were incensed by their freshly shredded tires in this wilderness. Their response was outrage rather than retreat, and the escalation took the form of fire.

Cabins are precious here and often built one load at a time. Windowpanes, woodstoves, door hinges, and other components are hand carried long distances to small clearings cut from the forest. The greatest attack one can level at enemies in northern Primorye, one with implications that can last years, is to set a cabin aflame. And so, one by one, most of the hunting cabins along the Maksimovka River, including the one at Ulun-ga, were doused with gasoline and burned to the ground. Zinkovskiy had rebuilt a much smaller structure where the schoolhouse had once stood, but now nothing of the original Old Believer village remained.

We parked the Hilux near the Ulun-ga clearing. Katkov stayed at the Maksimovka River to bore holes in the ice and fish while the rest of us split up at the mouth of the Losevka River to look for the resident pair's nest tree. Shurik and Sergey pushed north into the Losevka valley on skis while I walked farther up the road a few kilometers, then cut through the forest to the largely frozen Maksimovka River and looped back toward the truck.

Walking the road, I saw some roe deer and was happy that at least here there was still some life; I'd hardly seen any tracks in the snow at all in the Terney and Amgu areas. As I approached the river, three carrion crows cawed excitedly from the forest edge. Two of them flew over to me, circled, then returned from where they had come. I followed their flight with my eyes and caught motion among the pines below: a wild boar. Had the crows purposely alerted me to its presence, hoping to feast on the offal a hunter typically leaves behind? I watched the wild boar amble along and out of sight, unaware that he had been betrayed.

The river ice was hard and flat like a sidewalk, so I took off my skis and slung them over my shoulder. Not two hundred meters downriver I saw more movement on the riverbank: first a pale rump, then a good view of the roe deer buck it belonged to, with antlers in velvet. The animal was thin and walked cautiously, with sharp toes sinking deep into the snow. The deer finally noticed me: a camouflaged, white abomination crunching along the river ice. He bolted toward the forest, but the deep snow changed his mind, and he reversed to the river, using the firm ice underneath to gain speed in escape. I watched through binoculars as the buck loped downstream, surprised that he actually paused in one place to nibble on a passing branch. After putting some distance between us, the deer inexplicably hooked right in a break across the river ice, perhaps headed for the trees on the far side. However, his escape route led directly toward a stretch of open water. The deer saw this—he must have—but did not slow down. He leaped as though to cross it, but crashed headlong into the water instead. He flushed a brown dipper, which chattered past me upstream like a bullet. I paused and lowered my binoculars, stunned by what I was witnessing, then raised them to my eyes again. Surely he would make it out. I could see the deer pawing at the water—it must have been too deep for him to stand—and he was swimming toward the icy bank. When he got there, however, the deer discovered that the water was flowing not at ice level but rather nearly a meter below it. The deer could not pull himself free. He swam around the patch of water, testing each corner for a way out, but found none. Then he stopped moving, succumbed to the current, and let it take him to the lower lip of the open water patch. The current was strong. The deer was going to drown.

My stomach sank as I realized that the deer was in a situation that he could not extract himself from. I started skiing forward hesitantly and then faster, yelling, hoping to scare some strength into him, but even as I stood on the bank just a few meters away, he continued to tread water and lunge impotently against the vertical bank of ice. It was clear to me that this deer, after weathering a vicious winter and avoiding prowling poachers, was going to drown in the Maksimovka River on the cusp of spring because I had startled him. I dropped one of my skis onto the ice and lay flat, using my other ski like a pole to stretch out, over the water, to reach his torso and pull him toward me. Once he was close, I leaned down and grabbed him by his antlers with both hands, hoisting the limp, soaked, and defeated deer onto the safety of the ice.

Deer experience "capture myopathy," meaning that a capture by a predator can trigger an irreversible physical decline that they cannot recover from: they simply die even if they manage to free themselves. Nearly drowning had been traumatic

enough for the deer, and I did not want him to perish from capture stress after all this. The second I had him on the ice, I was
gone. I collected my skis and moved downriver at a steady pace
without looking back. Once I'd walked several hundred meters,
I turned and raised my binoculars. The deer was where I had left
him, panting deeply. I watched for a few moments more, until he
swung his heavy head and looked in my direction, as if trying to
understand why I had not eaten him yet.

I continued downriver with the adrenaline still screaming
through me. I did not have high hopes that the deer would
survive—perhaps if he had been healthy, he might have been
able to withstand the stress of the near drowning, the frigid water, and his inexplicable brush with a predator. But this deer was
skin and bones. The experience was probably too much, and he
would likely die where I left him, to be picked at by foxes, wild
boar, and ravens until the ice melted and his carcass drifted with
the current into the Sea of Japan. However, about an hour later,
when Shurik walked to the river and followed my trail back to
our rendezvous point, he noted that he'd seen something strange:
a soaking-wet deer in the forest. That the animal still had energy
to run from my companion was a good sign; there were only a
few more weeks until all the snow and ice would be gone and the
forest would start to become green again. Perhaps the deer
would make it through after all.

When we returned to Saiyon, the snow came hard and the
snow came long, despite the approach of spring. The two-day
blizzard left behind a knee-deep layer of wet, heavy snow, which
likely sealed the fate of the deer I had rescued. When the storm
moved on, it took the deep cold of winter with it: everything,
including the river ice, began melting rapidly. Our traps were
ineffective in the turbid, murky water, and as if a switch had
been flipped, our capture season went from active to over. Spring

had once again arrived a little earlier than we would have liked, and we did not have the time to capture all of the owls we wanted to. We were filthy; our clothing was stained, rank, and torn. Our arms were covered with scrapes both old and fresh from chopping wood, repairing prey enclosures, fighting through the understory, and forest life in general. There were cracks in our rough hands so deep that they had assimilated the dirt of our surroundings; even a robust scouring was ineffective, and the stains remained. We packed up camp and moved our caravan south, driving slowly through the slush and mud of the thawing road, 320 kilometers to Terney.

30

Following the Fish

WITH THE FIELD SEASON OVER, I was able to turn my full attention to the GPS data we had been collecting and quickly began seeing patterns in how the owls interacted with the landscape. Each owl territory clearly had a "core" area centered on a nest tree, and where and how owls moved away from those core areas changed based on the time of year. Owls were closely tied to the core area in winter, which was intuitive especially during breeding seasons, when females sat firmly on their nests while males stood watch and brought mates their food. In spring, the owls tended to shift their focus downstream to the edges of adjacent fish owl territories or natural borders such as the coast of the Sea of Japan. In summer their attention switched, with most fish owls pivoting upstream of their core territories to haunt the upper reaches of main river channels and smaller side tributaries as well. Movements in autumn were the most unexpected, with some owls leaving the core area entirely for the extreme upper reaches of the waterways in their territories and not returning to the area around the nest until winter. I showed a map of this seasonal data to Sergey, who tapped on the computer screen at the autumn locations.

"That's where the trout go to spawn," he said. "They're following the fish."

If the owls were indeed shadowing fish migration and spawning, I'd expect to see a lot of fish movement in summer and autumn to account for the owl patterns I was seeing. I started looking into salmonid life histories. I found five species of particular interest. Masu (or cherry) and pink salmon arrived in summer to spawn, while Dolly Varden trout, white-spotted char, and chum salmon laid their eggs in autumn. This last species spawned in side channels and tributaries of major rivers, while the trout and the char spawned in the upper reaches of rivers during autumn. The seasonal movements of these fish were in fact consistent with what we saw fish owls doing in their territories from summer to autumn. This was good evidence that outside the breeding season, fish owls were tracking their protein-rich prey. Like a hinge centered on the nest tree, they pivoted downstream in summer to meet the arriving migrants and in autumn swiveled upriver to catch the breeding fish, which were vulnerable during spawning.

AFTER A FEW MONTHS at home in Minnesota, in August 2009 I headed back to Russia. North Korea had recently issued a threat against South Korean airplanes, and since Korean Air had already been shot down once by a foreign military, they took the threat seriously. Instead of the usual flight path that traced the eastern coast of North Korea to arrive in Vladivostok from the southwest, we boomeranged clear across the Sea of

Japan before looping back and arriving from the east. This added an hour to the final leg of my flight.

I had two objectives this summer. The first was to describe the vegetation around fish owl nest trees to learn if there was something other than the obvious about those locations—their massive trees—that fish owls found attractive for nesting. I'd do this by comparing the characteristics of a nest site with random sites in the forest. I had practiced my vegetation sampling methodology at the mouth of the Samarga River in April 2006 and had refined the process further with run-throughs in Minnesota. This part of the field study required knowledge of local tree species and a few special tools, such as a hypsometer to estimate distances and tree heights and a densiometer to estimate canopy cover.

My second objective was similar to the first, except that it was related to prey rather than nesting. I would compare river stretches where I knew fish owls hunted with random river stretches in an owl's territory. The methodology largely consisted of me squeezing into a black, full-body neoprene wet suit and donning a mask and snorkel to crawl a hundred meters up shallow rivers identifying and counting fish. Collecting such information about vegetation and fish might reveal important disparities in habitat and give me a better idea of what we needed to protect to help save these owls.

Surmach met me at the airport in a T-shirt and jeans, his shock of hair wafting. The first thing he commented on was my clean-shaven face. I typically wear my beard only in winter, so he and many others in Russia I'd worked with in recent years had never seen me without one. We chatted as we sped toward Vladivostok in the frenzied traffic the locals considered normal. Along the way, Surmach took a detour to check in on Katkov, who was working for him and living in the purple domik while monitoring a yellow bittern nest. This was the first known record of the species breeding in Russia. The wetland Katkov had staked as his home the past few weeks was adjacent to the main highway into town and surrounded by a horseshoe of train tracks; from what I could tell, it was a passing loop that allowed a lower-priority train to move out of the way while a higher-priority one passed.

"You get used to it," he yelled as another train rolled in and eased to a stop, with its engineer smoking and leaning out the window to eye us inquisitively. I understood that Katkov and his wetland were almost constantly encircled by the rhythmic din of train clatter. Katkov's time swapping camera batteries and reviewing footage in the marsh was coming to a close. After a few days consulting with Surmach in Vladivostok, Katkov and I drove north to Terney County in the domik for data collection.

OTHER THAN THE FACT that Katkov ran the domik off the road just as much in summer as he did in winter, and that for some reason he stockpiled newspaper and buckwheat in the back of it, I found him to be an excellent field assistant. He dutifully collected data, took the job seriously, and did not complain. The man really did have the best of intentions, and I felt bad about how he'd been treated the previous winter. I saw that he was genuinely interested in the work, cared about the owls, and valued my company. In Terney, we based ourselves out of the Sikhote-Alin Research Center and drove each day to record vegetation and river characteristics from the five nearby fish owl territories: three where we had captured fish owls and two where we had not.

I had not been to Primorye in summer for years, not since my master's work with songbirds, and it was dizzying. Forests that I was accustomed to seeing frozen, open, and silent were claustrophobic with vegetation and deafening with the symphony of birdsong. Diminutive Pallas's leaf warblers, sounding like crazed machine gunners, perched in the highest reaches of the canopy to spray volleys of sharp trills across the valley. Blue-and-white flycatchers sang from the dark, damp corners of the forest, ethereal calls that flitted along the edge of my senses like memories. Closer to the river I surprised a Siberian weasel, a small and lithe predator and a blaze of rust-colored fur, which disappeared among the branches of a logjam. I saw few other mammals—most knew to avoid humans in the forest—but the soft mud of the riverbanks was latticed with a multitude of animal tracks, including brown bear, river otter, and raccoon dog.

IT TYPICALLY TOOK US TWO DAYS to complete data collection at a territory, as each required five surveys: three of the vegetation and two of the waterway. For vegetation, we first surveyed right around the nest tree, then in an area in proximity to the nest tree, and finally at a random location within the owl's territory. For the river surveys, we collected information from where we knew the owls hunted and also from a random stretch of river within their territory. If there were any features specific to where the owls nested or hunted, these comparisons should make such distinctions clear.

For vegetation surveys, Katkov usually stayed at the center of the plot to record relevant data while I fought my way around him in a circle, counting all the trees and noting their species and size and other data within a twenty-five-meter radius, information I shouted to Katkov to write down. This work was tedious and hot and left my skin raked with scrapes and peppered with infected dots from *Eleutherococcus* thorns.

The fish surveys were considerably more fun, at least for me. After fighting into a wet suit purchased more for the slimmer body I wished I had rather than the heftier form I actually hauled around, I'd slip into the water. As most of the river stretches where fish owls hunt were shallow, I would crawl upriver just barely submerged and tally fish species and their numbers in my head. Each survey was a hundred meters long; I'd stop every twenty meters to yell my observations to Katkov on the bank, and he would record them on paper, then walk the next twenty meters upriver to stand as a visual indicator of where I should stop next. There were only a few different fish species, and all were fairly easy to tell apart. After the first few surveys Katkov suggested that we switch roles, but we could not fit him into the wet suit. With the water too cold to work without one, I stayed in the river and he on the bank. The atmosphere of these surveys was markedly different from that of my winter field seasons: there were no time pressures, no looming winter storms, and no concerns about captures. Just Katkov and me counting fish.

At one point I saw two fish about half a meter long hiding under a submerged log in a deep pool. I had completed only a handful of surveys by then, and this species was new to me. I popped up just as a fisherman was walking by in a camouflage jacket and hip waders, smoking and carrying a fishing pole. He was trying his best to ignore me.

"Hey," I called out in Russian. "What's a fish about yea big, silvery and with small black spots?"

"Lenok, of course," he answered impassively and without stopping, as though he often fielded pop quizzes on fish identification from lurking foreigners in wet suits. I returned to the water.

At one site south of Terney, where we'd heard fish owls but

not seen them, we worked in a veritable downpour. Katkov stood on the bank, miserable and dutifully recording on waterproof paper the notes that I called to him from the water. His saturated hood was cinched tight around his head in an ineffective attempt to keep out the rain. Meanwhile, the river here was deeper and I turned and rolled in it like a delighted seal. Once back in Terney, Katkov silently crawled to bed, shivering, wrapped himself in blankets, and did not appear until the next morning.

Katkov had a particularly rough day at the Serebryanka site, our last day of work in the Terney area. At one point I looked up from the water with my head full of salmon and trout numbers to see Katkov stumbling downriver, swatting at his head. He had apparently disturbed a European hornet's nest, vindictive monsters when threatened, and he was swollen with stings. At the end of our surveys that day, we crossed back over the Serebryanka River where several channels merged. Sections of the river there were relatively deep, perhaps four or five meters, but a sandbar snaked most of the way across, allowing one to wade in water that was waist high at its deepest. Katkov followed this while I, still in my wet suit and mask and diving down to explore the deep pool, monitored his progress from the water. He was about halfway across the river, waist deep and clutching his backpack over his head, when I noticed his trajectory led to a precipice. I surfaced and blew water out of the snorkel.

"Katkov—you need to go more to the left. The water gets deeper where you are headed."

Irritated from his experiences that day and pulsing with pain from his hornet encounter, he ignored me and stayed his course. I looked under again.

"Seriously, man, you're about to get dunked."

"I can see where I'm going," he responded curtly, so I shrugged and ducked underwater for a better view of the impending disaster. He hit the abrupt lip and his full body, submerged and surprised, with mouth open in a silent scream, came into my aquatic view. He surfaced, held on to his pack, and swam the rest of the way.

I did not feel it was necessary to say anything, and neither did he, so I changed out of my wet suit and into the clothes I had left on the bank while Katkov rummaged through his pack for something dry. He had stripped to tight-fitting maroon underwear, and I could see that his arms were angry from hornet stings and his legs were latticed with athletic tape to cover the diverse scrapes and thorn wounds he had accrued thus far in our work. He found no suitable change of clothes, as everything in his bag was soaked from the crossing, so he squatted in the river with as much dignity as he could muster to wring out his badly torn and stained shirt. He cinched back into it, remained pantless, and we walked to the domik. Low on fuel, we detoured to the gas station on the way back to Terney. There, emotionally done for the day, Katkov pumped gas in his underwear and ripped blue shirt, which hung from him as a wet rag. A few days later, Katkov and I drove to Vladivostok, where he was to start a new job at a local oil refinery heading their environmental compliance office. He still holds that position today, his days of suffering in Primorye's forests now in the distant past.

31

California of the East

S
URMACH DROVE me out to the Vladivostok airport to meet
Rocky Gutiérrez, my Ph.D. adviser, who was coming to
Primorye for a visit with his wife, KT, to help with fieldwork in Amgu. As we waited for them to emerge from the customs line, Surmach voiced concern about the itinerary I had
generated for their trip. Our plan was to drive a thousand kilometers north of Vladivostok to the Amgu and Maksimovka
River drainages with Sergey to complete the remainder of my
vegetation and river surveys. Surmach had not met Rocky before, but his past experiences with foreigners had taught him
that most were doughy, pampered, and unable to bear the discomfort of the insect swarms, the catholes, and the insect swarms
at catholes that awaited them in northern Terney County. I assured Surmach that Rocky took a perverse pleasure in suffering
of all kinds and viewed discomfort as an adversary best ignored.
Still, doubts lingered until they met, when Rocky's rough hands
and KT's ropy physique showed him they were a pair accustomed

to an honest life outdoors. Rocky, in his sixties, resembled a snowy owl: short, with large eyes under a mop of white hair. KT was about Rocky's age, slight, quiet, and highly observant.

We traveled north toward Amgu with Sergey, who had been in Vladivostok to buy spare parts for the Hilux. Floods had taken out more than a dozen bridges between Terney and Amgu that spring, left the roads pitted with ruts, and isolated the citizens of Amgu from the rest of the world for more than a month. True, a few supplies came in by helicopter or ship, but for the most part the unfazed villagers continued with their lives, hunting for meat and distilling *samagon*, or moonshine, until the supply chain was restored. As Amgu didn't really have a road until the mid-1990s, the people there still remembered how to live without one.

We drove on the freshly graded road over new bridges of earth and wood. The recent cosmetic attention surfaced a number of particularly sharp rocks, and we twice passed vehicles with sullen occupants smoking and changing tires before one of our own punctured. Sergey and Rocky patched the flat while I cracked sunflower seeds with my teeth and squinted at them in the sun. As we began piling back into the car, Rocky noticed a speck in the sky; we all trained our binoculars on it to reveal a mountain hawk eagle soaring unhurriedly in the warm air. This was a raptor instantly recognizable by its large size and its heavily banded tail. Not much was known about their distributions in Primorye, but they seemed especially common in the Kema and Maksimovka River drainages, where Sergey and I had often found their feathers or remains of their kills while looking for fish owls in 2006.

We arrived in Amgu late and headed straight to the house of Vova Volkov, the man whose father had been lost at sea. He and his wife, Alla, met us warmly and put Rocky and KT up in a back room. The next morning we were greeted by a typical Volkov meal, but one that Rocky still heralds as among the best breakfasts he has ever eaten. Fresh bread, butter, sausage, tomatoes, and fried fish crowded a giant bowl of red salmon roe, a serving plate heaped with steamed king crab legs, and a wide dish piled high with cubed and seasoned moose meat. These were items common to the ocean, rivers, and forests near Amgu but were delicacies to us outsiders.

After breakfast, Rocky pulled me aside with a look of confusion on his face.

"Is that guy's name really Vulva?" he said in a loud voice, although meaning to be discreet. He suffered hearing loss from his time in the military and could not always discriminate linguistic nuances or appropriate volumes.

"No, Rocky, it's V-o-v-a."

He seemed relieved.

Rocky and KT had spent decades living in Northern California prior to moving to the Midwest and the University of Minnesota, and throughout their trip to Primorye they regularly commented on the physical similarities between their California home and this place. Interestingly, there was also a myth perpetuated among Primorye's residents that Vladivostok was "the San Francisco of the East," given that both cities are situated in hilly, North Pacific bays, and curious Russians would often ask me if that was true. I usually lied and said I had never been to San Francisco, which was gentler than the reality. Vladivostok, a cosmopolitan darling of early-twentieth-century imperial Russia, had not aged well in the Soviet Union. The city closed itself off to protect the secrets of the Soviet Pacific Fleet; foreigners were banned from this city once celebrated for its international influences. Memories of the czar were similarly suppressed, sometimes crudely: a massive, onion-domed church was demolished by the Soviets on Easter Sunday in 1935. When I first arrived in Vladivostok in the mid-1990s, once-white building facades were gray and crumbling from neglect, I saw a dead body in the bushes by the train station, and open pits pocked the streets where manhole covers had been pilfered for scrap. Thankfully, things have markedly improved in Vladivostok since then. Buildings have been repaired, and many of the beautiful imperial landmarks have been rebuilt. It is quite a lovely city, with promenades, restaurants, and culture.

AFTER LEAVING THE VOLKOVS, we described the vegetation at five fish owl sites in the Amgu and Maksimovka areas, camping along the way. Rocky and KT did a lot of the legwork for the vegetation surveys, and Sergey and I took turns in the wet suit counting fish. Sergey carried a trident with him in the water in case he encountered a salmon large enough to stab at and was disappointed to never come across such a prize. In one location, I raised my head out of the water to see a roe deer doe a dozen paces away on the riverbank, staring at me with blank incomprehension. In my sleek black suit, protruding mask, and blue snorkel, I looked nothing like anything she had ever seen. Perhaps finally recognizing the human underneath, she bolted into the forest.

We spent a few days up the Sherbatovka River. At the Amgu River the bridge had once again been called to sea, so we pushed through the shallow water to the far side to stop at Vova's cabin, where we had been in 2006, to spend the night. It was almost hidden among the tall grasses. I found a scythe in the cabin eaves and cleared a wide space in front of the hut; we did not want to unnecessarily accumulate ticks, and Sergey and I needed somewhere to pitch our tents. We would sleep outside while Rocky and KT would occupy the sleeping platforms inside. We had a dinner of *ukha*, fish soup made with potatoes, dill, onions, and trout Sergey had caught that afternoon, along with an even spacing of vodka and good conversation.

After describing the vegetation and river conditions of the Sherbatovka fish owl pair the following day, we continued up the river along a new logging road, curious to see if we could find any suitable fish owl habitat there. This road was in good condition, and Sergey was surprised to see that it ran right past Vova's second cabin, so we stopped to inspect it. When we were last in the area in 2006, this was a good five kilometers' walk from where the road ended, and the sparse decor reflected this: the few furnishings must have been carried there on Vova's back. The lower cabin was like a resort in comparison; the interior here consisted of a low sleeping platform nailed to braces above a dirt floor, a stump to sit on, and a small iron woodstove. A slit of a window just large enough for light to find its way inside illuminated the squalor. I thought I might contract hantavirus just by looking at the cabin, and Rocky and KT refused to sleep in it. We therefore made camp at a clearing nearby, close to the bank of the Sherbatovka River.

After erecting our tents, we set off to explore. We passed timeworn brown bear tracks in the mud of a skid trail and watched a Eurasian three-toed woodpecker probe the trunk of a fir with deliberate taps. The forest was very different from the diverse bottomlands I was accustomed to seeing; here the tree species dwindled largely to fir and spruce. Pure stands of them, draped by bearded lichens, rolled unchallenged across slopes of pillowy moss. Everything was soft and aromatic. This was the classic habitat of the Siberian musk deer, strange, shy animals that forage on the lichens in these quiet forests. They are small creatures with large ears, weigh about what a dachshund does,

and seem perpetually hunched forward given their disproportionately large back legs. Rather than antlers, male musk deer
have elongated canines that curve from their upper lips like
fangs. This smattering of exaggerated features makes them
seem like an elaborate prank, the Northeast Asian version of a
jackalope, and whenever I see one I'm reminded of a vampire
kangaroo.

On our way back to camp, by the river, Rocky discovered the
faint but certain imprint of a fish owl track in the sand, the closest he would come to seeing a fish owl on that trip. I noted few
suitable trees for nesting: my guess was that the Sherbatovka
pair used this periphery of their territory only sparingly, perhaps mostly in autumn, when the trout spawned. That evening,
not yet ready for sleep and looking to entertain themselves,
Rocky and Sergey took turns mimicking Ural owl hoots and testing Sergey's red deer horn. This was an instrument used by Russian hunters to attract male red deer and was constructed by
peeling a long swath of white birch bark from a tree and rolling
it into a tube. The haunting sound, resembling the powerful and
otherworldly roar of a testosterone-laden male during the autumn rut, resounded throughout the still valley.

Sergey had become fond of Rocky and was tremendously impressed by his hunting ethic and stubborn unwillingness to put
up with any guff. In addition to their shared knowledge and love
of hunting, Rocky and Sergey bonded over their military service.

"I spent some time in Japan, monitoring Russian transmissions," Rocky said once when Sergey asked if he had served. I
interpreted this answer for Sergey.

"Oh yeah?" came the interested response. As it turned out,
Sergey had served in Kamchatka, not far from Japan, where he
monitored American transmissions. They nodded at each other,
smiling over their mirrored Cold War vocations.

THE INFORMATION WE COLLECTED from nest sites and hunting sites was revealing. For nesting, our data showed that big trees really were the best descriptor of a fish owl nest site; it didn't matter too much what else was around. We'd found nest trees both deep in the forest and near villages. All that seemed to matter was that the tree had a large enough hole to provide the owls with a safe location to incubate their clutch.

The river data gave us more unexpected results. They showed that fish owls tended to hunt in locations that had old-growth trees near the rivers themselves. It made sense that fish owls needed large, ancient trees to nest in, but why did the owls care about forest age along rivers? After some thought and a lot of reading, I came up with a possible answer: it wasn't so much the owls that needed big trees, it was salmon.

When a small tree falls into a big river during a storm or otherwise, it typically flows with the current without fanfare. Conversely, when a large tree falls into a small waterway or narrow channel, the water notices. These trees can sometimes entirely block the river's current, causing the rushing water to seek alternate routes. The water might mass behind a blockage and then flow over it as a cascade, or it might reroute entirely across the forest floodplain, following the path of least resistance. Where there might have been a single, uniform channel before an old-growth tree fell into the water, its influence can catalyze the development of an aquatic tapestry of deep pools, backwaters, and shallow, rushing water. This diversity of river habitats is exactly what salmon look for. Young masu salmon fry and smolt, probably the most important fish owl prey in winter, need the safety and calm of backwaters and side channels to grow. Adult masu salmon, mobile feasts for fish owls when they migrate from the Sea of Japan in summer, require the pebbly substrate of main channels to lay their eggs in the rushing water. By hunting along the river's edge surrounded by old trees—some of which eventually fall into the water—the owls were merely going where the fishing's good.

WITH OUR WORK DONE in the Amgu area, we headed south toward Terney. We were about halfway back, having seen nothing but forest and the dirt road for hours, when suddenly a stranger sprang into view, waving his arms wildly. Sergey slammed on the brakes. We were too far from any settlement to disregard such a clear plea for help. I rolled down my window and the man approached, panting.

"Guys!" he shouted with vibrant panic in his eyes. "Guys! Do you have any cigarettes?"

I could smell the vodka on his breath. Sergey tapped a few out of his pack and leaned across me to hand them over.

"To your health," he said, using a common Russian response to a request that was peculiar under these circumstances.

The man looked at Sergey, frowning. "That's all you can spare?"

Sergey handed him the rest of the pack.

"So," the stranger said, calmer after lighting a cigarette and inhaling deeply. "You folks up for drinking some vodka?"

We continued on, Sergey and I unfazed by the interaction, and Rocky and KT trying to understand what had just happened.

THE MORNING AFTER we returned to Terney, a friend arranged for Rocky, KT, and me to tour the Sea of Japan coast north of Terney in a small motorboat. Under normal circumstances one would need a permit to do this since the coast is a border area, but the pilot was retired FSB, or Federal Security Service, so he had the necessary permissions. The sea was calm as we motored out of the Serebryanka River mouth and turned up the coast, scattering Temminck's cormorants and passing the rusty wrecks of two ships that didn't quite make it back to port. This was the same striking coast I had seen from the helicopter in winter 2006 on my way to Agzu, and in summer I could see trickles of water-falls twisting down narrow ravines and disappearing among the boulders piled on the water's edge. A juvenile Steller's sea eagle, the largest eagle species in the world, soared in the still air above the cliffs, then tucked its wings and vanished. Adults are overall black but gilded with snow-white shoulders, tail, and legs and breed along the fringes of the Sea of Okhotsk. They can be seen as far south as Primorye, Japan, and the Korean Peninsula.

About six kilometers from Terney, our light blue boat passed Abrek, a section of the Sikhote-Alin Biosphere Reserve that pro-tects the habitat of the long-tailed goral, a strange and rare goat-like animal that lives along coastal cliffs. We flushed a family group of seven of them, the most our retired FSB guide had ever seen at one time. As we continued along the coast, he smoked and pointed out the capes we could see on this exceptionally clear afternoon: Russkaya, Nadezhdy, and Mayachnaya. He gave special weight to this last cape and held my gaze longer than I thought he should after he said it. I nodded in acknowl-edgment. Cape Mayachnaya, sure.

"You remember Mayachnaya?" He was yelling over the en-gine's drone and maintained a curiously intense stare.

"No," I conceded. This conversation was weird, but I did not understand why.

"Cape Mayachnaya. You were there in 2000 with Galina Dmitrievna at the Uragus summer camp."

I nodded and smiled as though thankful for the jogged memory, but in fact his words froze me inside; if not for the wind, he would have seen the hairs bristle on my arm. I had spent two weeks at that cape nearly a decade ago while in the Peace Corps. I'd certainly forgotten about it, but the FSB, in an announcement cloaked as friendly conversation, were telling me they had not. We had to take a break onshore not long after to dump buckets of accumulated water from the leaky craft; I spent this time wondering what else the FSB knew about me.

32

Terney County Without Filter

BOUT A WEEK BEFORE I arrived in Russia for the 2010 field season, a tiger killed and partially ate an ice fisherman in the heart of the Serebryanka fish owl territory. The poor villager's daughter, worried when her father did not come home, tracked him to his favorite fishing hole. There, she discovered his headless body on the river and a tiger in the bushes gnawing on his skull. The tiger then attacked a logging truck before being shot and killed by a fireman who happened to be nearby. Roman Kozhichev, the Terney County wildlife inspector, gave me this information over coffee my first morning back in Terney.

"The fisherman's teeth are still on the ice," he said in a calm voice but with horrified eyes. "It's a good fishing hole, so people still go."

An analysis of the tiger's brain tissue eventually revealed that the man-eater had been infected with canine distemper virus, a highly contagious disease that, among other things, causes tigers to lose their fear of humans. This tiger was only one of many that succumbed to an outbreak of that terrible virus in the southern Russian Far East in 2009–2010: an epidemic that decimated the tiger population in the adjacent Sikhote-Alin Biosphere Reserve. But at the time of the killing, the tiger's motivation remained unknown. And since tiger attacks in Russia are very rare—and unprovoked ones such as this essentially unheard-of—the unfortunate death instigated a wave of paranoia and anti-tiger backlash in Terney. Phantom sightings abounded, some residents believed that all tigers should be tracked down and shot, and I even knew a woman who slipped a knife into her coat on outhouse runs, just in case.

I SETTLED into this final field season like a handshake with an old friend. With dozens of successful captures since 2007, Sergey and I were veterans and, in most cases, could catch a fish owl with minimal effort. The value of our capture methodology extended beyond Blakiston's fish owls: in the off-season, we'd written and published a scientific paper describing the prey enclosure and how it might be a useful tool for anyone trying to catch a fish-eating raptor when traditional methods failed.

We worked as a lean team of three people to recapture all seven of our target owls in the Terney and Amgu areas over the course of eight weeks. Fish owls lead difficult lives, and the birds unwillingly recruited into this project had undoubtedly suffered stress and discomfort at our hands. So it was satisfying to cut the straps from these owls one last time, leaving them with only leg bands and bad memories. At Saiyon, when I scraped the silicone sealant off the connector port and plugged the data logger into my computer, the screen was blank. The unit had not worked at all, and it was like a punch to the gut. We'd devoted so much time and energy to this territory last year—Katkov had almost gone crazy—and we had nothing to show for it. I was also distressed that the Saiyon male had worn the harness all this time for absolutely no reason. He had forgone comfort and dexterity for a year on the faulty promise that his sacrifice would help us protect his species. It was not even evident why the data logger had malfunctioned. The event record showed that it had tried to connect with satellites nearly a hundred times, but none of the attempts were successful. This type of technology was still relatively new, and sometimes the things just didn't work.

At Kudya, the tagged male had managed to snip one of the harnesses at some point over the year and pull his data logger around to the front of his body. It hung from him like a necklace, and with the unit in reach of his beak he'd picked at the sealant protecting the plug and exposed the internal components. Water sloshed inside the rusty data logger when we retrieved it; it would not even turn on. I sent this unit back to the manufacturer, hoping they might be able to miraculously retrieve some of our GPS fixes, but the wiring was too corroded for anything to be salvaged. Thankfully, the remaining five data loggers we retrieved that season had, on average, several hundred GPS locations each. This was enough to work with: I had the data I needed, for both my Ph.D. and the fish owl conservation plan.

THREE INTERACTIONS with fish owls that season made lasting impressions on me. The first was my final encounter with the Sha-Mi female, the owl I'd probably spent more time with than any other, having seen her every year for half a decade. This was the owl we'd kept overnight in a box in 2008 for fear she'd freeze to death otherwise. I'd posed with her for a photograph the next morning, right before her release, a trout hanging from her beak as she stared impassively at the river. Now, in 2010, I looked up at the colossal poplar that held her and her nest. She looked down for a moment, largely hidden among the flecks of brown and gray of the surrounding bark, before tucking back into the cavity, knowing she was out of my grasp.

The following year, the logging company widened the muddy, rutted road leading up the Sha-Mi River in anticipation of harvesting trees from the upper reaches there. The improved surface meant people could drive faster along it, and in 2012 an Amgu local found a dead fish owl next to the road. His photographs of the leg band showed that this was the Sha-Mi female, and that her injuries were consistent with a vehicular strike. She may have been safe from me, but she could not escape the march of human progress I was trying to shield her from.

The second memorable encounter was at Serebryanka, the site of the fatal tiger mauling earlier that winter. The fishing hole where the man died was within sight of our camp. It had snowed several times since then, so any direct evidence of the attack was hidden, but our work was tainted by the specter of this horror. The final recapture of the Serebryanka male—and his hundreds of data points—should have been joyous, but the air of that place seemed poisoned. Both Sergey and I were glad to move on.

The third moment that has stayed with me was at Faata, the last site where we needed a recapture. Here, the male had lived alone since at least late 2007, when his mate abandoned him for the neighboring territory. Night after night, year after year, his single call was a melancholy plea for her to return or for a new owl to fill the void. We were therefore surprised and excited to hear a pair of fish owls actively vocalizing there. It was fitting that we ended our field season, and our fieldwork overall, specifically with the Faata male. This was the first owl Sergey and I had ever caught, after weeks of self-doubt and missed opportunities. As we released him back into the wild, I watched the last bird captured for this project disappear into the darkness over the river. It occurred to me that an era was over. We'd spent a total of twenty months in the forest since 2006, mostly in winter, tracking and catching fish owls. The finality of it all saddened me, but I also felt invigorated: we had data, information that should help save the species.

When we packed up and left Terney, heading south, we drove up the north side of Whale Rib Pass under a radiant sun on a clear, early April day that did not reflect my mood. For the first time in a decade, I had no specific plans to return to this place that I loved. The spring mud yielded to the heavy truck, as did gray wagtails that trilled in alarm as they flitted out of our way. When we reached the crest that served as the county line, I removed my sunglasses and looked over my shoulder, taking in Terney County one last time without anything between us. If you know when to watch for it, there's a spot among the trees where the landscape reveals a final flash of coastline and cliff before again disappearing behind the forest lining the road. I absorbed this snapshot in silence, then settled pensively back into my seat. I was bound for Minnesota and a year of data analysis and dissertation writing, and after that: the unknown. Primorye is not a hotbed of employment for foreign biologists; it would not be easy to find a job that kept me coming back here. I shared these thoughts with Sergey. Freshly shaven, as he always was the moment a field season ended, he was in good spirits. He pulled on his cigarette before cutting me off, telling me to stop being so melodramatic.

"It's your second home, Jon. You'll be back."

33

Blakiston's Fish Owl Conservation

I T TOOK ABOUT A YEAR for me to process the data and complete my dissertation, most of this time dedicated to analysis. In fact, it was months before the information I'd gathered over four field seasons was even in the proper format for the necessary computer program. To define which resources were important for fish owls, I first estimated a home range, like a territory, for each bird. I did this by plotting GPS points from a given owl onto a map, and then, by assessing the distributions of those points, I determined the statistical probability of where else that specific owl might go. As these probabilities dwindled to zero, farther from the clusters of GPS points, the boundaries of the home range were formed. Next, I identified the most important resources within a home range by comparing where an owl spent its time in relation to the proportions of different habitats (or other potentially important elements such as distance to water or a village) within the home range. It was immediately clear, just from looking at the raw data, how vital valleys were to fish owls: of the nearly two thousand GPS locations collected from the backs of these birds, a mere fourteen points—0.7 percent—showed one outside of a valley.

I was new to this type of analysis and clumsy with the programming language. I frequently ran into problems, spending weeks resolving one issue only to immediately be confronted with another. Then, suddenly, everything clicked. My outputs were beautiful: fish owl home ranges snaked along given waterways and fit neatly between the valley walls. The resource selection analysis showed that fish owls were most likely to be found in valley forests close to multichanneled rivers (rather than those with a single course) and that they stayed near areas where rivers didn't freeze year-round. The average home range was about fifteen square kilometers, although this varied a lot by season. The birds moved around least in winter when nesting (the average winter home range size was only seven square kilometers) and most in autumn when they moved to the upper reaches of rivers (the average autumn home range size was twenty-five square kilometers).

I then extrapolated the combined data of all tagged owls to create a predictive map of eastern Primorye that showed the locations where fish owls were most likely to be found and, consequently, the most important places to protect for them. Going from a few square kilometers for each specific territory to twenty thousand square kilometers for the whole study area meant that my computer calculations were much more complex, and some analyses took a full day or more to run. I happened to do the bulk of this analysis in summer, and my computer kept overheating and shutting down in my hot apartment, and I'd have to start over. Eventually, I brought my laptop into the only room with an air conditioner, propped it up on books for better ventilation, and kept a box fan blowing on it at all times.

The results were fascinating. Only about 1 percent of the landscape in our section of Primorye was considered valley, so fish owls stick to an extremely narrow niche even before taking human threats into account. I overlaid my predictive map of the best fish owl habitat on a map of human land use to see which areas were already being protected and which were most vulnerable. Only 19 percent of the best fish owl habitat was protected by law, mostly within the four-thousand-square-kilometer Sikhote-Alin Biosphere Reserve; everything else was unprotected. Now I knew exactly which landscape features were important for fish owls, and the maps pinpointed the specific forest and river patches the owls needed most.

AFTER RECEIVING MY DEGREE, I began working for the Wildlife Conservation Society's Russia Program full-time as a grant manager. The basic duties of the job weren't really related to my research or expertise, but it allowed me to keep working in Primorye and still be involved in fieldwork. I've continued my work with fish owls, but the primary focus of my organization's efforts in Russia has long been Amur tigers and Amur leopards. So for years, my avian interests have been overshadowed by the needs of large mammalian carnivores. I write grant proposals, generate reports, and assist in data analysis for a range of species from tigers to deer.

I've had to find creative ways to stay engaged with fish owls. For example, I led a tiger prey field study in the Maksimovka River basin for two winters. I hired Sergey as a field assistant, and we tracked deer and boar during the day. Then, while the rest of the field crew made dinner and relaxed at camp, Sergey and I grabbed our headlamps and a thermos of hot tea and headed back out to the woods to look for fish owls. We found new pairs along the Maksimovka River and took day trips to Saiyon to check on our owls there.

More recently, I've expanded my avian conservation work all across Asia, traveling everywhere from the Russian Arctic to China, Cambodia, and Myanmar. This shift came with the understanding that while we can do the best possible work to protect the nesting habitat of northern-breeding birds such as spoonbilled sandpipers and Nordmann's greenshanks in Russia, these efforts mean little if we don't coordinate conservation action with strings of researchers elsewhere on the continent. This is because many species that breed in Russia and Alaska migrate to Southeast Asia for the winter, where they are confronted by habitat destruction, hunting, and other threats. A holistic approach that addresses specific pressures at different stages of avian annual cycles is the best chance conservationists have to curb steep population declines in these birds.

AS TIME HAS ALLOWED, I've worked with Surmach to advance some of the conservation recommendations that evolved from the Ph.D. study and allowed us to structure a fish owl conservation plan. We focus on stabilizing or increasing local fish owl populations by reducing mortality and protecting their breeding and hunting sites.

Given the potential importance of the Sikhote-Alin Biosphere Reserve for fish owls, as the only protected area of consequence in our study area to contain them, Sergey and I surveyed it extensively in 2015. We found only two pairs there, with possible habitat for only another two or three more. There were plenty of good, old-growth trees for fish owls to nest in, and no human disturbance, but in winter nearly all rivers froze solid: there was nowhere to hunt. This single season of fieldwork there did yield one remarkable finding: both pairs of fish owls we discovered fledged two chicks at a time. This was twice the reproductive rate we were accustomed to seeing in Russia; this pattern was prevalent only in Japan, where many fish owls are fed artificially.

It was striking to me that in a protected area where no fishing was allowed, both pairs produced two chicks. I was reminded that we often found two eggs in a clutch but later only one chick in the brood. I also thought of Yuriy Pukinskiy's records from the Bikin River in the 1970s: half of the nests he found had two chicks, and he noted even earlier records of two to three chicks per brood. He speculated that the decline from two or three chicks in the 1960s to one or two chicks in the 1970s was the result of increased fishing pressure on the Bikin. Could we be seeing a continuation of this same pattern? Perhaps fish owls in Primorye today laid two eggs because biologically they were accustomed to, but in reality most pairs had enough food to raise only one chick. Could overfishing of salmon and trout in recent decades be depressing the reproductive potential of fish owls? If true, this would have tremendous implications for fish management and for fish owl conservation. I hope to follow this line of research more closely in the future.

Our habitat analysis found that nearly half of the best fish owl habitat in our study area (43 percent) was leased to logging companies, meaning that direct engagement with industry was essential to fish owl conservation. While this may seem like a potential setup for confrontation between wildlife and commercial interests, reminiscent of the spotted owl controversy in the Pacific Northwest, there is an important difference. The trees that fish owls need—the rotting poplars and elms—are almost worthless commercially. In contrast, a single sequoia in California, where a spotted owl might nest, can be worth $100,000. The loggers in Primorye simply don't have the same economic motivation to target fish owl nest trees and largely do so only by mistake (if the trees happen to be where the loggers want to lay a road) or for convenience (to use the trees for a makeshift bridge). Either way, there was an opening to adapt logging methods that mitigate threats to fish owls and have a negligible impact on company income.

We shared our findings with Shulikin and the logging company that operates in the Amgu and Maksimovka River drainages, and he agreed to stop harvesting large trees for their bridges. This was an easy win for him: good public relations at little cost. It didn't matter to Shulikin too much what his bridges were made from. He had a history of building berms across roads to deter deer and boar poachers; modifying his bridge-building technique was just another wildlife-saving step that will save countless fish owl nest trees from destruction.

We are also working on a larger scale to protect pockets of quality fish owl habitat—also commercially worthless old-growth forest patches—from any logging or other disturbance. When this project was conceived, we already knew that fish owls and their habitat were protected by law. The problem, and the excuse used by logging companies, was that they didn't know where the owls or their habitats were. Our work identified more than sixty patches of forest likely important for fish owls within the logging leases of a single timber company, which is officially in receipt of this information. Ignorance is no longer a valid excuse for logging at key fish owl sites.

Throughout this project I'd seen time and time again that the threats to fish owls in Primorye could all be linked by a single common denominator: roads. As nearly all the roads in the Sikhote-Alin mountain range run through river valleys, fish owls are disproportionately vulnerable to the threat posed by roads.

They provide river access to salmon poachers, who reduce the number of fish the owls can catch and set nets that the owls can drown in, and they increase the risk of fatal vehicular collisions, as we saw with the Sha-Mi female. In fact, in 2010, another fish owl—one that was not part of our study—was hit and killed by a car along the road to Amgu. So we began working with logging companies in 2012 to limit the number of forest roads left accessible to vehicles after the companies are done logging an area. Roads were either blocked by creating earthen berms such as the ones Sergey and I encountered on the Maksimovka in 2006 and the Sherbatovka in 2008 or by removing bridges at strategic locations. In 2018 alone, five logging roads were closed, representing nearly 100 kilometers rendered inaccessible to vehicular traffic and limiting human access to 414 square kilometers of forest. This benefited the bottom line of logging companies by preventing illegal logging and also protected fish owls, tigers, bears, and Primorye's biodiversity in general.

In 2015, after being unable to find a suitable nest tree at the Saiyon territory when our last one was felled in a storm, Sergey and I borrowed a strategy from our colleagues in Japan and erected a nest box. We used a plastic two-hundred-liter barrel that once contained soybean oil, cut a hole in the side, and secured it eight meters up a tree near the Saiyon River. The pair found it in less than two weeks and have fledged two chicks there, one in 2016 and another in 2018. We've since expanded this project to about a dozen other patches of forest, mostly potential fish owl sites that have good fishing but lack nest trees.

With this better understanding of the habitat the owls need, we have been able to update global population estimates. While in the 1980s there were believed to be 300 to 400 pairs, our analysis suggests there are likely more, perhaps twice as many (735 pairs, for 800 to 1,600 individuals), many of them (186 pairs) in

Primorye. If we take the owls in Japan into consideration, and allow for a few pairs hiding in the Greater Khingan Range of China, we believe that the global population of Blakiston's fish owl is fewer than 2,000 individuals (or 500 to 850 pairs total).

Fish owls lack the name recognition and star power of Amur tigers. While more people know about fish owls because of our work, and we are acting to bolster their populations, interest in tigers has also increased. The highest levels of the Russian government are engaged with tigers: President Vladimir Putin has visited Primorye several times to oversee conservation efforts and personally hosted a global tiger summit in Moscow that attracted the likes of Leonardo DiCaprio and Naomi Campbell. Conservation organizations devote entire funding drives to Amur tigers, with millions of dollars a year raised for their protection. With fish owls, funding is limited to whatever grants Surmach and I have time to cobble together.

While modest in comparison with the efforts to protect tigers, our work to promote fish owls and disseminate our results has had an impact, especially with respect to fish owl research elsewhere in the world. Scientists in Japan had been reticent to attach transmitters to the highly endangered island subspecies, given that there were fewer than two hundred individuals left in the wild. Our project showed that tags had no evident impact on survival or reproduction: all of our owls in the Terney and Amgu regions survived the project, and all territories with paired and tagged owls successfully fledged chicks. Based on our successes, Japanese fish owl biologists now conduct their own GPS telemetry studies of fish owl movements, which will increase our understanding of the species. We also consult with researchers and wildlife managers across fish owl range in Russia from the Kuril Islands in the east to the middle Amur region in the west, offering advice on how to bolster fish owl populations. Finally, tawny fish owl researchers in Taiwan read our paper on the use of the prey enclosure for captures and adopted it.

Primorye is, more so than most of the temperate zone, a place where humans and wildlife still share the same resources. There are fishermen and salmon, loggers and fish owls, hunters and tigers. Many parts of the world are too urban or overpopulated for such natural systems to exist; in Primorye, nature moves in a flow of interconnected parts. The world is richer for it: Primorye's trees become floors in North America, and seafood from its waters is sold throughout Asia. Fish owls are a symbol of this functioning ecosystem, a demonstration that wilderness can still be found. Despite the ever-increasing network of logging roads pushing deeper into fish owl habitat, and the resulting threats to the owls, we continue to actively collect information to learn more about these birds, share what we discover, and protect them and the landscape. With proper management we'll always see fish in the rivers here, and we'll continue to follow tracks of tigers that weave among pine and shadow in search of prey. And, standing in the forest under the right conditions, we'll hear the salmon hunters too—the fish owls—announcing like town criers that all is well: Primorye is still wild.

Epilogue

I N LATE SUMMER 2016, a typhoon called Lionrock settled over Northeast Asia, bringing winds and rains that left hundreds of people dead in North Korea and Japan. In Primorye, gales reached near-hurricane levels, with the strongest gusts directly over the central Sikhote-Alin mountains, in the heart of fish owl habitat. It was the worst storm in Primorye in decades. Trees snapped at their bases or were uprooted entirely, then thrown onto one another in cluttered piles. Whole river valleys of oak, birch, and pine became fields of debris overnight, with surviving trunks solitary and conspicuous like gravestones in a neglected cemetery. In the Sikhote-Alin Biosphere Reserve, an estimated 1,600 square kilometers of forest was lost, or 40 percent of the reserve's total territory.

When I went to investigate the impact of Lionrock on our fish owls, I found a jumble of logs and broken branches in the poplar grove where the Serebryanka site used to be. At Tunsha, the nest was splintered on the ground, nearly buried under the wreckage left there by receding floods. Our greatest shock came at Dzhigit, a site that Sergey and I had found only in 2015, where the entire forest that had contained the nest tree was simply gone. During the storm, the Dzhigitovka River had broken its banks and sawed through the forest and a highway in a frenzied push toward the Sea of Japan. When the water retreated to its normal course, it left behind a scar through the valley, a wide bar of gray gravel and stone where poplar and pine used to be.

The birds at Faata have been silent since Lionrock, but in the few times I've been able to drive out to Serebryanka and Tunsha, I've heard fish owls calling from both sites. But the forests are so mangled that a search for a new nest would require more effort than I could spare on a weekend afternoon. My wife and I have two young children, so I spend far less time in the field. In March 2018, I set aside a week for fieldwork and focused on finding the nest at the Tunsha territory. I brought with me a woman named Rada, Sergey Surmach's daughter, whom I'd known since she was a child. Rada had just entered a graduate program to study fish owls and build on her father's legacy. The going was difficult; the forest was like the ruins of some intricate labyrinth, with all passageways choked with rubble. Almost every step was a challenge. Where possible, we balanced on fallen trunks to move a dozen paces at a time unimpeded over the carnage, but such opportunities were rare. Almost every step precipitated a pause to decide where to go next: through, over, under, or around the obstacle. Our GPS tracks from that week show drunken meanders through the Tunsha River valley as we searched the floodplain for our prize but were constantly detoured by blockages. Along the way, I explained the characteristics of a good nest tree to Rada, although with the destruction of the forest, there were few suitable examples. We paused at river crossings— the Tunsha broke into many channels here—and I showed her one place where the river was too narrow and too crowded by vegetation for a fish owl to hunt and another spot where the shallow riffle and expansive gravel bar were perfect.

On the third day of searching, my forehead a mixture of sweat and dirt and my clothes stained by pine pitch, I spied an enormous poplar and knew instantly we'd found the nest. Everything about the tree was right: it was a thick, gray column rising above the surrounding canopy, maybe a dozen meters tall, capped by a yawning cavity and only a stone's throw from the river. Seconds after spotting the tree, I whispered to my companion to watch for a sentry, and almost immediately thereafter a fish owl flushed from a nearby pine: the male moving off with slow, steady wingbeats. As he flew, a handful of crows peeled from nearby trees; they chased him in a serenade of excited caws.

Worried that the nest tree was unguarded, I had hurried toward it to collect a quick fix with my GPS when the commotion must have panicked the female. Another owl appeared, this time emerging from the nest tree itself, an enormous ball of blurred brown wheeling above me in the sky. She landed on a branch, then hunched to get a better look at me; the crows pulsed around her like a swarm of summer insects. We locked eyes and she flew off, disappearing among the early-spring branches of the devastated Tunsha River valley.

As I'd learned years ago at Saiyon, the female would probably keep me in sight but would not return until I was gone. So I moved away, both concerned for her clutch and elated at the same time: the Tunsha owls were okay. They'd survived my Ph.D. project and the recent typhoon and had found a suitable nest tree several kilometers from their old one. They had adapted to the shifting dynamics of the river floodplain and didn't need our conservation interventions—for the moment, anyway. This was a species that would not go down without a fight: they shrugged off catastrophic storms, withstood subzero temperatures, and ignored gangs of crows. I was proud of their resilience. Surmach, Sergey, and I will continue to keep tabs on them, monitor the evolving human threats, and offer our assistance when needed. Like the owls, we'll have to stay vigilant.

Notes

EPIGRAPH

vii Vladimir Arsenyev, *Across the Ussuri Kray* (Bloomington: Indiana University Press, 2016).

PROLOGUE

3 *On a hike in the forest there in 2000:* My companion was Jacob McCarthy, a fellow Peace Corps volunteer and now a schoolteacher in Maine.

4 *Then, flying from Moscow:* At the time, my father (Dale Vernon Slaght) served as the minister counselor for the U.S. Commercial Service (a branch of the U.S. Department of Commerce). He was stationed at the U.S. embassy in Moscow from 1992 to 1995.

5 *It turned out that no scientist:* Aleksansdr Cherskiy, "Ornithological Collection of the Museum for Study of the Amurskiy Kray in Vladivostok," *Zapisi O-va Izucheniya Amurskogo Kraya* 14 (1915): 143–276. In Russian.

INTRODUCTION

7 *After completing a master of science:* Jonathan Slaght, "Influence of Selective Logging on Avian Density, Abundance, and Diversity in Korean Pine Forests of the Russian Far East," M.S. thesis (University of Minnesota, 2005).

8 *A fish owl nest was not discovered:* Found by Yuriy Pukinskiy along the Bikin River in Primorye.

8 *in the entire country:* V. I. Pererva, "Blakiston's Fish Owl," in *Red Book of the USSR: Rare and Endangered Species of Animals and Plants*, eds. A. M. Borodin, A. G. Bannikov, and V. Y. Sokolov (Moscow: Lesnaya Promyshlenost, 1984), 159–60. In Russian.

8 *Across the sea in Japan:* Mark Brazil and Sumio Yamamoto, "The Status and Distribution of Owls in Japan," in *Raptors in the Modern World: Proceedings of the III World Conference on Birds of Prey and Owls*, eds. B. Meyburg and R. Chancellor (Berlin: WWGBP, 1989), 389–401.

8 *Fish owls and other endangered species were protected by Russian law:* For Amur tigers, see Dale Miquelle, Troy Merrill, Yuri Dunishenko, Evgeniy Smirnov, Howard Quigley, Dmitriy Pikunov, and Maurice Hornocker, "A Habitat Protection Plan for the Amur Tiger: Developing Political and Ecological Criteria for a Viable Land-Use Plan," in *Riding the Tiger: Tiger Conservation in Human-Dominated Landscapes*, eds. John Seidensticker, Sarah Christie, and Peter Jackson (New York: Cambridge University Press, 1999), 273–89.

9 *No such approach for fish owls existed:* Morgan Erickson-Davis, "Timber Company Says It Will Destroy Logging Roads to Protect Tigers," *Mongabay*, July 29, 2015, news.mongabay.com/2015/07/mrn-gfrn-morgan-timber-company-says-it-will-destroy-logging-roads-to-protect-tigers.

9 *The Udege and Nanai:* V. R. Chepelyev, "Traditional Means of Water Transportation Among Aboriginal Peoples of the Lower Amur Region and Sakhalin," *Izucheniye Pamyatnikov Morskoi Arkheologiy* 5 (2004): 141–61. In Russian.

10 *We already had a general idea:* Mostly from research by Yevgeniy Spangenberg in the 1940s and Yuriy Pukinskiy in the 1970s.

10 *I was enthused:* See Michael Soulé, "Conservation: Tactics for a Constant Crisis," *Science* 253 (1991): 744–50.

11 *The Samarga River basin was unique:* For a detailed account of the Samarga River basin and the logging conflict there, see Josh Newell, *The Russian Far East: A Reference Guide for Conservation and Development* (McKinleyville, Calif.: Daniel and Daniel Publishers, 2004).

11 *In 2000, a council of indigenous Udege:* Anatoliy Semenchenko, "Samarga River Watershed Rapid Assessment Report," Wild Salmon

Center (2003). sakhtaimen.ru/userfiles/Library/Reports/semen chenko._2004._samarga_rapid_assessment.compressed.pdf.

1: A VILLAGE NAMED HELL

20 *The helplessness and distress:* Elena Sushko, "The Village of Agzu in Udege Country," *Slovesnitsa Iskusstv* 12 (2003): 74–75. In Russian.

22 *They had discovered some ten territorial pairs:* Sergey Surmach, "Short Report on the Research of the Blakiston's Fish Owl in the Sam-arga River Valley in 2005," *Peratniye Khishchniki i ikh Okhrana* 5 (2006): 66–67. In Russian with English summary.

24 *Yevgeniy Spangenberg:* For example, see Yevgeniy Spangenberg, "Observations of Distribution and Biology of Birds in the Lower Reaches of the Iman River," *Moscow Zoo* 1 (1940): 77–136. In Rus-sian.

24 *Yuriy Pukinskiy:* For example, see Yuriy Pukinskiy, "Ecology of Blakiston's Fish Owl in the Bikin River Basin," *Byull Mosk O-va Ispyt Prir Otd Biol* 78 (1973): 40–47. In Russian with English sum-mary.

24 *Sergey Surmach:* For example, see Sergey Surmach, "Present Sta-tus of Blakiston's Fish Owl (*Ketupa blakistoni Seebohm*) in Ussuril-and and Some Recommendations for Protection of the Species," *Report Pro Natura Found* 7 (1998): 109–23.

2: THE FIRST SEARCH

25 *Whereas most owl species:* Frank Gill, *Ornithology* (New York: W. H. Freeman, 1995), 195.

25 *This difference in hunting strategy:* Jemima Parry-Jones, *Understand-ing Owls: Biology, Management, Breeding, Training* (Exeter, U.K.: Da-vid and Charles, 2001), 20.

25 *This once made them a prized food source:* Yevgeniy Spangenberg, "Birds of the Iman River," in *Investigations of Avifauna of the Soviet Union* (Moscow: Moscow State University, 1965), 98–202. In Russian.

3: WINTER LIFE IN AGZU

32 *A typical owl, however, is almost completely silent:* Ennes Sarradj, Christoph Fritzsche, and Thomas Geyer, "Silent Owl Flight: Bird Flyover Noise Measurements," *AIAA Journal* 49 (2011): 769–79.

36 *I'd studied the sonograms:* For example, see Yuriy Pukinskiy, "Blakis-ton's Fish Owl Vocal Reactions," *Vestnik Leningradskogo Universiteta* 3 (1974): 35–39. In Russian with English summary.

36 *Fish owl pairs vocalize in duets:* Jonathan Slaght, Sergey Surmach, and Aleksandr Kisleiko, "Ecology and Conservation of Blakiston's Fish Owl in Russia," in *Biodiversity Conservation Using Umbrella Species: Blakiston's Fish Owl and the Red-Crowned Crane*, ed. F. Nakamura (Singapore: Springer, 2018), 47–70.

36 *This is an uncommon attribute:* Lauryn Benedict, "Occurrence and Life History Correlates of Vocal Duetting in North American Passerines," *Journal of Avian Biology* 39 (2008): 57–65.

4: THE QUIET VIOLENCE OF THIS PLACE

41 *These were Russian hunter skis:* In Primorye, hunting skis are often handmade following the Udege style, with the deck crafted from oak or elm. See V. V. Antropova, "Skis," in *Istoriko-etnograficheskiy atlas Sibirii* [Ethno-historical Atlas of Siberia], eds. M. G. Levin and L. P. Potapov (Moscow: Izdalelstvo Akademii Nauk, 1961). In Russian.

42 *Fish owls hoot at frequencies:* Karan Odom, Jonathan Slaght, and Ralph Gutiérrez, "Distinctiveness in the Territorial Calls of Great Horned Owls Within and Among Years," *Journal of Raptor Research* 47 (2013): 21–30.

43 *The frequency of duets follows an annual cycle:* Takeshi Takenaka, "Distribution, Habitat Environments, and Reasons for Reduction of the Endangered Blakiston's Fish Owl in Hokkaido, Japan," Ph.D. dissertation (Hokkaido University, 1998).

45 *But those owls had higher voices:* The mean fundamental (that is, lowest) frequencies for the Eurasian eagle owl (*Bubo bubo*) in one study were 317.2 hertz, or about 88 hertz higher than the fish owls we've recorded. See Thierry Lengagne, "Temporal Stability in the Individual Features in the Calls of Eagle Owls (*Bubo bubo*)," *Behaviour* 138 (2001): 1407–19.

45 *Fish owls are nonmigratory:* Jonathan Slaght and Sergey Surmach, "Biology and Conservation of Blakiston's Fish Owls in Russia: A Review of the Primary Literature and an Assessment of the Secondary Literature," *Journal of Raptor Research* 42 (2008): 29–37.

45 *These were long-lived birds:* Takeshi Takenaka, "Ecology and Conservation of Blakiston's Fish Owl in Japan," in *Biodiversity Conservation Using Umbrella Species: Blakiston's Fish Owl and the Red-Crowned Crane*, ed. F. Nakamura (Singapore: Springer, 2018), 19–48.

5: DOWN THE RIVER

48 *This is because unlike most birds:* Slaght, Surmach, and Kisleiko, "Ecology and Conservation of Blakiston's Fish Owl in Russia," in *Biodiversity Conservation Using Umbrella Species,* 47–70.

49 *In Japan, where fish owl extinction was narrowly avoided:* Takenaka, "Distribution, Habitat Environments, and Reasons for Reduction of the Endangered Blakiston's Fish Owl in Hokkaido, Japan."

49 *In Russia, a pair concentrates on a single chick:* Pukinskiy, *Byull Mosk O-va Ispyt Prir Otd Biol* 78: 40–47; and Yuko Hayashi, "Home Range, Habitat Use, and Natal Dispersal of Blakiston's Fish Owl," *Journal of Raptor Research* 31 (1997): 283–85.

49 *In contrast, a young great horned owl:* Christoph Rohner, "Nonterritorial Floaters in Great Horned Owls (*Bubo virginianus*)," in *Biology and Conservation of Owls of the Northern Hemisphere: 2nd International Symposium,* Gen. Tech. Rep. NC-190, eds. James Duncan, David Johnson, and Thomas Nicholls (St. Paul: U.S. Department of Agriculture Forest Service, 1997), 347–62.

51 *"frazil ice":* M. Seelye, "Frazil Ice in Rivers and Oceans," *Annual Review of Fluid Mechanics* 13 (1981): 379–97.

6: CHEPELEV

57 *Pyramid power, a pseudoscience with some popularity in western Russia:* Colin McMahon, "'Pyramid Power' Is Russians' Hope for Good Fortune," *Chicago Tribune,* July 23, 2000, chicagotribune.com /news/ct-xpm-2000-07-23-0007230533-story.html.

58 *The sausage magnate also owned a helicopter:* Ernest Filippovskiy, "Last Flight Without a Black Box," *Kommersant,* January 13, 2009, kommersant.ru/doc/1102155. In Russian.

7: HERE COMES THE WATER

62 *It is thought that, like the osprey's:* Alan Poole, *Ospreys: Their Natural and Unnatural History* (Cambridge: Cambridge University Press, 1989).

63 *I wasn't worried about this tiger:* A recent study examined fifty-eight cases of tiger attacks on humans over a forty-year period (1970–2010) and found that 71 percent of them were provoked. See Igor Nikolaev, "Tiger Attacks on Humans in Primorsky (Ussuri) Krai in XIX–XXI Centuries," *Vestnik DVO RAN* 3 (2014): 39–49. In Russian with English summary.

64 *Recent scientific data:* Clayton Miller, Mark Hebblewhite, Yuri Petrunenko, Ivan Serëdkin, Nicholas DeCesare, John Goodrich, and Dale Miquelle, "Estimating Amur Tiger (*Panthera tigris altaica*) Kill Rates and Potential Consumption Rates Using Global Positioning System Collars," *Journal of Mammalogy* 94 (2013): 845–55.

64 *occupying massive home ranges:* John Goodrich, Dale Miquelle, Evgeny Smirnov, Linda Kerley, Howard Quigley, and Maurice Hornocker, "Spatial Structure of Amur (Siberian) Tigers (*Panthera tigris altaica*) on Sikhote-Alin Biosphere Zapovednik, Russia," *Journal of Mammalogy* 91 (2010): 737–48.

64 *human overhunting and destruction of habitat are the true culprits:* Dmitriy Pikunov, "Population and Habitat of the Amur Tiger in the Russian Far East," *Achievements in the Life Sciences* 8 (2014): 145–49.

64 *Chepelev's steel elephant:* V. I. Zhivotchenko, "Role of Protected Areas in the Protection of Rare Mammal Species in Southern Primorye," 1976 Annual Report (Kievka: Lazovskiy State Reserve, 1977). In Russian.

66 *Burgess's invented language:* Robert O. Evans, "Nadsat: The Argot and Its Implications in Anthony Burgess' 'A Clockwork Orange,'" *Journal of Modern Literature* 1 (1971): 406–10.

67 *I found it very interesting:* Wah-Yun Low and Hui-Meng Tan, "Asian Traditional Medicine for Erectile Dysfunction," *European Urology* 4 (2007): 245–50.

67 *He knew that our goal was to find fish owls:* For example, see Semenchenko, "Samarga River Watershed Rapid Assessment Report."

8: RIDING THE LAST ICE TO THE COAST

75 *Their survival rate was a modest 66 percent:* Vladimir Arsenyev, *In the Sikhote-Alin Mountains* (Moscow: Molodaya Gvardiya, 1937). In Russian.

75 *In 1909, he described:* Vladimir Arsenyev, *A Brief Military Geographical and Statistical Description of the Ussuri Kray* (Khabarovsk, Russia: Izd. Shtaba Priamurskogo Voyennogo, 1911). In Russian.

77 *I was suspicious of village wells:* Chad Masching, a Peace Corps volunteer in Terney from 1999–2000; now a Colorado-based environmental engineer.

9: VILLAGE OF SAMARGA

80 *With only a few known records:* Sergey Yelsukov, *Birds of Northeastern Primorye: Non-Passerines* (Vladivostok: Dalnauka, 2016). In Russian.

80 *great gray owls are quite rare this far south:* Occasionally, in what are called "irruption years," low vole abundance drives great gray owls south of their normal range, and they can be seen in places such as northern Minnesota in high numbers. For example, in early 2005—an irruption year—a fellow graduate student at the University of Minnesota (Andrew W. Jones, now curator of ornithology at the Cleveland Museum of Natural History) saw 226 different great gray owls in a single day.

81 *a ship called the* Vladimir Goluzenko: See ship-photo-roster.com /ship/vladimir-goluzenko for a photograph and current location of the *Goluzenko.*

82 *I had adopted a standardized methodology:* See Jonathan Slaght, "Management and Conservation Implications of Blakiston's Fish Owl (*Ketupa blakistoni*) Resource Selection in Primorye, Russia," Ph.D. dissertation (University of Minnesota, 2011).

83 *Fish owls seem to prefer the "side cavity" nest:* Jeremy Rockweit, Alan Franklin, George Bakken, and Ralph Gutiérrez, "Potential Influences of Climate and Nest Structure on Spotted Owl Reproductive Success: A Biophysical Approach," *PLoS One 7* (2012): e41498.

83 *In Magadan:* Irina Utekhina, Eugene Potapov, and Michael McGrady, "Nesting of the Blakiston's Fish-Owl in the Nest of the Steller's Sea Eagle, Magadan Region, Russia," *Peratniye Khishchniki i ikh Okhrana* 32 (2016): 126–29.

83 *And in Japan:* Takenaka, "Ecology and Conservation of Blakiston's Fish Owl in Japan," 19–48.

10: THE *VLADIMIR GOLUZENKO*

89 *Hyundai also had eyes on the Bikin:* Newell, *The Russian Far East.*

90 *He spoke of the fishing villages:* Shou Morita, "History of the Herring Fishery and Review of Artificial Propagation Techniques for Herring in Japan," *Canadian Journal of Fisheries and Aquatic Sciences* 42 (1985): s222–29.

11: THE SOUND OF SOMETHING ANCIENT

96 *I'd spent several years bird-watching here:* These walks were with Sergey Yelsukov, who worked at the Sikhote-Alin Biosphere

Reserve from 1960 to 2005 (most of those years as the resident ornithologist).

96 *John Goodrich, then the field coordinator:* As of 2019, John is the chief scientist for Panthera, an international science-based nongovernmental organization dedicated to the study and conservation of wildcats.

99 *A reliable way to pinpoint:* See Gary White and Robert Garrott, *Analysis of Wildlife Radio-Tracking Data* (Cambridge, Mass.: Academic Press, 1990).

12: A FISH OWL NEST

105 *Dalnegorsk is a city of forty thousand inhabitants:* Rock Brynner, *Empire and Odyssey: The Brynners in Far East Russia and Beyond* (Westminster, Md.: Steerforth Press Publishing, 2006).

105 *The city, river, and valley were all called Tyutikhe:* See John Stephan, *The Russian Far East: A History* (Stanford, Calif.: Stanford University Press, 1994).

105 *When explorer Vladimir Arsenyev:* Arsenyev, *Across the Ussuri Kray.*

106 *The scarring is internal as well:* worstpolluted.org/projects_reports /display/74. See also Margrit von Braun, Ian von Lindern, Nadezhda Khristoforova, Anatoli Kachur, Pavel Yelpatyevsky, Vera Elpatyevskaya, and Susan M. Spalingera, "Environmental Lead Contamination in the Rudnaya Pristan—Dalnegorsk Mining and Smelter District, Russian Far East," *Environmental Research* 88 (2002): 164–73.

106 *We continued a short distance to Vetka:* Arsenyev, *Across the Ussuri Kray.*

111 *Tolya had not thought anything of it:* Stefania Korontzi, Jessica McCarty, Tatiana Loboda, Suresh Kumar, and Chris Justice, "Global Distribution of Agricultural Fires in Croplands from 3 Years of Moderate Imaging Spectroradiometer (MODIS) Data," *Global Biogeochemical Cycles* 1029 (2006): 1–15.

111 *These fires are particularly destructive in southwest Primorye:* Conor Phelan, "Predictive Spatial Modeling of Wildfire Occurrence and Poaching Events Related to Siberian Tiger Conservation in Southwest Primorye, Russian Far East," M.S. thesis (University of Montana, 2018), scholarworks.umt.edu/etd/11172.

13: WHERE THE MILE MARKERS END

115 *We continued over Beryozoviy Pass:* Anatoliy Astafiev, Yelena Pimenova, and Mikhail Gromyko, "Changes in Natural and An-

thropogenic Causes of Forest Fires in Relation to the History of Colonization, Development, and Economic Activity in the Region," in *Fires and Their Influence on the Natural Ecosystems of the Central Sikhote-Alin* (Vladivostok: Dalnauka, 2010), 31–50. In Russian.

116 *We would not see another road sign:* Erickson-Davis, "Timber Company Says It Will Destroy Logging Roads to Protect Tigers," news.mongabay.com/2015/07/mrn-gfrn-morgan-timber-company -says-it-will-destroy-logging-roads-to-protect-tigers.

119 *We had drawn the fish owls out of hiding:* For more on mobbing, see Tex Sordahl, "The Risks of Avian Mobbing and Distraction Behavior: An Anecdotal Review," *Wilson Bulletin* 102 (1990): 349–52.

120 *Hunters commonly kept cats:* Hiroaki Kariwa, K. Lokugamage, N. Lokugamage, H. Miyamoto, K. Yoshii, M. Nakauchi, K. Yoshimatsu, J. Arikawa, L. Ivanov, T. Iwasaki, and I. Takashima, "A Comparative Epidemiological Study of Hantavirus Infection in Japan and Far East Russia," *Japanese Journal of Veterinary Research* 54 (2007): 145–61.

14: THE BANALITY OF ROAD TRAVEL

127 *There is a belief:* K. Becker, "One Century of Radon Therapy" *International Journal of Low Radiation* 1 (2004): 333–57.

132 *This was the last evidence:* Aleksandr Panichev, *Bikin: The Forest and the People* (Vladivostok: DVGTU Publishers, 2005). In Russian.

140 *I found an eagle feather:* I. V. Karyakin, "New Record of the Mountain Hawk Eagle Nesting in Primorye, Russia," *Raptors Conservation* 9 (2007): 63–64.

141 *While not typically aggressive:* John Mayer, "Wild Pig Attacks on Humans," *Wildlife Damage Management Conferences—Proceedings* 151 (2013): 17–35.

15: FLOOD

145 *Sakhalin taimen:* For more information on species distribution and causes of local extinctions, see Michio Fukushima, Hiroto Shimazaki, Peter S. Rand, and Masahide Kaeriyama, "Reconstructing Sakhalin Taimen *Parahucho perryi* Historical Distribution and Identifying Causes for Local Extinctions," *Transactions of the American Fisheries Society* 140 (2011): 1–13.

145 *A nature reserve along the Koppi River:* See wildsalmoncenter.org/2010 /10/20/koppi-river-preserve.

148 *Sometimes Sergey used climbing spurs:* See David Anderson, Will Koomjian, Brian French, Scott Altenhoff, and James Luce, "Review of Rope-Based Access Methods for the Forest Canopy: Safe and Unsafe Practices in Published Information Sources and a Summary of Current Methods," *Methods in Ecology and Evolution* 6 (2015): 865–72.

150 *I harbored no illusions:* Other raptors are known to take deer; see, for example, Linda Kerley and Jonathan Slaght, "First Documented Predation of Sika Deer (*Cervus nippon*) by Golden Eagle (*Aquila chrysaetos*) in Russian Far East," *Journal of Raptor Research* 47 (2013): 328–30.

152 *the La Pérouse Strait:* A forty-kilometer-wide passage between Hokkaido island, Japan, and Sakhalin island, Russia.

16: PREPARING TO TRAP

161 *There were dozens of options:* For example, see H. Bub, *Bird Trapping and Bird Banding* (Ithaca: Cornell University Press, 1991).

161 *Then they reach out of the darkness:* Peter Bloom, William Clark, and Jeff Kidd, "Capture Techniques," in *Raptor Research and Management Techniques*, eds. David Bird and Keith Bildstein (Blaine, Wash.: Hancock House, 2007), 193–219.

161 *Some species are easier to ensnare:* Ibid.

162 *Udege hunting fish owls for meat:* Spangenberg, in *Investigations of Avifauna of the Soviet Union*, 98–202.

162 *others shot and killed by scientists:* V. A. Nechaev, *Birds of the Southern Kuril Islands* (Leningrad: Nauka, 1969). In Russian.

162 *Sergey had his bird:* Jonathan Slaght, Sergey Avdeyuk, and Sergey Surmach, "Using Prey Enclosures to Lure Fish-Eating Raptors to Traps," *Journal of Raptor Research* 43 (2009): 237–40.

162 *There, immature fish owls had been trapped using nets:* Takenaka, "Ecology and Conservation of Blakiston's Fish Owl in Japan," 19–48.

162 *This was possibly due to a history in Japan:* Ibid.

163 *The transmitters attached to the owls like backpacks:* Robert Kenward, *A Manual for Wildlife Radio Tagging* (Cambridge, Mass.: Academic Press, 2000).

163 *We'd then approximate an owl's location:* Josh Millspaugh and John Marzluff, *Radio Tracking and Animal Populations* (New York: Academic Press, 2001).

163 *This process, called "resource selection":* Bryan Manly, Lyman McDonald, Dana Thomas, Trent McDonald, and Wallace Erickson,

Resource Selection by Animals: Statistical Design and Analysis for Field Studies (New York: Springer, 2002).

165 *The first method:* Bub, *Bird Trapping and Bird Banding.*

166 *I knew of one fish owl pair in Japan:* Takenaka, "Distribution, Habitat Environments, and Reasons for Reduction of the Endangered Blakiston's Fish Owl in Hokkaido, Japan."

17: A NEAR MISS

168 *Each trap was modified:* For example, see telonics.com/products /trapsite.

168 *With coyotes or foxes:* Anonymous, *California Department of Fish & Wildlife Trapping License Examination Reference Guide* (2015), nrm .dfg.ca.gov/FileHandler.ashx?DocumentID=84665&inline.

171 *"it is the human encounters . . . that are the nastiest":* Arsenyev, *Across the Ussuri Kray.*

18: THE HERMIT

175 *eighth-century Balhae-era temple:* Also spelled "Boha"; see Stephan, *The Russian Far East.*

178 *Regardless, in addition to the noose carpets:* Bub, *Bird Trapping and Bird Banding.*

19: STRANDED ON THE TUNSHA RIVER

183 *Our modification, something novel:* Slaght, Avdeyuk, and Surmach, *Journal of Raptor Research* 43: 237–40.

184 *The masu have the most constricted range:* Xan Augerot, *Atlas of Pacific Salmon: The First Map-Based Status Assessment of Salmon in the North Pacific* (Berkeley: University of California Press, 2005).

20: AN OWL IN HAND

186 *others, like falcons, twitch and fight:* Lori Arent, personal communication, June 24, 2019.

187 *To be safe:* The vest was made by Marcia Wolkerstorfer, a volunteer at The Raptor Center for more than thirty years.

187 *Female fish owls are larger than males:* Malte Andersson and R. Åke Norberg, "Evolution of Reversed Sexual Size Dimorphism and Role Partitioning Among Predatory Birds, with a Size Scaling of Flight Performance," *Biological Journal of the Linnean Society* 15 (1981): 105–30.

187 *the first record of a fish owl weight:* See Sumio Yamamoto, *The Blakiston's*

Fish Owl (Sapporo, Japan: Hokkaido Shinbun Press, 1999); and Nechaev, *Birds of the Southern Kuril Islands*.

187 *Following established protocol:* Kenward, *A Manual for Wildlife Radio Tagging*.

188 *There was, however, regional precedent:* For example, see Linda Kerley, John Goodrich, Igor Nikolaev, Dale Miquelle, Bart Schleyer, Evgeniy Smirnov, Howard Quigley, and Maurice Hornocker, "Reproductive Parameters of Wild Female Amur Tigers," in *Tigers in Sikhote-Alin Zapovednik: Ecology and Conservation*, eds. Dale Miquelle, Evgeniy Smirnov, and John Goodrich (Vladivostok: PSP, 2010): 61–69. In Russian.

192 *Fish owls seemed to prey upon frogs:* Slaght, Surmach, and Kisleiko, "Ecology and Conservation of Blakiston's Fish Owl in Russia," 47–70.

21: RADIO SILENCE

197 *There, we found a single white egg:* The average size of fish owl eggs measured by Sergey Surmach was 6.3 by 5.2 cm (length by width).

199 *bear gallbladders at a good price:* Jenny Isaacs, "Asian Bear Farming: Breaking the Cycle of Exploitation," *Mongabay*, January 31, 2013, news.mongabay.com/2013/01/asian-bear-farming-breaking-the-cycle-of-exploitation-warning-graphic-images/#QvvvZWi4ro C1RUhw.99.

200 *Chukotka:* A province in the Russian east Arctic.

202 *it takes a young owl three years to reach sexual maturity:* Pukinskiy, *Byull Mosk O-va Ispyt Prir Otd Biol* 78: 40–47.

202 *This type of scenario was possible:* Takenaka, "Ecology and Conservation of Blakiston's Fish Owl in Japan," 19–48.

203 *Amur tigers, for example:* Dale Miquelle, personal communication, June 26, 2019.

22: THE OWL AND THE PIGEON

204 *the workhorse of the raptor capture world:* Bub, *Bird Trapping and Bird Banding*.

204 *Sometimes the lure is a large predator:* Peter Bloom, Judith Henckel, Edmund Henckel, Josef Schmutz, Brian Woodbridge, James Bryan, Richard Anderson, Phillip Detrich, Thomas Maechtle, James Mckinley, Michael Mccrary, Kimberly Titus, and Philip Schempf, "The Dho-Gaza with Great Horned Owl Lure: An anal-

ysis of Its Effectiveness in Capturing Raptors," *Journal of Raptor Research* 26 (1992): 167–78.

204 *In other cases the lure is prey:* Bloom, Clark, and Kidd, in *Raptor Research and Management Techniques*, 193–219.

207 *In a 2015 study:* Fabrizio Sergio, Giacomo Tavecchia, Alessandro Tanferna, Lidia López Jiménez, Julio Blas, Renaud De Stephanis, Tracy Marchant, Nishant Kumar, and Fernando Hiraldo, "No Effect of Satellite Tagging on Survival, Recruitment, Longevity, Productivity and Social Dominance of a Raptor, and the Provisioning and Condition of Its Offspring," *Journal of Applied Ecology* 52 (2015): 1665–75.

208 *GPS data loggers:* See Stanley M. Tomkiewicz, Mark R. Fuller, John G. Kie, and Kirk K. Bates, "Global Positioning System and Associated Technologies in Animal Behaviour and Ecological Research," *Philosophical Transactions of the Royal Society B* 365 (2010): 2163–76.

209 *Mikhail Gorbachev's anti-alcohol campaign:* See Jay Bhattacharya, Christina Gathmann, and Grant Miller, "The Gorbachev Anti-Alcohol Campaign and Russia's Mortality Crisis," *American Economic Journal: Applied Economics* 5 (2013): 232–60.

214 *holy to Chinese inhabitants:* Arsenyev, *Across the Ussuri Kray*.

23: LEAP OF FAITH

223 *Mist nets are a standard bird-trapping tool:* Bub, *Bird Trapping and Bird Banding*.

225 *If the bird ejaculated, it was a male:* F. Hamerstrom and J. L. Skinner, "Cloacal Sexing of Raptors," *Auk* 88 (1971): 173–74.

227 *After the several hundred years:* Slaght, Surmach, and Kisleiko (in *Biodiversity Conservation Using Umbrella Species*, 47–70) found that fish owls used a nest tree for 3.5 ± 1.4 (mean ± standard deviation) years.

231 *The mergansers are interesting birds:* Diana Solovyeva, Peiqi Liu, Alexey Antonov, Andrey Averin, Vladimir Pronkevich, Valery Shokhrin, Sergey Vartanyan, and Peter Cranswick, "The Population Size and Breeding Range of the Scaly-Sided Merganser *Mergus squamatus*," *Bird Conservation International* 24 (2014): 393–405.

231 *Once, Surmach had even found a tree:* Sergey Surmach, personal communication, June 10, 2008.

232 *In the 1960s, the naturalist Boris Shibnev:* Shibnev (1918–2007) was a schoolteacher in a small village along the Bikin River, and an amateur naturalist who made important ornithological discoveries

along that river and established a natural history museum there. He also acted as a guide for visiting researchers such as Yuriy Pukinskiy. Boris's son, Yuriy Shibnev (1951–2017), would become a well-known ornithologist and wildlife photographer in Russia.

232 *Boris Shibnev reported two or three chicks:* Boris Shibnev, "Observations of Blakiston's Fish Owls in Ussuriysky Region," *Ornitologiya* 6 (1963): 468. In Russian.

24: THE CURRENCY OF FISH

236 *An article about the project appeared in the local Terney newspaper:* Nadezhda Labetskaya, "Who Are You, Fish Owl?," *Vestnik Terneya,* May 1, 2008, 54–55. In Russian.

236 *to talk to a reporter from* The New York Times*:* Felicity Barringer, "When the Call of the Wild Is Nothing but the Phone in Your Pocket," *The New York Times,* January 1, 2009, A11.

25: ENTER KATKOV

245 *In fact, one estimate suggested:* See globalsecurity.org/intell/world /russia/kgb-su0515.htm.

26: CAPTURE ON THE SEREBRYANKA

248 *tracked tigers and bears on the slopes:* For example, see blogs .scientificamerican.com/observations/east-of-siberia-heeding-the -sign.

248 *I began asking around Terney:* Some riverine fish exhibit seasonal, short-distance migrations. Brett Nagle, personal communication, July 3, 2019.

255 *International Women's Day:* Temma Kaplan, "On the Socialist Origins of International Women's Day," *Feminist Studies* 11 (1985): 163–71.

27: AWFUL DEVILS SUCH AS US

259 *While not endangered, they are prized:* Judy Mills and Christopher Servheen, *Bears: Their Biology and Management,* vol. 9 (1994), part 1: *A Selection of Papers from the Ninth International Conference on Bear Research and Management* (Missoula, Mont.: International Association for Bear Research and Management, February 23–28, 1992), 161–67.

28: KATKOV IN EXILE

265 *The waters at Saiyon:* At the Tyopliy Kyuch ("Hot Spring") sanatorium south of Amgu, the waters are much warmer, reportedly a stable 36 to 37 degrees Celsius (or 97 to 99 degrees Fahrenheit). See ws-amgu.ru.

29: THE MONOTONY OF FAILURE

272 *The explorer Arsenyev wrote:* Arsenyev, *Across the Ussuri Kray.*

276 *Deer experience "capture myopathy":* Jeff Beringer, Lonnie Hansen, William Wilding, John Fischer, and Steven Sheriff, "Factors Affecting Capture Myopathy in White-Tailed Deer," *Journal of Wildlife Management* 60 (1996): 373–80.

30: FOLLOWING THE FISH

279 *Movements in autumn were the most unexpected:* Slaght, "Management and Conservation Implications of Blakiston's Fish Owl (*Ketupa blakistoni*) Resource Selection in Primorye, Russia."

280 *This last species spawned in side channels:* Anatoliy Semenchenko, "Fish of the Samarga River (Primorye)," in *V. Y. Levanidov's Biennial Memorial Readings*, vol. 2, ed. V. V. Bogatov (Vladivostok: Dalnauka, 2003), 337–54. In Russian. See also Augerot, *Atlas of Pacific Salmon.*

280 *a threat against South Korean airplanes:.* See "N. Korea Threats Force Change in Flight Paths," *NBC News*, March 6, 2009, nbcnews.com /id/29544823/ns/travel-news/t/n-korea-threats-force-change-flight -paths/#.XaJ_VUZKg2w.

280 *Korean Air had already been shot down once:* Alexander Dallin, *Black Box: KAL 007 and the Superpowers* (Berkeley: University of California Press, 1985).

281 *Surmach took a detour:* Tatiana Gamova, Sergey Surmach, and Oleg Burkovskiy, "The First Evidence of Breeding of the Yellow Bittern *Ixobrychus sinensis* in Russian Far East," *Russkiy Ornitologicheskiy Zhurnal* 20 (2011): 1487–96. In Russian.

31: CALIFORNIA OF THE EAST

289 *"the San Francisco of the East":* Courtney Weaver, "Vladivostok: San Francisco (but Better)," *Financial Times*, July 2, 2012.

289 *Memories of the czar were similarly suppressed:* B. I. Rivkin, *Old Vladivostok* (Vladivostok: Utro Rossiy, 1992).

292 *jackalope:* A mash-up of the words *jackrabbit* and *antelope,* a jackalope is a fearsome mythical creature of the American West. It has
the body of a rabbit and the antlers of a deer. For a scientific description, see Micaela Jemison, "The World's Scariest Rabbit
Lurks Within the Smithsonian's Collection," *Smithsonian Insider,*
October 31, 2014, insider.si.edu/2014/10/worlds-scariest-rabbit
-lurks-within-smithsonians-collection.

293 *The information we collected from nest sites:* See Jonathan Slaght,
Sergey Surmach, and Ralph Gutiérrez, "Riparian Old-Growth
Forests Provide Critical Nesting and Foraging Habitat for Blakis-
ton's Fish Owl *Bubo blakistoni* in Russia," *Oryx* 47 (2013): 553–60.

32: TERNEY COUNTY WITHOUT FILTER

297 *About a week before I arrived in Russia:* Nikolaev, *Vestnik DVO RAN* 3:
39–49.

298 *This tiger was only one of many:* Martin Gilbert, Dale Miquelle, John
Goodrich, Richard Reeve, Sarah Cleaveland, Louise Matthews,
and Damien Joly, "Estimating the Potential Impact of Canine
Distemper Virus on the Amur Tiger Population (*Panthera tigris
altaica*) in Russia," *PLoS ONE* 9 (2014): e110811.

298 *And since tiger attacks in Russia are very rare:* For a compelling account of a fatal tiger attack in Primorye, see John Vaillant, *The
Tiger* (New York: Knopf, 2010).

298 *The value of our capture methodology:* See Slaght, Avdeyuk, and Surmach, *Journal of Raptor Research* 43: 237–40.

33: BLAKISTON'S FISH OWL CONSERVATION

302 *It was immediately clear:* See Jonathan Slaght, Jon Horne, Sergey
Surmach, and Ralph Gutiérrez, "Home Range and Resource Selection by Animals Constrained by Linear Habitat Features: An
Example of Blakiston's Fish Owl," *Journal of Applied Ecology* 50
(2013): 1350–57.

303 *The average home range was about fifteen square kilometers:* Slaght,
"Management and Conservation Implications of Blakiston's Fish
Owl (*Ketupa blakistoni*) Resource Selection in Primorye, Russia."

303 *I then extrapolated the combined data:* Jonathan Slaght and Sergey
Surmach, "Blakiston's Fish Owls and Logging: Applying Resource Selection Information to Endangered Species Conservation in Russia," *Bird Conservation International* 26 (2016): 214–24.

304 *I write grant proposals, generate reports, and assist in data analysis:* For

example, see Michiel Hötte, Igor Kolodin, Sergey Bereznuk, Jonathan Slaght, Linda Kerley, Svetlana Soutyrina, Galina Salkina, Olga Zaumyslova, Emma Stokes, and Dale Miquelle, "Indicators of Success for Smart Law Enforcement in Protected Areas: A Case Study for Russian Amur Tiger (*Panthera tigris altaica*) Reserves," *Integrative Zoology* 11 (2016): 2–15.

305 *This is because many species:* For example, see Mike Bamford, Doug Watkins, Wes Bancroft, Genevieve Tischler, and Johannes Wahl, *Migratory Shorebirds of the East Asian–Australasian Flyway: Population Estimates and Internationally Important Sites* (Canberra: Wetlands International—Oceania, 2008).

306 *In contrast, a single sequoia in California:* Howard Hobbs, "Economic Standing of Sequoia Trees," *Daily Republican*, November 1, 1995, dailyrepublican.com/ecosequoia.html.

308 *In 2015, after being unable to find:* Takenaka, "Ecology and Conservation of Blakiston's Fish Owl in Japan," 19–48.

309 *If we take the owls in Japan:* Jonathan Slaght, Takeshi Takenaka, Sergey Surmach, Yuzo Fujimaki, Irina Utekhina, and Eugene Potapov, "Global Distribution and Population Estimates of Blakiston's Fish Owl," in *Biodiversity Conservation Using Umbrella Species: Blakiston's Fish Owl and the Red-Crowned Crane*, ed. F. Nakamura (Singapore: Springer, 2018), 9–18.

309 *The highest levels of the Russian government:* Anna Malpas, "In the Spotlight: Leonardo DiCaprio," *Moscow Times*, November 25, 2010, themoscowtimes.com/2010/11/25/in-the-spotlight-leonardo-dicaprio-a3275.

309 *Scientists in Japan:* Slaght et al., "Global Distribution and Population Estimates of Blakiston's Fish Owl," 9–18.

309 *Based on our successes:* Ibid., 19–48.

309 *Finally, tawny fish owl researchers:* Yuan-Hsun Sun, *Tawny Fish Owl: A Mysterious Bird in the Dark* (Taipei: Shei-Pa National Park, 2014).

EPILOGUE

311 *In late summer 2016, a typhoon called Lionrock:* Aon Benfield, "Global Catastrophe Recap" (2016), thoughtleadership.aonbenfield.com/Documents/20161006-ab-analytics-if-september-global-recap.pdf.

Acknowledgments

To Jenna Johnson, Lydia Zoells, Dominique Lear, and Amanda Moon at FSG for their masterful editing. My text came to them ragged like the ear tufts of a fish owl; their comments and suggestions polished it smooth like the surface of a frozen river (although they didn't appreciate every single metaphor or attempt at humor). To Diana Finch, my literary agent, who saw promise in this book's first draft and devoted considerable time to the edits that led us to FSG.

To my mentors Dale Miquelle and Rocky Gutiérrez, who made me a better scientist, conservationist, and writer. To Rebecca Rose, retired now from the Columbus Zoo and Aquarium, the first person to encourage me to turn my experiences with fish owls into a book. To Sergey Surmach, my collaborator of nearly fifteen years, whose friendship, expertise, and guidance were indispensable. To the field assistants—those named in this book and those whose sections were cut (sorry, Misha Pogiba)—for the discomforts they endured to see the project to a successful end.

To the many funders of this work—including the Amur-Ussuri Center for Avian Biodiversity, Bell Museum of Natural History, Columbus Zoo and Aquarium, Denver Zoo, Disney Conservation Fund, International Owl Society, Minnesota Zoo Ulysses S. Seal Conservation Grant Program, National Aviary, National Birds of Prey Trust, University of

Minnesota, U.S. Forest Service International Programs, and Wildlife Conservation Society—for believing in me, the mission, and the owls.

To my wife, Karen, who allows me to slip off periodically to the woods and rivers of Primorye; I know it is not easy for her. To my two children, Hendrik and Anwyn, who've never known a father who didn't disappear for weeks or months at a time. I hope that, when they're older, they will assess this text and decide that my absences were worth it. And finally to my mom, Joan, and especially my dad, Dale. He was proud of me, my work, and my writing; I wish he'd lived long enough to hold this book in his hands.

Index

Page numbers in *italics* refer to illustrations.